D1055303

THE LEARNING DISABLED ADOLESCENT

Learning Success in Content Areas

Dolores M. Woodward
Assistant Superintendent of Schools
Connecticut

Dolores J. Peters
St. Joseph's College
Glastonburg, Connecticut

MERCYHURST COLLEGE LIBRARY
ERIE, PA. 16546

AN ASPEN PUBLICATION®
Aspen Systems Corporation
Rockville, Maryland
London
1983

Library of Congress Cataloging in Publication Data

Woodward, Dolores M.
The learning disabled adolescent.

Includes bibliographies and index.
1. Learning disabilities.
2. Remedial teaching.
3. Mainstreaming in education.
4. Programmed instruction.
I. Peters, Dolores J.   II. Title.
LC4704.W659   1983   371.9   83-2740
ISBN: 0-89443-875-1

Publisher: John Marozsan
Editorial Director: R. Curtis Whitesel
Executive Managing Editor: Margot Raphael
Editorial Services: Jane Coyle
Printing and Manufacturing: Debbie Collins

Copyright© 1983 by Aspen Systems Corporation

All rights reserved. This book, or parts thereof, may not be
reproduced in any form or by any means, electronic or
mechanical, including photocopy, recording, or any
information storage and retrieval system now known or
to be invented, without written permission from the
publisher except in the case of brief quotations embodied
in critical articles or reviews. For information, address
Aspen Systems Corporation, 1600 Research Boulevard,
Rockville, Maryland 20850.

Library of Congress Catalog Card Number: 83-2740
ISBN: 0-89443-875-1

Printed in the United States of America

1 2 3 4 5

To all those students who have taught us

Table of Contents

Acknowledgments

The authors wish to acknowledge the pioneering work of Dr. Harold Herber. His view of the reading/thinking process and suggested instructional strategies was most influential in the development of Part II of this book. The intent of Part II was not to paraphrase Dr. Herber's work but rather to demonstrate that this view, combined with a directive teaching approach, can be most effective with learning disabled readers. An attempt has been made to bridge the gap that exists between reading specialists and special educators by integrating the efforts and philosophies of the two disciplines into a more comprehensive and effective instructional approach for these students.

The authors give a special note of appreciation to those students and teachers who have developed and field tested the various activities suggested in this book and to George Herrera for his personal commitment and expertise in graphics.

Preface

The adolescent with a learning disability poses a complex instructional challenge for educators on the secondary level. Effective education of older learning disabled students makes demands on both special and regular education teachers and requires collaboration by both groups in all instructional endeavors.

Variables in the learning situation that must be addressed include the instructional environment, educational methodologies, and instructional materials for content subjects, basic skills, and career and vocational education.

The secondary learning disabled student must be individually and interactively incorporated into teaching-learning planning. Educators must have the necessary strategies, techniques, and approaches to enhance the learning potential of the learning disabled adolescent.

For people working with the learning disabled student in the secondary school, this book attempts to provide an arsenal of information and effective instructional tools.

In order to describe the book in a comprehensive manner, it is simpler to state what the text is not.

This book is not primarily a comprehensive treatise on the teaching of secondary subjects, although there are major chapters that present methods for effectively teaching math, English, and social studies to learning disabled adolescents; outline models to follow; provide guidelines for program construction and evaluation; and list resources for materials and sources for further reading.

This book is not a textbook on learning disabilities although it is intended for learning disabled adolescents. The text does *not* trace the etiology of learning disabilities, present major theories or theorists, or cover the various types of learning deficits included under the label of learning disability. However, the educational handicaps manifested by these students have been considered in the presentation of every guide, model, program, and strategy throughout the text. An arsenal of information and resources is provided to enable the secondary educator to effectively provide instruction to this population.

Although the problems involved in instructing adolescent students are stressed throughout the book, the text does not deal primarily with adolescence. However, the methods recommended have been used successfully with an adolescent population.

This book is not primarily a theoretical or philosophical discourse although the material presented is predicated upon solid, proven theoretical foundations. The philosophy espoused is that it is incumbent on educators to know themselves and know their students as individuals. Educators should then use this knowledge to bring together in an interactive mode the student, environment, and educator to work toward predetermined goals. This book's intent is to assist and facilitate this accomplishment.

This is not primarily a methods book although the delivery of instruction is a major emphasis throughout the text. Every chapter offers guides, suggestions, and strategies for the effective presentation of subject matter. This information is specifically tailored for use by regular or special education teachers on the secondary level who are working with learning disabled adolescents.

Although the authors believe that underlying psychosocial factors should be considered along with academic instruction, this book is not a text on affective education. However, the text does describe how feelings, attitudes, values, and beliefs of both teachers and students influence learning. Suggestions, strategies, exercises, and guidelines are offered for the teacher to use in constructively capitalizing on the affective domain within the learning situation.

Even though this book is not primarily about mainstreaming the potential audience was conceived to be the secondary mainstream teachers. The nature of the secondary school and the demands made on teachers in this setting (time, numbers of students seen, size of classes, curricular requirements) were very real considerations throughout the development of this text.

This book is not primarily a text on curriculum. However, both general and specific curriculum suggestions and guidelines are offered in major subject areas and in career and vocational areas.

If this book is not all of the aforementioned, what, then, is it?

This book is about the teaching-learning process. It is about the educator who teaches, about the student who learns, and about the effective integration of both. The text suggests how people within an educational setting can work together effectively and harmoniously. The book is predicated upon the belief that effective education depends on individualization of material and method; integration of the facets of the learning process into a composite entity of teacher, student, and setting; and lastly, collaboration toward common educational goals.

This *is* a "how to" book designed to make the individualization, the integration, and the collaboration become a reality.

Foundations for Effective Instruction on the Secondary Level with the Learning Disabled Adolescent: Theory, Principles, Guidelines, Application

The first part of this text addresses the secondary school learning environment and its related teaching and learning expectations. It presents cogent organizing guidelines, principles, and information targeted toward enhancing students' potential success in the content areas.

It is intended to provide:

- a comprehensive, yet specific, understanding of the secondary curriculum, its demands on learning disabled students, and possibilities for its adaptation;
- an understanding of the learning disabled student as a learner or individual and as a group member and how to effectively present instruction from this knowledge base;
- an understanding of the major subject areas required of all secondary students: math, social studies, and communications and how to enhance a student's concept and skill acquisition; and
- an awareness of the interrelationships of career and vocational education with the core academics.

In summary, upon completion of Part I, the reader should possess the foundations essential for effective instruction of the learning disabled student in the content areas.

Chapter 1

The Learning Disabled Student and the Secondary Curriculum

INTRODUCTION

The curriculum of an educational system defines what a society requires to be taught and encompasses cognitive skills, attitudes, and values. The goals of the educational process are to prepare the American youth to function successfully in the life roles defined within the societal structure. These roles include learner, citizen, family member, producer, consumer, and individual.

Under the mandates of the Education for All Handicapped Children Act of 1975 (PL 94-142), each student must be provided with a free, appropriate public education—one that enables each child to derive benefit from the educational experience. Adaptations and/or special provisions must be made within the secondary educational structure in order for learning disabled adolescents to gain academic success and self-esteem.

In light of the aforementioned considerations, this chapter seeks to accomplish the following objectives:

1. present curricular models appropriate for instructing learning disabled secondary students
2. suggest strategies for preparing the learning disabled student to derive maximal benefit from the educational process
3. discuss student learning styles along with recommendations for accommodating instruction to individual student differences.

LEARNING DISABILITIES: DEFINITION AND DESCRIPTION

The term *learning disability* refers to a handicapping condition associated with the inability of a child to perform school tasks at an expected level (Hobbs, 1975). Some 40 different terms have been used to describe this condition, which affects about 7,000,000 children under the age of 19 (Hobbs, 1975). Despite the differing foci that appear in the literature, there does exist a core of agreement among different professionals that includes the following four elements:

1. There should be a significant discrepancy between expected and actual development. Some authorities state that learning disabled students at the secondary level must lag two or more years behind grade placement in basic math and language arts skills and in all cases fall below the seventh grade level in basic skills (Goodman & Mann, 1976).
2. The learning disability should be specific and not a correlate of other primary handicapping conditions such as general mental retardation, emotional disturbance, sensory impairment, or cultural disadvantage.
3. The deficits formed must be of a behavioral nature: impairments in thinking, conceptualization, memory, speech, language, perception, reading, writing, spelling, arithmetic, and related abilities.
4. The primary focus of identification should be psychoeducational for it is almost impossible to directly examine the brain (Kirk, 1972). Learning disability programs at the secondary level should be reserved for students who have failed to master the academic skills usually acquired during elementary school (Goodman & Mann, 1976).

On April 6, 1963, Dr. Samuel Kirk, in a speech at a conference sponsored by the Fund for Perceptually Handicapped, Inc., used the term *learning disabilities* in a public forum. He had introduced this term in *Educating Exceptional Children* (1962, p. 763).

A commonly selected definition of learning disability is one used in PL 94-142 (USOE, 1977):

> "Specific learning disability" means a disorder in one or more of the basic psychological processes involved in understanding or in using language, spoken or written, which may manifest itself in an imperfect ability to listen, think, speak, read, write, spell, or do mathematical calculations. The term includes such conditions as perceptual handicaps, brain injury, minimal brain dysfunction, dyslexia, and developmental aphasia. The term does not include children who have learning problems which are primarily the result of visual, hearing, or motor handicaps, of mental

retardation, of emotional disturbance, or of environmental, cultural, or economic disadvantage. (p. 65083)

THE LEARNING DISABLED ADOLESCENT

The term *learning disability*, thus, is applicable to those children and youths who are experiencing educationally related problems in learning. They are unable to maximally profit from the education provided unless modifications of the learning environment are made on an individualized basis.

In dealing with the learning disabled adolescent, consideration must be given to the way in which adolescence itself affects a youth's role as a student.

The term *adolescence* is derived from the present participle of the Latin verb *adolescere,* meaning "to grow up."

The adolescent's growing up is observed in:

- physical growth in stature and appearance
- cognitive growth through the development of abstract or formal thinking abilities
- greater active involvement with the environment
- a low tolerance for boredom
- self-motivation
- sexual maturation
- attempts to develop unique identity
- greater mobility
- greater influence of the peer group on the adolescent
- development of emotional and economic independence

The policy and procedures used in the identification, prescriptive planning, and program implementation for the adolescent must include careful consideration of the student's specific disability, chronological age, and educational setting.

The product of such considerations is the design of a model that integrates cogent factors relating to adolescence, specific learning disabilities, and the educational setting. Such a model also enables the effective and efficient delivery of services to handicapped youth. The authors posit an example of one such model.

A Service Delivery Model

In delivering educational services to the learning disabled adolescent, the following four points should be considered:

1. Procedures for identifying eligible adolescents must be developed and implemented. These procedures should ensure the identification of students in accordance with the definition as stated above.
2. The identified students should receive a formal assessment and diagnosis of their skills in addition to informal measures such as teacher observation.
3. The students eligible for special education should have Individualized Educational Plans (IEPs) written and approved. These plans should be consistent with the law.
4. Based on the IEP and diagnostic criteria, placement should be made within a continuum of services. The guiding principle in determining a child's appropriate placement is that it should always be in the least restrictive setting.

The educational system that delivers instructional services to the adolescent should allow the flexibility necessary to accommodate the innumerable differences among learning disabled students.

It is important to note that between the ages of 11 and 17 the range of individual differences in physical structure and physiological functioning at any given chronological age is greater than at any other time in the human life span (HEW Pub., 1976).

Differences in the rate of adolescent learning ability can be as startling as the variance in physiological development. This suggests that in addition to the cross-sectional differences, the vertical differences in the high school classroom must be considered.

Adolescents (as do all students) exhibit individualized learning styles. Styles are exhibited in the manner in which individuals approach tasks (trial and error vs. a purposeful approach); the preferred sensory channel for processing data (visual, auditory, kinesthetic); the ability to attend to tasks; the capacity to learn within a group setting, and interpersonal skills, among other things.

Despite individual developmental differences among adolescents, the common tasks that confront each adolescent may serve as a basis for developing appropriate educational services.

Although these tasks have been articulated by authors with variation in the number of tasks identified and the focus of each task, areas of agreement appear to include the achievement of independence from parents (economic and social); interpersonal skills requisite to effective societal functioning; development of a personal value system, and sexual role identification.

Havinghurst (1952), for example, delineated ten developmental tasks that impact on the youth's behavior during the state of adolescence (which within this text is defined as 13–18 years old).

Educators concerned with providing learning disabled students with appropriate educational programs should consider the stage of adolescence of students in formulating expectations for them. How do the goals defined for secondary education meet the needs of these exceptional adolescents?

PURPOSES AND OBJECTIVES OF THE SECONDARY SCHOOL

Rollins and Unruh (1964) indicated that the American secondary school should:

1. Provide opportunities for all boys and girls to receive at least a twelfth-grade education.
2. Attempt to help boys and girls to develop powers of independent, critical thinking.
3. Present boys and girls with opportunities to learn the traditions, the ideas, and the processes of American democracy.
4. Help boys and girls to understand and appreciate American and world society, their art, their literature, their history, their science, their customs, and their people.
5. Help boys and girls prepare for the roles they will assume after they leave it. (pp. 20–24. Reprinted with permission.)

These goals and objectives are articulated through the school's curriculum.

Curriculum

Stiles, McCleary, and Turnbaugh (1962) defined the curriculum "as what society requires to be taught, including intellectual skills, knowledge, attitudes and values" (p. 203).

There are numerous and varied measures that could be undertaken to assess the effectiveness of an educational system in providing educational services to its children and youth. In looking at the goal of preparing learning disabled adolescents for effective life functioning, academics appears to be but one measure.

The literature abounds with the articulation of criteria related to educational effectiveness. However, comprehensive efficacy evaluations involve the three significant factors in the teaching-learning process. These are the teacher, the learner, and the educational setting. A description of an effective school is provided by Thomas (1981).

Variables of Educational Effectiveness

The authors describe an effective school as one in which:

1. Conflict is resolved through collaboration and good will.
2. The attitude toward education of patrons and employers is positive.
3. Both school employees and patrons value education, appreciate its complexity, and keep current with educational trends.

A review of current literature in the field reveals the following trends:

1. increased attention to the needs of secondary level learning disabled students (Bailey, 1975; Goodman & Mann, 1976)
2. a trend away from categorical labeling reinforced by mainstreaming efforts
3. increased attempts to include learning disabled adolescents in the secondary curriculum, prepare them for specific vocational placement, and improve their general life skill capabilities
4. development of assessment techniques that isolate individual problem factors in special students
5. development of a "curricular" cascade of services that offers the individual a continuum of academic placement.

The educational system has several options available in the delivery of educational services to the learning disabled student within the secondary school.

EDUCATIONAL ALTERNATIVES FOR LEARNING DISABLED ADOLESCENTS

There are three distinct alternatives available for the educationally handicapped student within the regular classroom—remedial education, vocational education, and compensatory education.

Remedial instruction has as its objective the amelioration of the student's problems. This is accomplished by identifying specific weaknesses of the student and implementing instructional techniques to decrease these weaknesses.

Vocational instruction is the process of providing students with the job skills needed for specific occupations that generally are not considered "professional" and do not require college degrees.

Compensatory education is designed to help students learn by circumventing, to some extent, their handicaps. This process frequently involves modifying or adapting high school requirements. Examples of such modification include using an easier-to-read text, altering the manner of presentation, and varying testing methods.

All three approaches have the common goal of enabling the student to engage in meaningful learning.

The teacher can increase the material's relevancy by using the following modification techniques:

1. incorporating into unfamiliar material, wherever possible, aspects of familiarity with which students may identify
2. structuring the material into a familiar sequential order
3. relating unknown (new) material to the student's frame of reference
4. using associational techniques

Smith (1973) suggests additional strategies to increase meaningfulness of the instructional material presented by the teacher.

CURRICULUM FOR LEARNING DISABLED ADOLESCENTS

Typical High School Curriculum

A curriculum for junior and senior high school students consists of required courses and electives. The tradition of the Carnegie Unit is maintained. A student must earn credits in required and elective courses to be promoted and earn a diploma. A unit of credit is, in most cases, equivalent to two semesters of work.

The required courses ordinarily consist of three units of English or language arts, one or two units of history or social studies, two units of mathematics, and two units of science. Many schools permit "basic" courses in the required areas to suffice for credit. Some schools offer basic arithmetic, practical English, or applied science and math. Although these courses have simpler content, they can be used to qualify for graduation credit. Successful completion demands that the student attend classes regularly, maintain acceptable behavior, and complete course assignments to the satisfaction of the instructors.

A typical class on the secondary level is primarily presented in the lecture format of instruction. Individualization of instruction within a typical "mainstream" setting is, unfortunately, infrequent since the course objectives require the instruction to cover a predetermined amount of material each semester. The size of the classes and the number of students each high school teacher instructs (120–150 per day) serve to further mitigate against the individualization so needed by the learning disabled adolescent.

A third mitigating factor is the measurement of pupil progress. The letter grade, based on a normative scale, is used by the majority of junior high schools and senior high schools to evaluate students' performance. Simon and Belanca (1976) present an overview of the research relating to grading systems and discuss several alternatives.

Alternative modes of evaluation, however, lend themselves to a more individualized rating of student progress. Examples include criterion-referenced assessments, domain-referenced testing, and individually guided instruction. Refer to the chapter on evaluation for a description and an elaboration of these approaches.

The learning disabled student's acquisition of knowledge is enhanced if the material to be learned is presented in a structured approach, integrated into a model that allows for individualized tailoring of educational programs. Mainstream and special education teachers should be cognizant of the major curricular models utilized at the secondary level.

Curriculum Organization Models

In addition to content, the manner in which subject matter is organized is also important. The curriculum can be organized in the following four ways:

1. The *subject-centered* curriculum is organized round the traditional subjects taught in the secondary school and aims at helping the pupil to acquire specific knowledge and skills. Teachers are frequently concerned with developing skills in only one content area with the result that students instructed within this organizational framework often do not see the relationships between subjects. This is the most prevalent model used in secondary schools in America.
2. The *broad fields* curriculum attempts to correlate subjects by cutting strict subject matter boundaries. It allows students to discover the relationships of different facets of the educational program.
3. The *core* curriculum is defined by Douglass (1964) as one that "involves organizing two or more subjects around problems" (p. 25). This model attempts to provide a set of learning experiences that are

necessary for all pupils and encourages flexible instructional methods and the elimination of subject matter divisions.

4. According to Rollins and Unruh (1964) "The *experience* curriculum assumes that the skills and attitudes that are valuable to a pupil in solving a problem or satisfying a need are those that are learned best and most effectively by the pupil" (p. 52).

Learning disabled students require learning alternatives that will accommodate their unique learning preferences and needs. The design of the curriculum allows for this individualization of instruction.

Curriculum Design

A curriculum design is a statement that identifies the elements of instruction and their relationships to each other. The design also outlines the principles of organization and the administrative requirements for that organization. A design must reflect a curriculum theory that delineates the sources to consider and the principles to apply. In making consistent curriculum decisions, it is essential that there exist a congruence between the curricular foundation principles and practice.

The most prevalent curriculum design has been the separate subjects design. Such a design is organized to present such subjects as mathematics, physical education, communication, art, and so forth as separate and discrete.

The term *instructional design* refers to a statement of content students will learn, proposed ways of learning, and means of assessing learning. Instructional designs are developed prior to instruction and provide direction and suggested resources for instructional activity. Curriculum design refers to the overall school organization, but instructional designs are developed for specific classes, students, or courses.

Activities involved in instructional design include selection of content, sequencing of the content in the order in which it will be taught, specification of instructional objectives, and development of preassessment procedures, learning alternatives and resources, and postassessment procedures for each objective.

Curriculum Design for Exceptional Learners

In attempting to design a curriculum to meet the needs of a continuum of "student learners," consideration must be given to a number of variables. The following seven factors should be taken into account:

1. Since people learn at different rates and in different ways, the rate of material presentation as well as the manner of material presentation must be considered.
2. Individuals are to be accepted for their uniqueness as well as for their similarities to other individuals. The hypothetical "typical adolescent student" that has guided curriculum design should be replaced with "the individual adolescent student" as a guiding principle.
3. Schools are human inventions created to nourish individual differences and similarities and to assist students in their affective, cognitive, and psychomotor growth. The school's responsibility is not unidimensional in nature but integrative in serving the "total child."
4. Curriculum and instruction are the school environment's primary means of providing opportunities for student growth. The growth should be goal directed, related to the real world, and meaningful to the students.
5. A student's school experiences become more individualized and meaningful when the school environment offers a wide variety of curriculum and instructional alternatives. It is a school's responsibility to maximize the learning opportunities for all the students in its charge. Clearly, there is no single appropriate program.
6. Alternatives in curriculum and instruction must be related to the students being served and to the competencies of teachers and other education personnel. The deployment of staff within the educational setting should be reassessed, and the staff's expertise should be surveyed. In-service training should be provided when indicated.
7. Success experiences foster other success experiences; curriculum and instruction should be designed and implemented in such a way that each student has a good chance of being successful each day.

One of the first steps in the curriculum development process is to establish a base for decision making and a set of internally consistent beliefs that can be referred to for direction through the remainder of the process.

The potential of each learning disabled adolescent to succeed is predicated upon the teacher's ability to individualize the presentation of the secondary curricular content to effectively meet the unique learning needs of the students. Options exist within the area of course requirements, testing and evaluation, and course modifications. Suggestions for curricular modifications follow.

Curriculum Modifications for Secondary Learning Disabled Students

Esminger (1976) has provided some guidelines for curriculum modifications for learning disabled secondary students as follows:

1. Courses can be substituted.
    a. Credit should be given for completing an individualized course in English, math, reading, history, science, etc. under the supervision or direction of a regular class teacher, tutor, or learning disabilities specialist in any setting where the student works, i.e., learning resource center, resource room, etc.
    b. Substitutes are alternative courses such as business math for algebra, vocational basic electronics for physical science, etc.
2. Courses can be waived.
    a. If a severe disability would have a negative impact on the completion of a course, the substitution of a course in a related area of strength can be an excellent solution for avoiding failure.
    b. Examinations should be administered in such a manner as not to penalize the student.
3. Alternatives for testing and evaluation can be devised as follows:
    a. objective instead of essay tests
    b. oral instead of written tests
    c. retests in the same or alternate form
    d. tests with a readability level adjusted to the student
    e. frequent short testing on short units of material
    f. extra credits, projects, or bonus questions
    g. projects to demonstrate proficiency in lieu of tests
    h. adjustment of time factor to give the student additional time to complete a test
    i. cues in the form of additional information, i.e., spelling or lists of words from which to choose
    j. review and/or narrowing the scope of material to be studied for the test
4. Parallel courses can be developed. A regular course could be paired with any one of the following:
    a. a course individually programmed to fit the needs of the particular student
    b. course-directed study by the regular classroom teacher
    c. project-centered course perhaps taken outside the building, i.e., a social science project carried out in conjunction with the county department of family and children's services
5. Alternatives for a choice of major are already available in many high schools as follows:
    a. business education
    b. occupational education
    c. general studies program

     d. college preparatory program
     e. distributive education (work-study programs)
6. Joint enrollment with private schools specializing in services for the learning disabled or half-day programs may be useful for students unable to tolerate a full-day program.
7. Course credit can be given for experience study programs such as:
     a. summer jobs
     b. summer travel

In addition to the aforementioned possible alterations in courses and course requirements, ideas suggesting the manner in which teachers are able to provide learning options for learning disabled students that relate to modification of the curriculum within the classroom follow.

Modification of Classroom Experiences

Instruction in the classroom involves:

1. modification of course requirements by reducing the scope of material to be covered
2. adjustments through the use of individualized instruction such as:
     a. learning packets
     b. programmed materials
     c. independent study
     d. contracting
     e. competency-based instruction

Competency-based education relates to purposeful, measurable, and meaningful learning. The curriculum in the majority of our schools is a subject curriculum, one that is content focused, not student focused. As such, the material is frequently irrelevant to the student's life. Moreover, many schools continue to employ competition, coercion, and punishment to engage students in this meaningless instruction.

Significant (meaningful) education is defined in improved problem-solving ability rather than in memorized solutions; in sharpened and broadened insights and understandings rather than in the accumulation of isolated facts; and in improved behavior and increased significance in the life of the individual rather than in the ability to pass exams or make the honor roll.

Essentials of an effective educational program include:

1. a suitable curriculum with student involvement in the selection of educational experiences
2. a social situation conducive to maximum self-realization
3. effective guidance of the process by means of which students are to achieve their potentialities
4. a competent, sensitive, and dedicated teacher

Development of Emotional Health

Research has proven that education becomes meaningful to individuals when they are able to relate that learning to themselves and to reality as they are experiencing it in their lives (Rogers, 1969).

It is the teacher's responsibility to discover and make clear the relevance of the content to the needs and interests of individual learners.

Combs (1970) suggests seven changes that would afford students more personal meaning in their experiences with the curriculum as follows:

1. deemphasizing information and objectivity
2. valuing meaning
3. developing sensitivity to student meanings
4. accepting students
5. encouraging personal exploration
6. testing, evaluation, and rewarding meaning
7. Teachers, too, must be evaluated and rewarded for humanism. (pp. 177–178. Reprinted with permission.)

The effective teacher of the learning disabled adolescent is able to provide instruction in such a way that specific learning needs exhibited by individual students are met with consideration not only to cognitive factors, but the equally significant affective issues. Factors to be considered are presented in the following section.

CURRICULUM SUGGESTIONS FOR SECONDARY LEARNING DISABILITIES PROGRAMMING

1. Applied specific remediation is focused on specific skills deficits exhibited by the student.
2. The student should learn acceptable social and emotional behaviors through a balance between cognitive and affective curriculum components.

3. The curriculum must be a unified whole, i.e., there must be a clear relationship between the program components and program goals established for the adolescent.
4. The curriculum should include an adequate feedback system. This is essential for adjusting the teaching pace and techniques to fit the individual student; for identifying specific areas of difficulty that will require additional instruction; and for providing accountability data.
5. The curriculum materials should be adapted from the regular education program whenever possible.

Goodman and Mann (1976) suggest five criteria for assessing curricular systems:

1. The curriculum will include a comprehensive, structured, developmental sequence of the subject matter content.
2. The appearance and format of the program should be appealing to the older student.
3. The scope and sequence of the program should be clearly delineated and preferably presented in a behaviorally objective format.
4. The program should have an accompanying curricular management–evaluation system.
5. The program should focus on mastery of basic skills. (p. 134. Reprinted with permission.)

"Tailoring" educational programming to the educational needs of the educationally handicapped student is no longer a desirable option, but a mandate. Public Law 94-142 has mandated that handicapped children must be educated with their nonhandicapped peers whenever such placement will enable them to profit from the educational experience. This means that they must be educated within the least restrictive educational setting— within the regular classroom (mainstream) where possible.

It is important, however, to be aware that "least restrictive" placements occur on a continuum and are relative to a specific educational setting and the specific needs of the individual child.

The efficacy of the mainstream placement must be carefully monitored. Specific issues to be addressed are:

1. an evaluation of the effect of the time spent within the mainstream setting on the academic or nonacademic status of the students
2. the type and degree of instructional integration afforded the mainstreamed learning disabled students

3. a determination of whether the mainstream teachers possess the skills and expertise necessary to meet the unique learning needs of the integrated students
4. the specific modifications made in task presentations and the adaptation of instructional materials to accommodate to the varying learning styles of the mainstreamed handicapped adolescents
5. the existence of a pupil progress monitoring system that provides a continuous measurement

Edwin Martin, former head of the Federal Office of Health, Education, and Welfare, commented on the promise of mainstreaming in 1974 that "we must seek the truth and we must tolerate and welcome the pain such a careful search will bring to us. It will not be easy in developing mainstreaming, but we cannot sweep the problems under the rug." (p. 153)

Effective mainstreaming is not a matter of chance but rather the result of well planned and effectively implemented activity.

The National Education Association, in its Resolution 77-33 (NEA Resolution 77-33, 1977) stated that to implement Public Law 94-142 effectively the following conditions should be adhered to:

1. A favorable learning experience must be created both for the handicapped and nonhandicapped students.
2. Regular and special education teachers and administrators must share equally in planning and implementation for the disabled.
3. All staff members should be adequately prepared for their roles through in-service training and retraining.
4. All students should be adequately prepared for the program.
5. The appropriateness of educational methods, materials, and supportive services must be determined in cooperation with classroom teachers.
6. The classroom teacher(s) should have an appeal procedure regarding the implementation of the program, especially in terms of student placement.
7. Modifications should be made in class size using a weighted formula, scheduling, and curriculum design to accommodate the demands of the program.
8. There must be a systematic evolution and reporting of program developments using a plan that recognizes individual differences.
9. Adequate funding must be provided and then used exclusively for this program.

10. The classroom teacher(s) must have a major role in determining individual educational programs and should become members of school assessment teams.
11. Adequate released time must be made available for teachers so that they can carry out the increased demands upon them.
12. Staff reduction will not result from implementation of the program.
13. Additional benefits negotiated for handicapped students through local collective bargaining agreements must be honored.
14. Communication among all involved parties is essential to the success of the program. (p. 52)

In summary, the goals of the secondary learning disabilities program must consider legal requirements, professional responsibilities, the nature of the instruction, and the student. The role of the special educator is defined by authorities in the field in differing terms.

Lerner (1976) suggests that the secondary school needs several options for delivering educational services and that resource teachers in high school "must be familiar with the entire curriculum of the school" (p. 38). "Remediation must be closely tied to what is happening in the classroom" (p. 39).

Goodman and Mann (1976), on the contrary, propose a "basic education program" at the secondary level that restricts the activities of the specialist to the teaching of basics in mathematics and language arts. They would restrict enrollment of students to those who lack full sixth-grade competency.

All programs for learning disabled students must be planned and implemented within a framework of legal regulations and restraints since the advent of PL 94-142, the Education for All Handicapped Children Act of 1975. The general effects of the public law may be summarized as follows:

1. All handicapped children have a right to an appropriate free public education.
2. Identification and placement of children in special programs for the handicapped must include careful consideration of race, ethnic, and language differences and may dictate modified assessment practices in many instances.
3. In assessing students using either individual or group testing, the following considerations should be incorporated:
   a. The title of the test should be stated together with an accompanying test description. Sample test items would be helpful.
   b. Especially with adolescents, it is important that students be told the purpose of the test.

    c. Students and their parents should be told who will receive the test results and where the results will be stored.

    d. Information should be given, prior to testing, about how the test results will be used.

4. The Council for Exceptional Children (Nazzaro, 1976) suggests guidelines for the use of group and individual assessments. A list of rights should be provided. These include the rights:

    a. to review all records related to referrals for evaluations,

    b. to review the procedures and instruments to be used in the evaluation,

    c. to refuse to permit the evaluation,

    d. to be fully informed of the results, and

    e. to get outside evaluation at public expense, if necessary.

5. Placement must be in the least restrictive educational alternatives within which the child may be effectively instructed.

6. The principle of due process ensures procedures to protect the rights of children and their parents and provides a legal vehicle for resolving any conflicts that might arise between the parents and the schools.

It is important to recognize that educational delivery systems must be developed along a continuum of options. An appropriate system for a specific learning disabled student is determined by the planning and placement team. This team delineates the student's educational needs and the required educational responses necessary to meet those needs. Options include full-time placement in a regular classroom with instructional accommodations made by the regular classroom teacher; placement in the regular class with supportive assistance provided to the student and the teacher by the special educator; or part-time placement in a self-contained special class. Public Law 94-142 mandates placement in accordance with the sequence as delineated, i.e., from least restrictive to most as the student's needs warrant.

SECONDARY LEARNING DISABILITIES PROGRAMS

Irrespective of the specific nonmainstream option adopted, there are goals toward which all learning disabilities programs should be oriented in the secondary level. These programs should have the following goals:

1. The student should move toward full-time general education with nonhandicapped peers.

2. The adolescent should have an opportunity to earn the necessary credits toward high school graduation. Planning for the student should be specific and designed for the short term although long-term projections should also be considered.
3. Those students with a poor prognosis for academic success in extended formal academic programs should be scheduled for vocational training, functional skill development, and eventual job placement.

Modifying the Curriculum for the Learning Disabled Adolescent

In order to meet the needs of the secondary learning disabled adolescent, the curriculum must be modified. Modifications should include the following eight suggestions:

1. The student's program should reflect a balance between easy and demanding courses, in addition to providing the student with opportunities for substitution.
2. Special textbooks should be used where appropriate. Project Math (Cawley et al., 1976) (Educational Development Corporation, Tulsa, Oklahoma) is one example. In addition, Weiss and Weiss (1974) offer several examples of how a teacher may modify a standard curriculum.
3. The program should reflect a coordination of activities between the general classroom and the interventions of the learning disabilities specialist. The information exchanged in this liaison should be used in the selection of materials for the respective students and also in planning study schedules for them.
4. Monitoring systems should be incorporated to evaluate pupil progress in a consistent manner through the use of informal or criterion-referenced tests.
5. The program should allow for adjusting the difficulty level of a particular task and for incorporating information about the student's attitude, interests, and values into the instructional plan.
6. Groups of adolescents should engage in discussions or activities that explore school survival skills, values clarification, attitudes, and self-concepts.
7. Learning disabled adolescents should be provided with a program of occupational exploration and preparation that includes "hands on" experiences.
8. The program should be aligned with the "regular" program in both content and duration.

TEACHER AS ORGANIZER OF LEARNING ENVIRONMENT

According to Hugh and Duncan (1970), "Teaching is an activity—a unique professional, rational, and humane activity in which one creatively and imaginatively uses himself and his knowledge to promote the learning and welfare of others" (p. 2).

Teaching is a four-step process that includes: (1) curriculum planning; (2) instructing; (3) measuring; and (4) evaluating. Actual instruction involves creating, using, and modifying instructional strategies and tactics to help children learn.

Involvement is a key to learning. Jackson (1965) has described it as follows:

> More and more I have come to think of the teacher's work as consisting primarily of maintaining involvement in the classroom. The teacher hopes that involvement will result in learning. Learning becomes the by-product or secondary goal rather than the thing about which he is most directly concerned. (p. 10).

Although it is critical that an effective classroom climate be created for the majority of students, alternatives must be available for those students who do not learn optimally under the prevailing structure. The classroom organization influences curriculum balance, grouping and grading practices, and instructional strategies. When a new learning experience is encountered, the outcome derives in large part from the interaction of the following two conditions:

1. the status of the student's cognitive structure to acquire new learning; and
2. the organization of the new material to attract and satisfy the learner.

The teacher's task is to provide experiences that will prepare learners to learn new material because they understand and can apply their earlier knowledge.

Preparing the Learner

Teachers can find ingenious ways to integrate material, to make it interesting, and to involve students in the learning process. Some examples are:

- Simulation can be used with students manifesting language deficits. In this method the substitution of action for words facilitates student involvement.
- The class can study newspapers to learn about the content areas included and can subsequently publish their own weekly newspaper.
- Team learning can be used to emphasize the creative development of social and cognitive abilities. Each team (group) produces a tangible product relating to its particular body of content. All members of the team would receive the same grade.
- Students can be allowed to help at all levels below their own grade placement. This is an effective technique for improving motivation.
- Change can be integrated into the usual structure by having students select certain topics of interest to pursue.
- Community resource persons could be used to enliven the treatment of a topic by their participation as team members.
- Group size can be varied for particular activities and topics. Groups can be established that will as nearly as possible assure a place of importance for each participant.
- Students can be provided with guided opportunities for them to learn for themselves.

Accommodating Individual Differences in Content Classrooms

Hunt and Sheldon (1950) said, "High school teachers must . . . realize that much of their frustration is derived from attempting to teach forty pupils as if all the children were able to perform on the same level" (pp. 352–353).

It appears that this statement is valid in today's secondary schools. Although teachers theoretically and professionally agree that it is important to consider individual differences, the apparent lack of such individualization in the classroom appears to be due to the teacher's lack of workable techniques to facilitate the individualization. Some specific strategies suggested for use in the secondary classroom follow.

Vocabulary Strategies

Taba (1967) has offered the *List-Group-Label* lesson as a simple means to acquaint students with new vocabulary. In this approach:

1. Students are asked to categorize all their verbal concepts that are related to a topic under study. The lesson begins with the teacher

supplying some one-word stimuli associated with the materials the students are about to read.

2. Students then develop a list of words which they freely associate with each stimulus.
3. These associations are recorded and students then categorize smaller lists of words from their large list and label each new grouping. (Reprinted with permission.)

Structured Overview

This strategy presents students with a visual diagram of major vocabulary terms the students will encounter in their text material. It provides a framework of the interrelationships among major vocabulary terms.

Prediction Strategies

The anticipation guide (Herber, 1978) is designed to enhance comprehension by encouraging students to organize information and reasoning relative to the concepts to be found in the text material. The teacher creates statements that support some ideas in the text and refute others. Students are asked to agree or disagree with each statement and to defend their thinking. The purpose of this guide is to involve students with text material by focusing their thinking on concepts to be encountered in the text.

Survey Technique

The survey technique (Aukerman, 1972) is another prediction strategy that is used to modify students' experiential background before they deal with the text material. Students are asked to analyze the various parts of a chapter to formulate purposes for reading. This analysis includes the examination of the chapter title, subtitles, and visual aids. Additionally, the introductory and concluding paragraphs are read, all in an effort to derive a main idea statement about the topic of the material. The strategy objective is to enable the students to achieve cognitive readiness for the text material.

The Content Area Textbook

The mainsteam teacher must frequently instruct educationally handicapped students who present a myriad of learning needs using a designated textbook. As learning disabled students progress through the formal educational system, the academic demands made on them tend to increase not in an arithmetic ratio but rather on a geometric scale. Some of the major difficulties adolescents will encounter in using secondary content area textbooks are:

1. The vocabulary may be unfamiliar and difficult to decode.
    a. Pronunciation may present a problem. The student has trouble pronouncing new words because those words are not in the student's listening or speaking vocabulary. The student has no reference for correction, and so the teacher must remove the guesswork from the pronunciation of new vocabulary.
    b. The student may be unfamiliar with technical terminology, figures of speech, "idiosyncratic" word usage, and abbreviations used in textbooks.
    c. Density of unfamiliar and technical vocabulary in the secondary area textbook may create difficulty for the student.
2. Concept density may be a problem for the student since numerous concepts are packed into passages. Often, students must cope with these concepts without a frame of reference or experience from which to draw.
3. The organization of material may create a problem because information is typically presented with little elaboration or embellishment in a format that fragments the material on topical basis.
4. Each subject area has unique characteristics that may pose problems for the student. Each subject area has unique "coding presentation of the material" that the student must be able to readily decipher, for example, graphics in social studies, symbols in math, and diagrams in science.
5. Students may have deficient study skills. Textbooks may not be used effectively because the students may have not been sufficiently instructed in how to have the book work for them. The index and vocabulary definitions may aid a student in searching for information, and the questions at the end of a chapter in history could be used as a study guide for the student. However, the student must know how to use these book parts.

Teachers should provide specific instruction in the efficient use of a textbook. The objective should be that the student approaches the text in a more enlightened manner, viewing it as an aid to learning rather than an obstacle. The student's attitude toward textbooks frequently depends on the teacher's guidance.

Student Learning Style

Learning styles are characteristic cognitive, affective, and psychological behaviors that serve as relatively stable indicators of how learners perceive, interact with, and respond to the learning environment. Learning styles consist of observable behaviors that give clues to the cognitive qualities individuals use to interact with their environment and to gather and process data. Cognitive qualities appear as dualities. Abstract/concrete perception and inductive/deductive processing are two examples. Although these dualities are within everyone, they vary in strength and orientation. This is evident in learning disabled students. Learning environments make adaptive demands upon individuals' cognitive processing qualities. It is essential that learning disabled students in their roles as learners recognize their inherent mediation abilities and the demands being placed upon them so they may accommodate their environment accordingly.

As each student has a unique learning style, so teachers have a teaching style that is uniquely characteristic. Teaching style consists of the teacher's personal behaviors and the media technologies chosen to deliver and receive information. Teachers' energies appear to flow more easily when their natural personalities and teaching styles are parallel (matched). Prolonged periods of matched styles can result in a comfortable "path of least resistance." Teachers' efficiency is influenced by varying degrees of difficulty and frustration when their personal learning styles and teaching styles are mismatched. Teachers of the learning disabled student must be sensitive to "self-style" in the instructional process to enhance the efficacy of individualization of presentation to accommodate the styles of learners. Chronic periods of acute mismatch can result in major mental, emotional, and physical problems if the mismatch is not recognized and dealt with appropriately.

Learning Alternatives

The phenomenon of styles suggests that alternatives be developed that allow for the adaptation of curriculum presentation to the teacher's preferred style. Teachers are then able to maximize affective, cognitive, and psychomotor educational tasks to "fit" their most effective teaching mode as well as the preferred learning mode of the learning disabled student. These adaptations are possible through the exploration of types of learning options feasible within the secondary setting.

An instructional design must include a variety of learning alternatives to facilitate student growth. Learning activities are the proposed educational activities and materials from which students and teachers choose in order to achieve instructional objectives or accomplish educational plans. They are statements of what a student is to do, how he or she is to do it, and what can be done with results or products.

Learning alternatives are created to promote purposeful educational activity of students as they enjoy and learn more about a concept, theme, topic, or skill. Teachers and students must have a variety of activities to choose from in order to maximize individualization. Both teachers and students can create learning alternatives. Teachers develop alternatives as part of an instructional design and in planning and learning situations. Alternative statements should be fully developed and should enable the individual student to know the intent of and the procedures for completion of the alternative.

Alternatives can be created and developed for all ages and levels of ability. Students of some ages and ability levels will require careful explanation of the requirements and intent of the alternative. Learning alternatives are designed to accommodate curriculum intentions and will reflect affective, cognitive, and psychomotor areas of learning.

CURRICULUM MATERIALS: THE SIGNIFICANCE OF STUDENT DIFFERENCES

Alvin Toffler (1964) begins his book *Learning for Tomorrow: The Role of the Future in Education* with these sentences "All education springs from some image of the future. If the image of the future held by a society is grossly inaccurate, its educational system will betray its youth." (p. 3).

Students learn (i.e., benefit from the educational experience) as a function of the following factors:

- intellectual ability
- cognitive ability
- motivation
- experiences
- creativity
- social orientation
- verbal expression
- perceptual-motor skills

The differences in curriculum materials often parallel differences among pupils. The Annehurst Curriculum Classification System (ACCS), jointly developed and implemented by public school and university faculty during a six-year period, is a systematic and practical means of determining the compatibility of pupils and materials.

ACCS describes pupils and available curriculum materials as high or low in ten dimensions:

1. experience
2. intelligence
3. motivation
4. sociability
5. verbal expression
6. auditory perception
7. emotion-personality
8. creativity
9. visual perception
10. motor coordination

Curriculum materials are a prominent feature of classroom instruction with ACCS. Teachers are able to make better use of the materials they already possess and make better decisions about selecting and developing future materials.

INSTRUCTIONAL MATERIALS AND ADAPTATIONS FOR ADOLESCENTS

Most instructional materials available for teaching functional academics to adolescents require adaptation in one or more of the following areas:

1. the relevance of the instructional material to the student's life, i.e., interests, needs, etc.,
2. the readability level and vocabulary used in the instructional material,
3. the prerequisites that must be presented in order for students to use the materials successfully, and
4. modifications necessary to foster interest in the materials.

Readability

Readability is the term used to cover the various aspects of written materials that together determine the reading "difficulty" of a printed page. Readability thus is equated with difficulty. Those texts described as being of "low readability" are easy to read.

Components in readability formula include the following:

- length of sentences
- types of sentences
- complexity of sentences·
- abstractions
- vocabulary
- ambiguity
- polysyllabic words

There are several widely used readability formulae (refer to Fry within this text for example).

Measuring Readability

A method proposed by Aukerman (1972) in *Reading in the Secondary School Classroom* is as follows:

1. Select several representative 500 word samples from each text. If possible, choose samples from the same broad topics.
2. Count the number of actual words in each sample. Try to get them as close as possible.
3. Count the number of sentences in each sample.
4. For each sample, divide the number of words by the number of sentences to obtain the average sentence length.
5. Tally the number of subordinate clauses in each sample.
6. For each sample, tally the number of words of three or more syllables.
7. For each sample, tally the number of words that are found on the lists of words that create reading problems in a specific content area [lists of "impedilaxae" developed by Aukerman, pp. 31–44].
8. For each sample, complete a "readability resume." [An example is shown in Exhibit 1-1.]
9. Compare the readability resumes of all the samples designating each sample as being of "high," "medium" or "low" readability. (p. 42. Reprinted with permission.)

Samples of readability ratings are provided in Table 1-1, and examples of impedilaxae are given in Table 1-2.

A Child-Based Materials Evaluation (CBME)

CBME is an assessment of the worth of an instructional material based on the performance of the actual learners with whom it is intended to be

Exhibit 1-1 Readability Resume Form

Title of Textbook _____

Author(s) _____

Publisher _____ City _____ Copyright yr. _____

Subject matter area _____ Grade _____

Topic _____ Pages _____

Evaluation made by _____ Date _____

For each sample, record the following:

Number of words in selection: _____ Number of sentences _____

Number of words divided by number of sentences = _____ average sentence length

Number of subordinate clauses = _____ × 3 = _____

  (Multiply number of subordinate clauses times three.)

Number of words of three or more syllables = _____

Number of words on the list of impedilaxae = _____ × 5 = _____

                                           (add) _____

                "Weighted readability" total = _____

Source: Reprinted from *Reading in the Secondary School Classroom* by R.C. Aukerman by permission of McGraw-Hill Book Co., © 1972.

Table 1-1 Samples of Readability Ratings

	Book A	Book B	Book C	Book D
Average sentence length	19	23	21	17
Number of subordinate clauses × 3	11 × 3 = 33	20 × 3 = 60	20 × 3 = 60	8 × 3 = 24
Words of three or more syllables	42	53	60	49
Impedilaxae × 5	10 × 5 = 50	23 × 5 = 115	24 × 5 = 120	19 × 5 = 95
	144	251	261	185
Weighted readability level	(low)	(high)	(high)	(medium)

Source: Reprinted from *Reading in the Secondary School Classroom* by R.C. Aukerman by permission of McGraw-Hill Book Co., © 1972.

Table 1-2 Examples of Impedilaxae

Social Studies

aggression	alliance	aristocratic	colonization
aliens	annexation	blockade	hemisphere

English

audience	chronicle	gable	replete
brusque	deduction	knave	timorous

Science

atomic	dehydrated	gamma	magnetic
bacteria	factors	isotope	radiation

Mathematics

adjacent	decimal	segment	vertical
congruent	midpoint	theorem	variable

Vocational Education

advertising	commercial	governmental	occupational
business	economy	liability	placement

Source: Reprinted from *Reading in the Secondary School Classroom* by R. C. Aukerman by permission of McGraw-Hill Book Co., © 1972.

used. It is a short-term assessment tactic that employs a limited number of pupils and affords information on the nature and rate of their learning.

Depending on the specific purpose for which a CBME is intended, the teacher may select either a continuous daily monitoring test or a pre-post test mastery measure. If the purpose is to pinpoint specifically when learning occurs and determine the kinds of changes that will be necessary to make the material work better, a continuous monitoring system should be used. If the purpose is to determine if the material works with a specific group of students, a pre-post test tryout will suffice.

Materials Adaptation: A Three-Step Process

Modifications in instructional materials are made by employing a systematic, three-step adaptation strategy called the Consequence = Stimulus = Response (CSR) strategy. This strategy was identified by Henderson and Rovig (1977) and is described as follows:

Step 1: The teacher changes the reinforcement tactic (C) using the assessment data collected daily to determine if the modification was successful. This step involves the least teacher effort and has the highest probability of gaining results.

Step 2: If step 1 proves unsuccessful (the student appears to be working hard but not improving) the stimulus (S) properties of the materials themselves are modified, usually by providing an additional prompt or cue. Typically, this includes further instructions or demonstration and does not require excess time or effort.

Step 3: Finally, the response (R) the child makes in the materials is modified, usually by breaking down the tasks or improving the sequence of the program. Daily data is once again used to determine the effect of this modification. A positive change in child performance should be observed within three days. If not, the next step of the CSR strategy should be initiated. (Reprinted with permission.)

HOW TO CREATE AN EFFECTIVE CLIMATE FOR LEARNING

Alfred North Whitehead (1949) wrote "What we should aim at is producing [people] who possess both cultural and expert knowledge in some special direction" (p. 13). Stated in contemporary terms, the aim of the educational system is to produce adults who function successfully in their life roles. This goal is achieved through creating a climate for learning in the schools.

Suggestions to allow for a positive, growth-producing learning environment follow:

1. Priorities must be established. Schools are increasingly asked to broaden their scope of educational services while at the same time they are asked to engage in greater individualization. Schools must selectively state those objectives and programs they feel are essential to realizing their philosophy and goals.
2. Educational experiences should be personalized. The standards that are used should be for the guidance of students rather than for normative comparisons.
3. Attempts should be made to build into the curriculum activities and experiences that foster problem-solving skills and reasoning abilities

rather than a reliance on convergent thinking that requires the student to produce the "right" answer.

4. Effective group functioning skills should be taught. With learning disabled adolescents, whose inferential learning is deficient in comparison with their nonhandicapped peers, direct instruction must be provided on those skills necessary to function in the group situations which permeate our society.

5. Adults must accept personal responsibility for the guidance of their youth. As John Dewey (1938) stated:

> It is then the business of the educator to see in what direction an experience is heading. There is no point in his being more mature if, instead of using his greater insight to help organize the condition of the experience of the immature, he throws away his insight.

INSTRUCTIONAL PRACTICES

The American high school seems to stand at a crossroads. In a period of greater flexibility in life styles, the high school curriculum continues in its standardization. As society's problems become more complex, the curriculum remains rooted in minimum competencies and subject areas. Student electives diminish while life choices are on the rise.

The authors have suggested that curriculum planning is an attempt to assist students prepare for their life roles as consumers, producers, family members, citizens, and learners. Curriculum planning is also a response to current social pressures and social influences. The results of a study undertaken by Tubbs and Beane (1981) indicate that, while many forces attempt to influence the high schools, the curricular decision making is still largely a building level responsibility. Any change in high school curriculum will need support if not actual initiation by teachers and administrators.

The Lecture

One of the most prevalent methods of presenting instruction at the secondary level is through the lecture. The lecture has decided advantages that include the following:

• The lecture is an effective way to introduce a unit or build a frame of reference (Kyle, 1972).

- The lecture is a superior technique for demonstrating models and clarifying methods that are confusing to students (Thompson, 1974).
- The lecture is superior in its ability to set the atmosphere or focus for students' activities (Haley, 1972).
- The lecture is effective for introducing and summarizing the major concepts presented in a lesson.
- The lecture is useful for collecting related information into a manageable framework.

The lecture method also has some disadvantages that include the following:

- The lecture is not an effective method for stimulating interest, promoting creativity, or helping students develop responsibility.
- The lecture is not a good vehicle for assisting students to develop good synthesizing skills.
- The lecture is only effective for immediate cognitive gain.
- The lecture is significantly less effective for retention over a period of three weeks or later (Lucas, Postman, & Thompson, 1975).

Improving Lecture Effectiveness

The lecture continues to be the most extensively used teaching style at the high school. In addition to adapting the lecture to the individual student's learning style and modifying it through introducing listening guides and organizational aids, the teacher can significantly increase the lecture's effectiveness through the manner in which it is presented.

Suggestions to be considered by the teacher in delivering the lecture include:

- Mix the lecture with modeling demonstrations.
- Blend tutorials with lectures.
- Individualize the audio-tutorial for students with lower abilities.
- Build in student participation for relevancy and meaningfulness.

Henson (1971) provides additional information about the lecture.

Teaching Thinking Skills

Frequently, the literature about the goals of effective teaching states, "It is the goal of teachers to make their pupils successfully functioning learners independent from their instructors." Effectiveness implies facilitating the development of students who have the necessary skills to continue as learners throughout their lives within a formal educational setting and as adults functioning within society. Further, it implies that students engage in efficient and effective higher order cognitive processes (refer to Bloom's Taxonomy, 1956) such as the ability to transfer and generalize, analyze and evaluate, etc. Teachers should not assume that the evolution from lower to higher order thinking occurs automatically or inferentially. This assumption, in particular, should not be made about the learning disabled adolescent.

Problem Solving

The literature suggests that a systematic approach to the task of solving a problem has a direct correlation with increased effectiveness in problem solving. There are many methods and strategies proposed. One suggested step-by-step prescriptive method is offered by Nickerson (1981) as follows:

A Prescription for Problem Solving

1. Read and reread the problem carefully.
2. State the goal in your own terms.
3. List in short, declarative sentences the facts that are (explicitly or implicitly) given.
4. Try to make a picture (table, graph, diagram) that represents the known facts and relationships.
5. Try to infer some additional facts or relationships from those that are given; add to the list and incorporate it in the picture.
6. Determine what additional information would be sufficient to reach a solution; see if that information can be inferred.
7. Try to infer something about the solution (for example, it must be positive; it must be less than s; it cannot be y).
8. If it is a numerical problem, try extreme cases (for example, solve for o, 1, oo).
9. If you're stuck, try to find another way to think about the problem, generalize it; particularize it.
10. If you're still stuck, try to solve a similar but simpler problem.
11. If you're still stuck, do something else for awhile.
12. Check your work. (p. 23. Reprinted with permission.)

The cognitive skills necessary to solve a problem include:

1. Problem identification. In order to solve a problem, a student must be able to accurately identify the problem requiring resolution. The terminal goal must be identified, i.e., the problem in its entirety—not simply a facet of the whole—must be addressed, and the point at which the problem is solved must be determined.
2. Process selection. A student must be able to identify those activities that will yield an accurate resolution. This implies a reliance on relevant data and an ability to distinguish relevant activities from irrelevant ones.
3. Information encoding. The task here is to translate the information deemed relevant into a form so that it has a utilitarian value to the problem solver. Categorization, symbolic representation, concrete models, etc. are examples of varying form options.
4. Process sequencing. Sequencing involves the order of activities the problem solver will use in progressing toward problem resolution. The order of steps taken is as essential (most often) to an effective solution as is the process itself.
5. Process monitoring. Engaging in systematic assessments of the efficacy of each step (activity) undertaken enhances the potential for success. The student is able to pinpoint ineffectual actions more readily and attempt options with minimal loss of time. Ongoing monitoring with careful data collection also serves as an objective reference in reviewing steps and as a model for future activity in a similar sphere.
6. Feedback adjustment. Adjusting the approach on the basis of data that has been analyzed and evaluated expedites and maximizes effort.
7. Solution evaluation. It is important to validate the solution arrived at. The manner in which this is accomplished obviously relates to the specific type of problem undertaken.

In addition to the specific suggestions for enhancing the student's learning potential through a refinement and focus of his or her cognitive and processing skills, it is important (as in all aspects of educating the learning disabled adolescent) to ascertain how the student feels about the learning situation. Fox, Luszki, and Schmuck (1966) offer a model for evaluating the student's perception of the learning environment.

SUMMARY

This chapter has presented pragmatic methodologies and strategies for the secondary mainstream teacher to meet the significant challenge of educating learning disabled adolescents.

The material presented is predicated upon the belief that teachers' effectiveness in instructing the learning disabled student can be greatly enhanced. The authors have suggested that the key to teacher success with the learning disabled adolescent entails an understanding of the characteristics of the learning disabled student, an awareness of adolescent developmental tasks and needs, and a broad repertoire of interventions and strategies that would enable the teacher to accommodate instruction to the individual learning style of the student.

This chapter has sought to provide the teachers with an arsenal of relevant methods, materials, and recommendations to enhance the teacher's role as an engineer of the learning environment.

ANNOTATED BIBLIOGRAPHY

Arena, John. *How to Write an IEP with Pertinent Sections of PL 94-142 Having Relevancy for Teachers and Parents.* Academic Therapy Publications. Novato, CA, 1978.

This guidebook, with pertinent sections of Public Law 94-142, was developed to help special education teachers and others working with the learning disabled to know what is required under the law and "how to do it." Parents as well will find it useful in gaining an understanding of how an Individualized Education Program (IEP) is prepared, and the sequence of tasks required to properly state educational goals, short-term objectives, and evaluation procedures.

Council for Exceptional Children. *Implementing Procedural Safeguards— PL 94-142.* Association Drive, Reston, VA.

The intent of this media package is to provide a practical guide to administrators, parents, teachers, advocacy groups, and other interested groups of professional and lay persons in meeting the requirements of PL 94-142 as they pertain to the education, identification, evaluation, and placement of handicapped children.

DeWitt, Frances B. *Our Educational Challenge—Specific Learning Disabled Adolescents.* Academic Therapy Publications. Novato, CA, 1977.

This book was written to give teachers of secondary learning disabled students a solid foundation upon which to base their efforts to reach these teenagers. The substance of the program is presented in the section entitled "The Special Program." "Learning efficiency," "movement efficiency," and "communication efficiency" are all treated in detail. A final section offers a potpourri of techniques for using various materials and equipment.

Foundation for Exceptional Children. *Individualized Education Programs for Handicapped Children.*

This media package reviews the complete IEP process—from explaining the related components of PL 94-142, through assessment, monitoring, and administrative procedures. It was designed to help people meet federal legal requirements and to facilitate the development and writing of IEPs by portraying the participation of teachers, administrators, parents, and children in this process.

Greenberger, Sue M. *Second S.T.E.P.—Sequential Testing and Educational Programming for the Secondary Student.* Academic Therapy Publications. Novato, CA, 1977.

This program is designed to help teachers create IEPs for secondary students with learning difficulties. It identifies over 200 specific areas of ability, organizes them developmentally, and translates them into specific goals and objectives. The program also tells how to test and remediate each of the specific areas and presents over 650 commercially available materials and correlates them with the program goals and objectives.

Kronick, Doreen. *Three Families.* Academic Therapy Publications. Novato, CA.

These three case studies offer an inside look at three different families with learning disabled children. Through the case study approach, the author explores the relationship between learning disabled children and their parents and traces the social and intellectual growth of the children. Written from a perspective within the home, the book provides valuable insights into the relationship between family dynamics and learning disabilities.

Kronick, Doreen. *They Too Can Succeed: A Practical Guide for Parents of Learning Disabled Children.* Academic Therapy Publications. Novato, CA, 1969.

This book is useful to parents of learning disabled children since it is written by mothers of learning disabled children who are also leaders in the field of learning disabilities. This text takes a parent-to-parent approach to the problems of raising a child with special learning needs and provides practical advice on solving daily family problems.

Kronick, Doreen. *What About Me? The LD Adolescent.* Academic Therapy Publications. Novato, CA, 1975.

This is a manual concerned with every facet of the learning disabled adolescent's experience. Self-concepts, family, education, vocation, sex, interpersonal relationships, and emotional growth are discussed in depth, with empathy and a profound understanding of the educationally handicapped youth's plight.

Megen, Edward L. (ed.) Edmark Associates. *IBAS Objective Cluster Banks*. (Instruction-Based Appraisal System), 1976.

This collection of goals and objectives is designed to save teachers time. Although it is not a curriculum, the volumes contain objectives common to most curricula. By first identifying student deficits and needs and then locating the appropriate goals and objectives clusters, a teacher is provided with a starting point for planning.

Roberts, Joseph, and Hawk, Bonnie. *Legal Rights Primer for the Handicapped: In and Out of the Classroom*. Academic Therapy Publications. Novato, CA.

The authors put together a book that stipulates what the handicapped are entitled to and clarifies, in straightforward language, the vagaries and complexities of the law. It includes a lucid summary of §504 and the complete text of PL 94-142.

Rosenthal, Joseph H. *Hazy . . .? Crazy? and/or Lazy . . .? The Maligning of Children with Learning Disabilities*. Academic Therapy Publications, Novato, CA.

In this highly readable book, Dr. Rosenthal discusses the history, present status, therapies, and research relating to learning disabilities. He also describes concepts he has established through his clinical research, teaching, and consulting experiences with 2,500 learning disabled children.

School, Beverly, and Cooper, Arlene. *The IEP Primer*, Revised/Expanded. Academic Therapy Publications. Novato, CA, 1981.

This guide provides information on how to formulate an IEP meeting, how to write agreed-upon goals, and how to implement IEPs that are truly individualized. The authors have included sample IEPs and a section that answers sticky "What if" questions. The guide also includes checklists for skill acquisition in reading and math that will help the teacher select and design an appropriate curriculum for each student.

Stanfield, J., and Adams, B. *Hello Everybody!* Opportunity for Learning, Inc. Pasadena, CA, 1977.

This introduction to mainstreaming for children, teachers, and parents provides a compassionate and gentle approach to the problems of those children who may be rejoining their classmates as a result of PL 94-142. The material is suited for teachers, IEP workshops, and parent education programs.

REFERENCES

Aukerman, R.C. *Reading in the secondary school classroom.* New York: McGraw-Hill Book Co., 1972.

Bailey, E. Academic activities for adolescents. Evergreen, Colorado: Learning Pathways, 1975.

Bloom, B.S. et al. (Eds.). *Taxonomy of educational objectives: Cognitive domain.* New York: David McKay Company, Inc., 1956.

Cawley, J.F., Fitzmaurice, A.M., Goodstein, M.A., Lepore, A.U., Sedlak, R., and Althans, V. *Project math. Level I.* Tulsa, Okla.: Educational Progress, A Division of Educational Development Corp., 1976.

Combs, A.W. An educational imperative: the humane dimension. In M. Seobey and G. Graham (Eds.), *To Nature Humaness: Commitment for the 70's.* Washington, D.C.: Assoc. for Supervision and Curriculum Development; National Education Assoc., 1970.

Cornbleth, C. Curriculum materials can make a difference. *Educational Leadership,* 1981, *39*(7), 567–568.

Dewey, J. *Experience and Education.* New York: MacMillan Publishing Co., Inc., 1938.

Esminger, E.E. A Handbook on secondary programs for the learning disabled adolescent: some guidelines. U.S. Govt. Printing Office (ERIC Document Reproduction Services, No. 102454).

Fox, R., Luszki, M.B., & Schmuck, R. *Diagnosing Classroom Learning Environments.* Chicago: Science Research Associates, Inc., 1966.

Goodman, L., & Mann, L. *Learning Disabilities in the Secondary School: Issues and Practices.* New York: Grune & Stratton, 1976.

Haley, J.H., Lalonde, E., & Rovin, S. An assessment of the lecture. *Improving College and University Teaching,* 1972, *22,* 326–327.

Havinghurst, R. *Developmental Tasks and Education.* New York: Longmans, Green, 1952.

Henderson, H., & Rovig, T. Evaluating, selecting, and adapting instructional materials: a critical teaching competency. *NSPL Journal,* July, 1977, pp. 18–23.

Henson, K.T. Improving courses in methods of teaching. *Schools and Society,* 1971, *9,* 236, 413–415.

Herber, H. *Teaching Reading in Content Areas* (2nd ed). Englewood Cliffs, N.J.: Prentice-Hall, Inc., 1978.

Hobbs, N. (Ed.). Issues in the Classification of Children. (Vols. 1 and 2) San Francisco: Jossey-Bass, Inc., Pubs., 1975.

Hugh, J.B., & Duncan, J.K. *Teaching: Description and Analysis.* Reading, Mass.: Addison-Wesley Publishing Co., Inc., 1970.

Jackson, P.W. The way teaching is. *N.E.A. Journal,* 1965, *54,* 10–13.

Kirk, S.A. *Educating Exceptional Children.* Geneva, Ill.: Houghton-Mifflin Co., 1962.

Kirk, S.A. *Educating Exceptional Children* (2nd ed.). Geneva, Ill: Houghton-Mifflin Co., 1972.

Kyle, B. In Defense of the Lecture. *Improving College and University Teaching,* 1972, *20,* 325.

Leichter, H.J. *The Concept of Educative Style.* Unpublished paper, 1972.

Lerner, J.W. *Children with Learning Disabilities* (2nd ed.) Boston: Houghton-Mifflin Co., 1976.

Martin, E.W. Some thoughts on mainstreaming. *Exceptional Children*, 1974, *41*, 150–153.

Morasky, R.L. Learning Experiences in Educational Psychology, Unit 9. Dubuque, Iowa: William C. Brown Co., 1973.

Nazzaro, J. Comprehension assessment for educational planning. In F.J. Weintraub et al. (Eds.) *Public Policy and the Education of Exceptional Children*. Reston, Va.: Council for Exceptional Children, 1976.

NEA Resolution 73-33: Education for all Handicapped Children. *Todays Education*, 1977, *66* (4), 52.

Nickerson, R.S. Thoughts on Teaching Thinking. *Educational Leadership*, 1981, *39* (1), 22.

Rollins, S.P., & Unruh, A. *Introduction to Secondary Education*. Chicago: Rand-McNally, 1964.

Rogers, C.R. *Freedom to Learn*. Columbus, Ohio: Charles E. Merrill Publishing Co., 1969.

Simon, S., & Bellanca, J. (Eds.) *Degrading the Grading Myths: A Primer of Alternatives to Grades and Marks*. Washington, D.C.: Association for Supervision and Curriculum Development, 1976.

Smith, F. *Comprehension and Learning: A Conceptual Framework for Teaching*. New York: Holt, Rinehart & Winston, Inc., 1973.

Stiles, L.J., McCleary, L.E., & Turnbaugh, R.C. *Secondary Education in the United States*. New York: Harcourt, Brace & World, 1962.

Taba, H. *Teachers Handbook for the Elementary School Social Studies*. Palo Alto, Calif.: Addison-Wesley Publishing Co., Inc., 1967.

Toffler, A. *Learning for Tomorrow: The Role of the Future in Education*. New York: Vintage Books, 1974.

Thomas, M.D. Variables of educational excellence. *The Clearing House*, 1981, *54* (6), 251–253.

Thompson, R. Legitimate lecturing. *Improving College and University Teaching*, 1974, *22*, 163–164.

Tubbs, M., & Beane, J. Curricular trends and practices in the high school: a second look. *The High School Journal*, 1981, *64* (5), 203–208.

The Education of Adolescents: The Final Report and Recommendations of the National Panel on High School and Adolescent Education. U.S. Department of Health, Education, and Welfare. Publication No. (OE) 76-00004. Washington, D.C.: U.S. Government Printing Office, 1976.

U.S. Office of Education. Assistance to states: procedures for evaluating specific learning disabilities. *Federal Register*, 1977, *42*, 65082-65085.

Weiss, H., & Weiss, M. *A Survival Manual: Case Studies and Suggestions for the Learning Disabled Teenager*. Great Barrington, Mass.: Treehouse Associates, 1974.

Whitehead, A. N. *The Aims of Education*. New York: New American Library, 1949.

SUGGESTED READINGS

Berauer, M., & Jackson, J. Review of school psychology for 1973. *Professional Psychologist*, 1974, *5*, 155–165.

Brown, V. A basic q-sheet for analyzing and comparing curriculum materials and proposals. *Journal of Learning Disabilities*, 1975, *7*, 10–17.

Bruner, J. *The Process of Education*. Cambridge: Harvard University Press, 1960.

Burton, W.H. Basic principles in a good teaching-learning situation. *Phi Delta Kappan*, 1958, *39*, 424–448.

Conant, J.B. *The American High School Today*. New York: McGraw-Hill Book Co., 1959.

Douglass, H.R. *Secondary Education in the United States* (2nd ed). New York: The Ronald Press, 1964.

Frymier, J. *Annehurst Curriculum Classification System*. West Lafayette, Indiana: Kappa Delta Press, 1977.

Grant, W.V., & Lind, C.G. *Digest of Educational Statistics*. Washington, D.C.: HEW (OE), 1974.

Hunt, L., Jr., & Sheldon, W.D. Characteristics of the reading of a group of ninth-grade pupils, *School Review*, 1950, 58(6), 348–353.

Lucas, L.A., Postman, C.H., & Thompson, S.C. Comparative study of retention used in simulation gaming as opposed to lecture-discussion techniques. *Peabody Journal of Education*, July 1975, p. 261.

Shane, H. A curriculum for the new century. *Phi Delta Kappan*, 1981, *62* (5).

Simon, H.A. Problem solving and education. In D.T. Tuma & F. Feif (Eds.), *Problem Solving and Education: Issues in Teaching and Research*. Hillsdale, N.J.: Lawrence Eribaum Associates, 1980.

Whimbey, A. Students can learn to be better problem solvers. *Educational Leadership*, 1980, *37*, 560–562.

Chapter 2

Effective Teaching and Learning Strategies for the Learning Disabled Adolescent in the Mainstream

In order for the mainstream teacher to succeed with the learning disabled student, it is important that the elements in the teaching-learning process be tailored for each student with regard to his or her learning needs.

The teacher has the task of creating a climate that enables the integrated learning disabled student to succeed while concomitantly providing effective instruction to the entire class.

This chapter provides the teacher with material relating to each of the elements in the teaching process:

- a guide to effective decision making
- mastery learning in the classroom
- developmental and remedial strategies
- program alternatives in the secondary school
- the teacher as a change agent
- classroom instructional strategies

The authors' presentation of the material is predicated on the premise that teaching is a dynamic/interactive process and that in addition to the teacher having competence in the content matter and delivery of instruction, the manner in which the discrete elements are integrated is also of significance.

Upon completion of this chapter, teachers should be able to enhance the degree of their instructional effectiveness with learning disabled students as well as these students' nonhandicapped peers.

THE TEACHING-LEARNING PROCESS

Classroom Teaching Skills

Smith (1960) defines teaching as "a system of actions intended to induce learning" (p. 230). Learning is often defined as a process by which behavior is either modified or changed through experience or training.

A teacher's effectiveness as a facilitator of other's learning is dependent upon a knowledge of the major variables that influence the success of the teaching-learning process. This process involves the student, the environment, and the teacher in an interactive relationship.

It is the teacher who has the responsibility of bringing together the student and the task within a classroom climate conducive to effective learning. Toward this goal the teacher effects outcomes through an ongoing series of decisions.

The Teacher as Decision Maker

Each decision a teacher makes is inherently integrated with other decisions. Hunter (1971) suggests that the following list of interrelated decisions be considered.

1. "What learning task can the student handle at the entry stage in his learning?
2. "What learner behavior is relevant to the task and to the learner's characteristics?
3. "What is the primary instructional objective of the lesson?
4. "What principles of learning can a teacher apply to the learning task?
5. "What modifications does a particular learner require?
6. "How can a teacher use his competencies and personality to translate teaching decisions into effective action?
7. "What is the best method to accomplish the instructional objective?
8. "How will a teacher synthesize the preceding decisions into the teacher-learning process?
9. "How successful was the teaching-learning process?
10. "What happens now?" (Reprinted with permission.)

A Guide for Decision Making

The following list provides a ten-point guide to the teaching-learning process:

1. Determine the student's entry level of behavior relative to the academic task through teacher-made criterion-referenced pretests (refer to testing section).
2. Ascertain what specific student behaviors are necessary to the successful completion of the presented task through a task analysis approach.
3. State clearly and precisely in behavioral terms (measurable and observable) the primary objective of the lesson.
4. Decide which principles of learning should be applied to the task.
5. Relate the student's learning style to the task (i.e., prefers quiet setting, works better independently, etc.).
6. Adapt the lesson to the particular student's needs. Adjust the task, manner of presentation, mode of response, classroom climate, etc. to meet the adolescent's need for competence, power, or independence.
7. Consider your personality in relation to the student's learning style and the task.
8. Determine and apply the method deemed most effective to attain the stated objective.
9. Group students where commonalities in style and level of functioning exist. Apply one of the personality questionnaire inventories suggested in addition to measures of academic functioning.
10. Use an evaluation plan that reliably measures the success of the teaching-learning process and apply this information to adjust subsequent lessons.

In attempting to evaluate the efficacy of the lesson, the teacher should keep detailed notes on both his or her behavior in addition to the student's behavior during the lesson.

Particular note of the following should be made:

1. Did the teaching focus on a particular learning target?
2. Was the objective appropriate for the particular group of students?
3. Was the objective achieved?
4. What problems arose during the lessons? How were these problems dealt with?
5. In what ways could the lesson be improved?

Theoretical Foundations of Teaching-Learning Decisions

Specific recommendations extracted from Piaget's and Ausubel's theories of learning are offered as an additional guide for the teacher.

Each of the theorists addresses the motivation of the learner, the method of presentation, and the nature of the task. However, in the final analysis, it is the teacher's task to synthesize the information into an effective teaching-learning process.

Piaget (1964) states:

1. Be conscious of the developmental level of the learner.
2. Analyze tasks within the curriculum to determine the level of reasoning required for successful solution of each task.
3. Motivate learners by emphasizing problems and trying to jolt them out of their ordinary way of looking at things.
4. Whenever possible have learners perform some relevant physical action on an object (concrete learning). (Reprinted with permission.)

Ausubel (1960) says,

1. Learning new knowledge will be meaningful to the degree that the learner can relate it to the ideas that she already understands.
2. Good intent on the part of the learner ensures the probability that learning will be meaningful.
3. A good strategy, for both you and your students, that reduces the possibility of rote learning is to adopt the practice of constantly paraphrasing new ideas. This exercise will encourage you and your students to concentrate on the substance of the material rather than on its literal meaning.
4. Organize lessons according to the process of progressive differentiation, moving from the general to the specific.
5. Help the learner discriminate between old and new ideas.
6. Relate concepts and principles presented early in the course to those ideas presented later in the course. (Reprinted with permission.)

The teacher facilitates and guides the learning process through the activities planned and implemented for the learner. Objectives, i.e., stating what is to be accomplished in behavioral terms, are the key to effectiveness.

Instructional Objectives

Objectives provide guidelines for making decisions about the selection of student activities. As part of instructional designs, objectives should:

- reflect the desired intentions and outcomes of a school's faculty and students;
- be based upon the beliefs and values a school faculty holds regarding students, the society, and the world, the nature and sources of subject matter, how human beings learn, and other areas that affect curriculum and instructional decisions;
- be developed and written by teachers and students, or they can be secured from objective banks;
- be based on a humanistic approach, that is, objectives should reflect what is important for and needed by a particular student group and should be written to include opportunities for growth in the affective, cognitive, and psychomotor areas of learning;
- be designed and arranged so that students can choose from alternative objectives, i.e., learning task levels, scopes, presentation methods, etc.;
- communicate to students what is expected of them, thus eliminating an element of game playing from the instructional process;
- help teachers set levels of classroom performance, based on student ability, age, and content or subject areas;
- help teachers to reflect on the worth and feasibility of content to be taught and the appropriateness of a particular instructional process for teaching that content;
- improve procedures for assessing student growth since assessment procedures flow directly from instructional processes;
- help manage student progress within an individualized classroom;
- provide motivation through the establishment of objectives with a clear goal; and
- ensure accountability for the performance of both the students and the teachers.

Objectives are easily grouped (bound) into a scope of instruction if they are carefully selected within the cognitive or affective hierarchy structures of the relative domain or within the skill structure of the subject matter.

Unit Development

A unit may be considered an organizational pattern of sequential activities geared to develop the understanding of specified relationships that yield to generalizations. A unit may be broken down into the following three components:

1. Objectives. The objectives establish the guideposts for the unit in terms of specific skills as well as the ultimate achievement of generalizations.
2. Activities. Selection of appropriate activities depends to some extent upon the receptivity of students, available resources, and teacher judgment.
3. Evaluation. This should measure the degree of fulfillment of the stated objectives.

Generalization of Learning

In addition, in the development of units of study the transfer of student learning to new situations should be stressed. The formation of generalizations should take into account the nature of the adolescent's learning disability.

It is important that the student's generalization capacity be measured through testing his or her ability to verbally express the generalization, provide explanations, predict outcomes given factual data and events, and apply generalizations to a new situation. Opportunities for the development of generalizations should be offered as a culminating experience and should be integrated within every instructional unit wherever possible.

MASTER LEARNING: A MODEL FOR SYNTHESIZING THE ELEMENTS IN THE TEACHING-LEARNING PROCESS

Bloom (1968) defined mastery for a subject area in terms of specific instructional objectives that students are expected to achieve by the course's completion. The subject is broken down into a number of smaller learning units, and objectives are defined for those units whose mastery is essential for mastery of the subject's major objectives.

The units, taught by usual classroom procedures, are supplemented with feedback and corrective procedures, and brief diagnostic tests are administered at each unit's completion.

Each test covers all of a particular unit's objectives and reveals what a student has learned from instruction for that unit.

Morasky (1971, 1973) suggests a systems process of program development in learning disabilities.

A Mastery Learning Approach

Bloom (1968) states that "most students (perhaps over 90%) can master what we have to teach them" (p. 2). An outline of Bloom's mastery learning strategy is as follows:

1. The course is broken down into small units covering one or two weeks of instruction.
2. The instructional objectives are clearly specified for each unit.
3. The learning tasks within each unit are taught using regular group instruction.
4. Diagnostic tests (formative tests) are administered at the end of each learning unit to determine whether each student has mastered the unit and, if not, what he still has to do to master it.
5. Specific procedures for correcting learning deficiencies, such as working with other students in small groups, rereading specific pages, and using programmed materials and audio-visual aids, as well as additional learning time are prescribed for those who did not achieve unit mastery. Retesting may be done after the corrective study.
6. When the units are completed, a final test (summative test) is administered to determine course grades. All students who perform at or above the predetermined mastery level receive a grade of A in the course. However, grades are also assigned on the basis of absolute standards that have been set for the course. (Reprinted with permission.)

Block (1973) has stated that mastery learning programs develop students' positive interests, positive attitudes toward the subjects in which they are used, and greater confidence in their ability to learn.

Instructional Assignments: A Guide for Effectiveness

The teacher should communicate the learning task to be completed by the student and the expected student outcome in every assignment. This is accomplished by adhering to the following guidelines:

- Provide an example of the task and related outcome that is common to the experiences of all class members.
- Present the assignment diagrammatically. This is very important for learning disabled adolescents who lack the essential cognitive strategy necessary for completing the task successfully.
- Restate the assignment by providing an explanation of why the task is to be completed and then discussing what is to be done.
- Use demonstration techniques for clarification purposes.
- Use illustrations (diagrams and pictures to clarify techniques).

Table 2-1 Classifying Students for Instructional Purposes

Learner Classification	Functioning Level	Educational Strategy	Curriculum Selection
Developmental	Nonfunctional to low fourth grade level	Continued presentation of basic skills: mastery of basic math and language skills.	Core curriculum for math and/or language skills
Remedial	Solid fourth to sixth grade level	Remediation of gaps in knowledge and skills while boosting achievement to the integration level.	Core curriculum, particular attention to pretest information, supplementary material for specific skill development tied to specific skills sequences.

Source: Reprinted from *Learning Disabilities in the Secondary School: Issues and Practices* by L. Goodman and L. Mann by permission of Grune and Stratton, © 1976.

Denton and Matheny (1980) offer additional suggestions and discussion on instructional assignments.

Effective instruction involves an appropriate diagnosis of the student's academic, cognitive and affective levels of functioning. One approach classifies students based on their academic functioning level as learners requiring either a developmental or a remedial instructional approach. Goodman and Mann (1976) offer a model that compares developmental and remedial instructional approaches as shown in Table 2-1.

In Goodman and Mann's model, remedial approaches are suggested for those students who are functioning from a fourth to a sixth grade level irrespective of the student's chronological age or grade placement.

REMEDIATION WITHIN THE SECONDARY CLASSROOM

Remediation or remedial teaching refers to those activities, techniques, and practices that are directed primarily at strengthening or eliminating the basic source(s) of a weakness or a deficiency that interferes with a student's learning. The focus is on changing the learner in some way so that he or she may more effectively relate to the educational program as it is provided and administered for all students.

This approach differs from accommodation and compensatory teaching that refer to a process whereby the learning environment of the student (either some of the elements or the total environment) is modified to promote learning. The focus is on changing the learning environment or the academic requirements so that the student may learn in spite of a fundamental weakness or deficiency. This may involve the use of modified instructional techniques, more flexible administrative practices, modified academic requirements, etc.

It is important in either approach used that the adolescent student be actively involved in both the design as well as the implementation of the program. The school counselor is a valuable resource to provide significant complementary services to the student and his teachers through:

- assistance with the transition to secondary classrooms
- referral to community services
- consulting/collaborating with the mainstream teacher
- providing vocational, postsecondary, and career information to assist the student in making informed choices
- assisting parents, students, and teachers with related aspects of testing

Principles for the Establishment of an Effective Remedial System

In order for an effective remedial approach to be implemented in the secondary schools, the following eight basic principles should be considered in the planning of the program design:

1. Every effort should be made to identify the learning disabled students as early in their formal education as possible. The earlier the attempted remediation of specific learning problems, the more potentially effective are the interventions.
2. The attempt should be made to establish a direct relationship between assessment data and instructional practices and materials.
3. Diagnosis should be undertaken with an objective of providing instructional information rather than simply a "label."
4. Remedial efforts should be predicated on specified skill deficits that preclude a student's learning success. Task analysis is an important requisite to the process.
5. The focus and evaluative measures should be on a criterion basis.
6. Peer tutors should be used where possible.
7. Nonteaching staff (volunteers, parents, aides) should be used to supplement the teacher's services.

8. Develop objective banks to aid the teacher in pinpointing specific remediation skill areas. Morasky and Johnson (1977) offer additional suggestions.

Compensatory Strategies

According to Marsh, Gearheart, and Gearheart (1978), learning modification employing a compensatory approach is: "A process whereby learning environment of the student, either some of the elements or the total environment, is modified to promote learning" (p. 85).

Some of the possibilities of learning modifications include:

- Supplemental prosthetic devices can be used to compensate for skills that are either absent in the learning disabled student or of a problematic nature. Such devices include calculators to aid students' computational skills and tape recorders to enable review and/or reinforcement of lecture presentations.
- Course requirements for the learning disabled students should be selectively chosen with consideration of the degree of abstraction required in the subject matter, prerequisite skills required, class size and class composition.
- Modifications can be made in test-taking. Allowances can be made for projects instead of reports, oral instead of written tests, group tests, etc.
- Material can be modified through varying instructional techniques (manner of presentation/mode of response) and adjusting the amount of material presented.

Smith and Payne (1980) offer additional suggestions.

Both compensation and remediation efforts have as a common element the attempt to individualize instruction such that each student is able to derive maximal learning possible from an instructional unit.

The Learning Activity Packet

One technique which has been found effective in further promoting individualization is the learning activity packet (LAP). This is suggested as an extremely useful tool in enhancing the delivery of instruction to learning disabled students. The LAP provides relevant materials and activities in package form and is typically written to cover a unit of work. It allows students opportunities for review and reinforcement on an individual basis.

The LAP is made up of the following six components:

1. an introduction to let students know what is expected, what the terminal task is, and what materials will be made available to them,
2. student objectives that state the terminal task in behavioral terms,
3. a list of appropriate reading selections from varied multilevel texts,
4. a list of available library materials on the subject,
5. a list of required and optional activities, and
6. an evaluation section.

For the learning disabled student, LAPs should include:

- achievable tasks that should be based on the teacher's knowledge of the student's learning strengths and weaknesses,
- simple, concise, readable directions that delineate a sequence of actions for the student,
- manipulative activities that reduce the degree of abstraction through the use of concrete models to assist learning disabled students in comprehending the concepts offered, and
- immediate reinforcement that provides students with feedback about their performance as immediately as possible following task completion in order to minimize errors, enhance motivation, and help build feelings of success.

Some advantages of LAPs include:

- The LAP gives each student a chance to work at his or her own speed.
- It enables the student to experience a feeling of accomplishment as each packet is completed.
- Once developed, the LAP is available for use by any child needing the extra work on the particular concept.
- The LAP can meet the needs of students functioning at different levels within the mainstream class.

The LAP is but one suggestion from among countless possibilities for providing individualized instruction.

LEARNING-RELATED BEHAVIORS IN THE SECONDARY SCHOOL

The teacher's task is to enhance the student's ability to benefit from the learning experience. Teachers can significantly influence specific student behaviors that relate to learning. These behaviors include review, note taking, underlining, questioning, and goal setting.

Review

For the adolescent with a learning disability it is important to review previously presented material prior to the presentation of new concepts. It is not uncommon for teachers to lament that students have forgotten what they appeared to have mastered the previous day. The practice of using review provides students with a sense of security in knowing that there will be opportunities for the material to be re-presented. It gives students additional opportunities to ask questions or gain greater understanding of the concepts. The authors' experience has indicated that spaced reviews result in greater retention than consecutive reviews.

The mode of review is as important as the temporal spacing. When students are asked to paraphrase information rather than simply recite material, their retention is enhanced. Paraphrasing requires that students "translate" the material into their own vocabularies, and the more personal articulation of the information makes its retention greater. Refer to Kurth and Moseley (1978) and Pio and Andre (1977) for additional reading on this issue.

Note Taking

The most prevalent mode of presenting academic instruction at the secondary level is the lecture. Students listening to the presentations must in some manner "capture" the important ideas and concepts presented. The teacher may provide a lecture outline with main ideas stated, and the student is responsible only for adding additional information. This approach enables the student to attend to the total lecture rather than to be preoccupied with selectively attending to only a portion. It has been documented that students who take notes during a lecture or while reading remember more than students who do not take notes (Carrier & Titas, 1979).

The teacher should provide direct instruction to the learning disabled students in how to effectively take notes. In this instruction, the quality of the note taking should be stressed. "More is not necessarily better" applies as a guide toward efficient note taking. In fact, Howe (1970) found that the fewer words it takes a student to place information into notes, the better the recall. Teachers may prompt effective note taking by providing the student with key terms or phrases that indicate important information that should be included in the student's notes.

Underlining

Student learning is facilitated if students underline important and relevant information (Richards & August, 1975). It is preferable that the student utilize the course textbook. However, if this is impossible, teacher-prepared study guides and abstracts may be substituted.

Questioning

Anderson and Biddle (1975) suggest that the teacher "ask questions during the course of instruction about each point that is important for students to master rather than depend upon a general, indirect consequence from questioning " (p. 92).

Goal Setting: A Student Guide

It is important that students have goals toward which to orient their behavior. Frequently, students experience anxiety or frustration because they have set goals (expectations) for themselves that are beyond their capacities. Students may set goals that are significantly below their potential because of low self-esteem, or they may set goals significantly beyond their capabilities because of parental pressure, group influence, or unrealistic insights. Teachers can assist these students in establishing viable goals.

A guide adapted from Sharp and Cox (1970) offers the following eight suggestions. A goal must be:

1. *Conceivable.* The student must be able to conceptualize the goal so that it is understandable and then identify clearly what the first step or two would be.
2. *Believable.* The student must believe he can reach the goal, and it should be consistent with his own personal value system.
3. *Achievable.* The goals the student sets must be accomplishable with his given strengths and abilities.
4. *Controllable.* If the student's goal includes the involvement of anyone else, he should first obtain the permission of the other person or persons involved.
5. *Measurable.* The goal must be stated so that it is measurable in time and quantity.
6. *Desirable.* The goal should be something he wants to do.
7. *Stated with No Alternative.* He should set one goal at a time.

8. *Growth-Facilitating*. The goal should never be destructive to
   the student, to others, or to society. (pp. 229–241. Reprinted
   with permission.)

In order to attain their goals, students must learn how to use time
effectively. Secondary learning disabled students frequently do not reach
their potential due to poor study habits, inefficient learning methods, and
poor scheduling of time in general.

Using Time To Enhance the Learning Disabled Student's Learning

Learning disabled students in the secondary school have four intimately
related types of time problems: (1) how to budget time; (2) how to study;
(3) how best to spend leisure time; and (4) how to deal with the time-
consuming nature of school subjects.

The school ocupies a most favorable position for helping youth solve
these problems. It is important to identify each pupil's time problems.

Little and Chapman (1953) offer a questionnaire to measure students'
use of time as shown in Exhibit 2-1.

An analysis of the student responses should be done with the adolescent.
One of the objectives is to assist the student to see if there is a balance of
time the student spends in leisure activities and school-related activities.
A critical factor in school success is the time spent studying. However,
time is only one of many factors to be addressed.

TECHNIQUES OF STUDY

The effectiveness of study is contingent upon many factors such as:

- Physical problems related to learning disabilities such as hyperactiv-
  ity, impulsivity, or distractibility can depress the student's study
  capacity.
- The student's inherent cognitive ability and academic aptitude relates
  positively with study effectiveness.
- A student's mastery of the techniques of cognitive processing peculiar
  to each field of study is significantly related to positive results of
  study.
- The ability of the student to engage in reading-related tasks with
  relative independence is strongly associated with study efficacy.
  Learning disabled students need direct assistance in order for them
  to derive the most learning possible from the reading task.

Exhibit 2-1 Time Use Questionnaire

Time Does March On

And each of us can work with time or against it. If we work with time, we can win. If we work mostly against time, we are tossed around aimlessly, much as a leaf in the wind, and we lose.

Time has an odd way of treating everyone alike. It is how a person uses time that counts. No one can take all the time he wants for everything he wants to do. This being true, each person needs to decide what he must do and learn how to use time so that he may do other things he wants to do.

Everyone has problems in the use of time. Fortunately, we now know some ways of learning how to work with time. But before anyone can be helped, it is necessary to know exactly what his time problems are.

Those listed below are time problems students generally worry about. Read them and place a check like this √ before those with which you would like some help. It will take only a few moments. Then something can be done about helping you.

I

1. It seems that I never have time to do the things I must do.
2. There are so many things to do that I have trouble when I try to plan my activities.
3. I do not know how to budget my time wisely.
4. I try to budget my time, but it doesn't work because I never know what to expect in the way of assignments by my teachers or parents.

II

5. I feel that I waste a lot of time because I don't know how to study some of my lessons.
6. It often takes me as long or longer to figure out how to study some of my lessons than it takes to do them.
7. I pass my courses but I feel that I waste a lot of time because I don't know how to study well enough.
8. I would like to have someone help me learn to study so that I can do better in school.

III

9. I often feel that I spend my spare time in useless ways.
10. I'd like to know how I can spend my leisure time wisely.
11. I'd like to know how to choose worthwhile things to do in my spare time.
12. I get tired of doing the same things over and over again for recreation.
13. I feel that when I have some free time there are not many really good things to do for pleasure and recreation.
14. I would like to know how to do many interesting things for fun when I have the time.
15. I would like to know how to find good books to read at home.
16. I would like to know about things I can do for pleasure at home so I won't feel that I must be going somewhere all the time.

Exhibit 2-1 continued

IV

17. Some of my teachers give such long assignments that we can't get through them the next day at class and understand them.
18. It seems to me that extra work in all my classes piles up at the same time. This keeps me from doing any of my work as well as I think I should.
19. I have to study late every night just to try to get by. No one can help me with my lessons at my home.
20. I often have homework that I can't do. Sometimes I get help, but I don't understand it very well.
21. Besides long homework assignments, some of my teachers assign so many books to be read outside the class that I never get enough sleep.
22. I can get some of my homework by myself, such as reading a story for English. But some of it I can't get by myself, for example, math.
23. It worries me that we have so many papers to write without any help. We just write them and turn them in and wonder what grade we'll get on them. I don't seem to get any better.
24. Some of my schoolbooks are so long that we have to hurry all the time just to get through them during the year, and I don't understand books we go through so fast.
25. My lesson assignments are often made in such a hurry that I do not understand what I am supposed to do and how I'm supposed to do it.

Name _____

Source: Reprinted from *Developmental Guidance in Secondary School* by Wilson Little and A.L. Chapman by permission of McGraw-Hill Book Co., Inc., © 1953.

- Effective study-related skills and study habits are essential, i.e., knowledge of the library facilities and skill in their use. It is important that the secondary learning disabled students be tested on their knowledge of study and reference skills.

- An exploration should be made of study conditions in the school in terms of availability and conduciveness. Quiet corners and study environments that are congruent with the individual student's learning style preferences should be considered.

- A reasonable and consistent study schedule should be established. The teacher should attempt to establish with the student a balance of work and recreational activities.

- Teachers should understand the psychological principles of study such as the best methods of memorizing. Traxler (1944) is a good reference in this area.

- The influence of peer pressure is a significant factor.

- Teachers should attempt to establish feelings of security through creating for the learning disabled student a learning environment that is consistent, predictive, and conducive to student success.

THE TEACHER AS A CHANGE AGENT

Secondary mainstream teachers must be aware of how to maximize their instructional effectiveness through the use of proven strategies and techniques. The teacher in this capacity is acting as a change agent. Teachers have available to them a wealth of opportunities to effect positive learning experiences for the students in their charge. They must be cognizant of specific classroom teaching skills that are amenable to improvement.

Guidelines for Improving the Lecture

One of the most prevalent teaching methods on the secondary level is that of the lecture. The following suggestions can be used to improve the lecture:

- Provide a lecture guide to aid the student in noting the main ideas of the material presented, important vocabulary, summary statements, and teacher-student summary paraphrasing. The lecture guide should state learner outcomes for the lecture itself.
- Consider taping the lecture for students to play again for the reinforcement of key concepts through repetition.
- Look at the seating arrangement of the students within the classroom. Attempt to seat those students with auditory processing difficulties nearer the front of the classroom.
- Present the lecture with audio-visual supplements to enable students to use more than one sensory modality in learning.
- Speak clearly and avoid the use of complex sentence structures or unneeded technical jargon.
- Attempt to maintain the students' attention throughout the lecture. Teacher behaviors that relate to student attention are offered by Cooper et al. (1977).

Travers (1979) provides additional suggestions for improving lecture presentations.

In summary, we have presented specific strategies relating to teaching behavior and learning behavior in the secondary classroom.

Most of the literature on learning disabilities focuses on (a) recognition, diagnosis, and testing; (b) working with the learning disabled student in a small group tutorial situation; and/or (c) working with the learning disabled student in a self-contained elementary classroom situation. Little of the available literature is addressed to the middle school or secondary school teacher.

Some general strategies to assist teachers of adolescents with learning disabilities are offered in the following lists:

- Be sure that presentations are organized in sequential order.
- Keep the student focused on the task through minimizing background noise.
- Present key points in the lesson at the beginning and summarize them again at the end.
- Incorporate experiential activities into lesson plans whenever possible. Remember that students learn effectively by doing.
- Be flexible in the format options of tests, reports, and assignments.
- Structure assignments for the student to enhance the student's organizational skills (provide outlines, vocabulary lists, context clues, etc.).
- Work with the student in keeping an "assignment calendar" wherein he or she regularly notes assignments and due dates.
- Establish clearly defined expectations for classroom behavior and academic performance.
- Provide directions in a simple and clear manner.
- Speak in a distinct and comfortable classroom level.
- It is important to be consistent in both expectations and behavior.
- Attempt to maintain moderation in attitude. Avoid threats or punishments.
- Begin instruction at a point where the child is assured of success.
- Provide ongoing feedback and positive reinforcement for the student's successful performance.
- Encourage extra credit assignments to provide the learning disabled adolescent with alternate options.
- Consider a flexible, criterion-based grading system, and use untimed tests on occasion.
- Consider the use of contracting with the student.
- Remember that how students feel about themselves is vital to their success in learning.
- Nothing succeeds like success with adolescents. Ensure that they experience feelings of success daily.

SUMMARY

Effective teaching is the product of awareness, competence, and appropriate application of learning principles.

The awareness relates to knowledge of instructional options available for individualization within the mainstream class for learning disabled students. This chapter has presented the teacher with approaches for teaching learning disabled adolescents.

Teacher competence is a function of instructional effectiveness analysis. It involves both the teacher's subject area of expertise and the methods used to present this material to a diverse range of students. Teachers must adapt the delivery of instruction based on the analysis of feedback.

Material in this chapter provides recommendations for strategies to enhance the learning of mainstreamed learning disabled students.

Teaching is a process, and learning is a process. The teacher's task is to enhance both processes through a careful engineering of their respective elements. This chapter has sought to provide essential information, recommendations, and guides to help achieve the dual goals of effective teaching and effective student learning.

ANNOTATED BIBLIOGRAPHY

Basic Thinking Skills. Midwest Publications. Pacific Grove, Calif., 1977. (grades 5–10, remedial–adult)

This is a series of 13 nongraded booklets, each containing an average of 30 activities to sharpen the thinking skills. Reading level is roughly upper elementary in complexity. Included are analogies, antonyms and synonyms, following directions, and patterns.

Dabney Day, Cal Edland, and Adele Graham. *Learning to Remember— Procedures for Teaching Recall*. Academic Therapy Publications. Novato, Calif.

The program emphasizes the active learner through the use of respondent conditioning wherein students receive positive feedback for their success through various reinforcement programs. LTR consists of four major components: respondent conditioning, recall testing, baselining, and reinforcement all tied together by a daily program.

Interpretive Education. *Following Directions*. Kalamazoo, Mich., 1979. (grades 5–9, remedial 10–12)

This program provides essential help for young people who may have difficulty following directions.

Learner, Inc. *Following Written Directions*. 1980. (grades 5–9, remedial 10–adult)

This is a 48-page skills book that gives students skills in following, comprehending, and executing a wide variety of directions. Individual exercises focus on various organization and decoding techniques.

Thinking Skills Inductive Thinking Skills. Midwest Publications. Pacific
Grove, Calif., 1979. (grades 5–10, remedial–adult)
   This nongraded series is designed to sharpen thinking skills for better
reading comprehension, math, writing skills, social sciences, test taking,
etc. Using primarily class discussion, it covers drawing reasonable inferences, reasoning by analogy, and the ability to generalize. It also covers
spatial perception and discovery.

Interpretive Education. *How To Study.* 1979. (two color sound filmstrips)
   The first filmstrip explains the importance of choosing the best time
to study, the importance of sleep and nutrition, the necessity for adequate lighting, etc. The second filmstrip teaches techniques to reinforce
study habits, steps to take to understand an assignment, and the importance of listening and test taking.

Reading Laboratory, Inc. *Why Am I Reading This Book?* 1972. (cassette
module grades 7–adult)
   A cassette module presenting the steps required for surveying, pre-
reading, and critical questioning for direction and purpose in a two-
period unit. Students will be instructed in how to determine the basic
scope and intent of the book. Then they will learn how to use this
knowledge to define their own reading purposes and form a mental
framework to fit the book's contents.

Library Filmstrip Center. *Reference Collection.* Revised 1976. (filmstrip
grades 9–adult) Wichita, Kan.
   This filmstrip introduces the student to the use of the reference collection in any library. It will help each individual to understand the
contents of the resources available and will assist him or her in selecting
reference materials. Each type of book is explained in detail.

Studies Series. McIntyre Publications, Inc. 1978. (grades 7–12)
   This series shows students how to budget their time and how to
provide adequate study environments. Class preparedness, systematic
reading of daily assignments, and methods of note taking are emphasized
as the key to better study habits and better grades.

Study Skills. McDonald Publishing. St. Louis, Mo., 1978. (grades 6–8,
remedial 9–12)
   Book A—Expands student's knowledge by learning how to use reference material, take notes, outline, summarize, decode unfamiliar words,
organize material, write a bibliography. Book B—Teaches the following
skills: understanding technical material (maps, graphs, tables); locating
specific information (table of contents, index, glossary); library skills.

Teaching Resources Films. *Why Am I Studying This?* Hingham, Mass.,
1974. (four color sound filmstrips, grades 7–9, remedial 10–12)

This program illustrates many everyday applications of useful knowledge that comes from each of four major subject areas; analyzes career opportunities related to specific areas of study; and defines the characteristics, tastes, and abilities that are requisites in specific careers. Also included is a comprehensive occupations study guide and bibliography.

Test Taking Skills. McDonald Publishers. St. Louis, Mo., 1978. (grades 6–8, remedial 9–12)

The series Test Taking Skills—Language Arts and Reading includes exercises similar in format to those on standardized achievement tests.

Test Taking Skills—Mathematics includes computations, problem solving, simple algebra and geometry, and concepts of money, time, fractions, distance, measurement. It also includes hints for maximizing test scores.

REFERENCES

Anderson, R.C., & Biddle, W.B. On asking people questions about what they are reading. In G.H. Bower (Ed.) *The Psychology of Learning and Motivation: Advances in Research and Theory* (Vol. 9). New York: Academic Press, 1975.

Ausubel, D.P. The use of advanced organizers in the learning and retention of meaningful verbal material. *Journal of Educational Psychology*, 1960, *51*, 267–272.

Block, J.H. *Mastery Learning in the Classroom: An Overview of Recent Research.* Paper presented at the Annual Meeting of the American Educational Research Association, New Orleans, February 1973.

Bloom, B.S. Learning for mastery. *Evaluation Comments*, Vol. (No. 2), May, 1968. Los Angeles: University of California, Center for Study of Evaluation.

Carrier, C.A. & Titas, A. The effects of notetaking: a review of studies. *Contemporary Educational Psychology*, 1973, *65*, 326–334.

Cooper et al. *Classroom Teaching Skills: A Handbook.* Lexington, Mass.: D.C. Heath and Company, 1977.

Denton, J.J., & Matheny, C. Making instructional assignments: how easy, yet how hard! *Clearing House*, 53, 7, 1980, 327–330.

Goodman, L., & Mann, L. *Learning Disabilities in the Secondary School: Issues and Practices.* New York: Grune & Stratton, 1976.

Howe, M.J.A. Using student's notes to examine the role of the individual learners in acquiring meaningful subject matter. *Journal of Educational Research*, 1970, *64*, 61–63.

Hunter, M.C. The teaching process. In D. Allen and E. Seifman (Eds.) *The Teacher's Handbook.* Glenview, Ill.: Scott Foresman, 1971.

Kurth, R.J., & Moseley, P.A. *The Effects of Copying or Paraphrasing Structurally-Cued Topic Sentences on Passage Comprehension.* Paper presented at the Annual Meeting of the American Educational Research Association, Toronto, 1978.

Little, W., & Chapman, A.L. *Developmental Guidance in Secondary School.* New York: McGraw-Hill Book Co., Inc., 1953.

Marsh, G.E., Gearheart, C.K., & Gearheart, B.R. *The Learning Disabled Adolescent: Program Alternatives in the Secondary School.* St. Louis: C.V. Mosby Co., 1978.

Morasky, R. Progress report: phase 1, *Program Development in Learning Disabilities*. Grant 15MH 12713-01 CET. National Institute of Mental Health, 1971.

Morasky, R. *Learning Experiences in Educational Psychology*. Dubuque, Iowa: William Brown, 1973.

Morasky, J.S., & Johnson, S. *Learning Disabilities*, (2nd Ed.) Boston: Allyn & Bacon, Inc., 1977.

Piaget, J. Development and learning. In R.E. Ripple & V.N. Rockcastle (Eds.) *Piaget Rediscovered: A Report of the Conference on Cognitive Skills and Curriculum Development*. Ithaca, N.Y.: Cornell University, 1964.

Pio, C., & Andre, T. *Paraphrasing Highlighted Statements and Learning From Prose*. Paper presented at the Annual Meeting of the American Educational Research Association, New York, 1977.

Richards, J.P., & August, G.J. Generative underlining strategies in prose recall. *Journal of Educational Psychology*, 1975, *67*, 860–865.

Sharp, B.B., & Cox, C. *Choose Success: How to Set and Achieve All Your Goals*. New York: Hawthorne Books, 1970.

Smith, B.O. A concept of teaching. *Teachers College Record*, 1960, *61*, 229–241.

Smith, J.E., & Payne, J.S. *Teaching Exceptional Adolescent*. Columbus, Ohio: Charles E. Merrill Publishing Co., 1980.

Travers, J.F. *Educational Psychology*. New York: Harper & Row, 1979.

Traxler, A.E. *The Improvement of Study Habits and Skills*, Educational Records Bulletin, 41, 4–5, October, 1944.

SUGGESTED READINGS

Bloom, B.S. Mastery learning. In J.H. Block (Ed.) *Mastery Learning: Theory and Practice*. New York: Holt, Rinehart, & Winston, 1971.

Bruner, J. *The Process of Education*. Cambridge: Harvard University Press, 1960.

Chaffee, J., Jr., & Clark, J.P. (Eds.) *New Dimensions for Educating Youth*. Denver: U.S. Department of Health, Education, and Welfare, 1976.

Conant, J.B. *The American High School Today*. New York: McGraw-Hill Book Co., Inc., 1959.

Gallegos, R., & Phelan, J. Using behavioral objectives in industrial training. *Training and Development Journal*, 1974, 28, *4*, 42–48.

Gay, L.R. Temporal position of reviews and its effect on the retention of mathematical rules. *Journal of Educational Psychology*, 1975, *64*, 171, 182.

Markle, S. Some thoughts on task analysis and objectives in educational psychology. *Educational Psychologists*, 1973, 10, *1*, 24–29.

Wiederholt, J.L., & McNutt, G. Assessment and instructional planning: a conceptual framework. In D. Cullman and M.H. Epstein (Eds.) *Special Education for Adolescents: Issues and Perspectives*. Columbus, Ohio: Charles E. Merrill Publishing Co., 1979.

Chapter 3

Teacher, Student, and Group Communication Skills in the Mainstream Class

INTRODUCTION

Teaching is a process that involves effecting behavioral change in students toward predetermined goals. Teacher effectiveness is contingent upon many factors. Among them are knowledge of subject matter, familiarity with instructional methodologies, materials, and instructional delivery systems.

The vehicle that transmits concepts, skills, etc. from the teacher to the student is communications.

This chapter is intended to provide the mainstream teacher with communication skills and strategies designed to enhance instructional effectiveness.

Specific objectives include:

- to acquaint teachers with techniques proven effective in presenting secondary level curriculum to the learning disabled adolescent;
- to present strategies that will enable teachers to become more skillful in the transmission of words, ideas, and feelings via effective listening and sending skills and nonverbal expression;
- to provide an overview of classroom communication skills with an emphasis on effective verbal communication in a teaching format; and
- to suggest effective communication approaches with the learning disabled student (as an individual and within the group).

COMMUNICATION AND INTERPERSONAL SKILLS

Hurt, Scott, and McCroskey (1978) state, "Trying to teach without understanding its relationship to the communication process is a bit like

65

eating a chocolate sundae without the ice cream—a bit sticky, and not very satisfying'' (p. 10).

Basic Tenets of Communication

Communication is a process that is dynamic in nature and continuously changing in practice. Communication involves two processes: (1) *encoding* in which a message is formulated and adapted to the characteristics of the intended receiver(s) and then is transmitted to the designated receivers; and (2) *decoding* in which a message is interpreted. This entails four phases as follows:

1. A receptor's sensory mechanism is stimulated, i.e., the message is "picked up" by a sensory modality and is heard, seen, or felt.
2. The message is interpreted, i.e., meaning is assigned to the information transmitted.
3. The message is evaluated, i.e., a value is assigned to the communication.
4. Feedback is given to the sender. It is through this phase that the sender is made aware of whether the messages sent are appropriate and understood. From the feedback to the communicator, adjustments are made in some facet of the communication (modifications of sender, medium, or content).

The process of communication is transactional, i.e., people adapt and change their own communication behavior (even as it is occurring) in response to what they perceive the other person is receiving. Human communication is the symbolic means by which we relate our realm of experience to another human being. Thus, encoding symbols are learned as a result of our individual experiences with them and as such are arbitrary and flexible. This suggests that there will always be, to some degree, a distortion of the encoded message although effective communication minimizes the distortion.

Communication is multidimensional since people communicate on three reference dimensions as follows:

1. Cultural communication is based on the norms of the culture or the culture's accepted ways of behavior. In our communication, we reflect the values, attitudes, and mores of our cultural and ethnic structure.

2. Sociological communication is based on a person's reference group. We adjust our communication to the group setting (PTA, women's organization, church group, etc.).
3. Psychological communication is based on our knowledge of the unique characteristics of another person. We modify our communications with individuals based on our awareness of the receiver's values, attitudes, or beliefs and on whether we perceive these characteristics to be similar or dissimilar to our own.

EFFECTIVE COMMUNICATION

The specific skills essential to effective communication can be learned by teachers in their role as either a "sender" or a "receiver" within the communicating process.

Sending Skills Guidelines

The following list provides guidelines for sending communication:

1. It is important that the communication process be based in the present. The teacher as a sender should concentrate on the "here and now."
2. The teacher should talk directly with the student rather than about him or her. This is particularly important for the adolescent who needs to feel a "part of the action."
3. Every effort should be made to maintain an attitude of respect for students. They should be made to feel that they are important as persons.
4. The teacher should be aware of the verbal as well as the nonverbal messages within the communication transaction. Adolescents frequently say more through their body language than through a verbal medium. Be alert to manifestations of avoidance, defensiveness, etc. transmitted via eyes (downcast) or body posture.
5. Teachers should take responsibility for statements they have made. This is effectively done by keeping the focus on the teacher rather than projecting it to the student, i.e., use "I" rather than "you" in communication. For example, in lieu of pointing out a student's tardiness to class by a statement that "you are late to this class and your coming in disrupts the lesson," it is more effective to communicate the message as "I am disturbed by your coming to class because it disrupts the lesson I had planned for the class." This latter

approach has the additional advantage of specifying to the student the behavior the teacher feels is problematic and the effect that behavior has on him or her as a teacher.

6. The teacher should be careful to minimize the questioning aspect of communicating. Adolescents are particularly sensitive to teachers giving them "the third degree."

7. In presenting specific feedback to students, it is essential that the messages be delivered in an effective manner. This is accomplished by providing comments that relate to specific behaviors that are within the capacity of the student to change. Further, the feedback should be descriptive rather than evaluative in nature. It is critical that the comments relating to the behaviors be separated from the student as a person, i.e., "I am concerned with your tardiness" rather than "you're always late and insensitive."

Receiving Skills Guidelines

Teachers need to convey to their students that they are receptive to the students' messages and that they feel what students have to say is important.

Specific skills that enhance the effectiveness of a teacher's role as a communication's receptor include:

- The teacher can check perception. Using this technique the teacher attempts to validate assumptions regarding the communication. The teacher leads into the checks by phrases such as, "Do I understand that . . .? Are you saying . . .?" This approach enables the students to clarify their messages without having to engage in defensive or negating responses.
- Teachers must recognize that their feelings, attitudes, and beliefs may influence their responses to others. Teachers are well advised to acknowledge a personal bias or particular effect certain messages have on them such as "I get really upset when you call me _____.."
- Teachers should practice nonevaluative, empathic listening, a technique that is also called active listening or paraphrasing.

Within the educational system, schools have the responsibility of not only determining how to effectively instruct secondary students in the content areas but how to decide what to teach. Both areas involve decisions that impact on the classroom teacher and relate to communication.

COGNITIVE/AFFECTIVE CURRICULA

One of the important controversies in curriculum development is over the ascendancy of cognitive versus affective dimensions of learning. Brown (1971) has been involved in developing an educational process called *confluent education* in which the affective and cognitive dimensions of a program are interrelated. It is his belief that teachers are unable to isolate intellectual experiences from emotional experiences, and in fact teachers should make constructive use of the relationship. It appears that the American public has some rather definitive views on what should occur within the educational process.

In a survey undertaken by Spears in 1973, American educators ranked the importance of 18 educational goals from most to least important as follows:

1. Develop skills in reading, writing, speaking, and listening.
2. Develop pride in work and a feeling of self-worth.
3. Develop good character and self-respect.
4. Develop a desire for learning, now and in the future.
5. Learn to respect and get along with people with whom we work and live.
6. Learn how to examine and use information (thinking and reasoning abilities).
7. Gain a general education.
8. Learn how to be a good citizen.
9. Learn about and try to understand the changes that take place in the world.
10. Understand and practice democratic ideas and ideals.
11. Learn how to respect and get along with people who think, dress, and act differently.
12. Understand and practice the skills of family living.
13. Gain information needed to make job selections.
14. Learn how to be a good manager of money, property, and resources.
15. Practice and understand the ideas of health and safety.
16. Develop skills to enter a specific field of work.
17. Learn how to use leisure time.
18. Appreciate culture and beauty in the world. (pp. 31–32. Reprinted with permission.)

The response from the educators clearly indicated the importance they give to the art of communication. They rated the goals of learning to read,

Table 3-1 Student Rights and Responsibilities

Student rights

The right to all constitutional guarantees
The right to learn
The right to pursue an education without interference
The right to be respected and accepted as a human being
The right to be appropriately involved in one's own education on an equal basis

Student responsibilities

The responsibility to respect the constitutional rights of others
The responsibility to learn
The responsibility to be involved in setting up and observing necessary constraints
    to freedom

Source: Reprinted from "Two R's for Students: Rights and Responsibilities" by S.B. Neill in J. Chaffee and J.P. Clark (Eds.), *New Dimensions for Educating Youth.* U.S. Department of Health, Education, and Welfare, 1976.

write, speak, and listen first. This involves skills as a sender as well as a receiver within the communication exchange.

In the determination of these curriculum decisions, the focus must be on the student.

Rights and Responsibilities of Students

What are students entitled to receive within the American public school system?

Neill (1976) lists student rights and responsibilities as shown in Table 3-1.

These rights and responsibilities, as stated, suggest emphatically that adolescent learners should be actively involved in education.

Dr. Terrel H. Bell (1976), the former U.S. Commissioner of Education, has recommended that secondary education be "dejuvenilized." If we expect students to behave in a mature and responsible manner, we must program for this to occur.

This entails the participation of students in important decision-making groups in the school and community. Through this participation they also are able to experience a sense of ownership (i.e., responsibility) for the results of the decisions made.

THE RIGHTS OF THE LEARNING DISABLED STUDENT

In 1975, the federal government articulated the rights of handicapped students in the legislation passed into law as Public Law 94-142, the

Education for All Handicapped Children Act. (Refer to appendix for additional references.)

The five most significant mandates within the public law are:

1. Handicapped children must be provided a free, appropriate education.
2. The rights of the handicapped children *and* their parents must be protected.
3. Handicapped children must be educated with their nonhandicapped peers to the maximum extent possible. The law states this as "in the least restrictive educational environment."
4. Each handicapped child must have developed for him or her an individualized educational program (IEP). This plan must be developed by a multidisciplinary group called a Planning and Placement Team (PPT). The student's parent(s) must be involved as an active participant. The finalized plan must then be implemented as written.
5. Parents must be involved in all decisions made regarding their child's special education program.

Due Process

Due process may be defined as fairness in the way in which decisions are made. It involves candor, ongoing communication, and collaboration among the agents responsible for educating handicapped children and must involve the students' parents. It is the opinion of the authors that, where feasible, the adolescent should also participate in the PPT meeting. Such decisions should be made on a per case basis. Due process impacts on the child's diagnosis, educational prescription, and implemented plan. PL 94-142 requires the following:

1. Diagnostics undertaken with children must be nonbiased (i.e., nondiscriminatory) and must involve at least two evaluative measures.
2. Parental consent (approval) is required prior to a diagnostic evaluation, prior to placement in a special education program, or prior to placement in a private residential program. Any other changes require that the parents be notified.
3. Parents may seek an independent evaluation if they are dissatisfied with the testing undertaken by the child's school.
4. A child advocate (surrogate) must be appointed if the parents or guardian of the child are not known or available.

5. The school must communicate with the parents in a manner that enhances the ability of the parents to understand the communication (i.e., in the parents' native language, in clear language, etc.).
6. Schools are responsible for informing the parents of their rights regarding the education of their child.

Any parent dissatisfied with the educational program provided by the school may request a due process hearing.

The Individualized Education Program (IEP)

The IEP is a written educational program agreed upon by parents and specialists who meet within a Planning and Placement Team meeting.
The IEP must include the following four parts:

1. a statement of the child's educational level or performance;
2. a statement of annual goals, including short-term objectives;
3. a statement of the anticipated duration of the special educational services, appropriate objective criteria, and evaluation procedures; and
4. a stated review date of the educational program (at least on an annual basis).

The IEP is the product of at least four individuals:

1. the parent(s) or guardian,
2. the child's teacher,
3. a representative of the local educational agency who is qualified to provide or supervise special education, and
4. the child, whenever possible.

The IEP is the definition and description of an appropriate program as defined by the local educational agency responsible for providing the child with an education. The obvious focus of the IEP is on the child.

THE LEARNING DISABLED STUDENT AS A LEARNER

In the literature about the teaching-learning process much attention has been given to the teacher's role, responsibilities, expectancies, and skills. Yet, teaching is only one-half of the teaching-learning phenomenon. The student is equally significant in the learning process.

Many variables affect the student's ability to accurately and effectively "take in" classroom instruction as presented by the teacher. Teachers must assess the student's entering behaviors and use this information in planning and implementing teacher activities.

Student Variables

Sensory limitations are cogent considerations with the learning disabled student, yet on the secondary level the most widely used teaching method is the class lecture. The teacher should consider a multisensory approach using overheads, color, and/or sound to increase the number of sensory channels available for students to use in the processing of information. However, although in the combined experience of the authors this approach has proven to enhance the degree of learning of most students (both learning disabled and regular students), for a minority of students the "bombardment" of excessive stimuli may result in an overloading. Again, as with all other interventions suggested, it is essential for teachers to know their students as individual learners.

Perceptual levels differ among students. Perception, defined as the meaning imparted to a stimulus, suggests that experience enters into an individual's interpretation of the stimulus. The teacher must be aware of perceptual differences among students as a result of differing cultures, varying degrees of exposure to life situations, and sensory deficits, as well as perceptual differences resulting from the emotional nature or connotation of the message (information) being transmitted.

Students' learned habits greatly affect their interpretation and understanding of the information transmitted. Generalizing impressions among similar stimuli is a rather common occurrence. For example, a student may feel that "all math teachers are boring." The similarity or contrast between present and previous learning environments experienced by the student will also influence interpretation and understanding, as well as receptivity.

Students tend to behave in accordance with the expectations placed on them. It is essential that both students and teachers behave under a common set of expectations and that exhibited behavior (in particular that of the teacher as a role model) be congruent with these expectations, i.e., what teachers profess to believe in and what they say is important must be observable in their behavior.

Anxiety and stress tend to negatively influence a student's performance. These emotional conditions may be minimized by clearly stating classroom rules and behavioral and academic expectations; building in feedback mechanisms on an ongoing, frequent basis; and consistently adhering to these established ground rules. Students must be involved in the development of the rules.

Teachers must recognize that there is a relationship between learning and evaluation. Students "learn" for many reasons beyond the acquisition of the knowledge or skill being imparted, and often these other reasons take precedent as motivators for learning. For instance, the cogent motivating factor may be the need to do well in front of peers or to gain parental approval. With learning disabled students, the teacher must structure the learning environment such that these very real needs can be met through some measure of academic success.

In light of the history of learning problems experienced by the adolescent with a learning disability, it is essential to consider the attitudes and values the student possesses relative to education and the educational setting in general.

The Human Factors of Communication

Curriculum adaptation must take into account that teaching and learning are dynamic in nature and that the essence of the process involves human beings who, above all else, are individuals. This fact has a significant influence on the transmission and reception of instruction. Several human factors that influence communication include:

- The level of communication skills that teachers possess as adults is considerably different from the skills level of their adolescent students. With the incidence of a learning disability, this already existent gap is frequently widened.
- Teachers must be aware that their attitudes mediate the manner in which messages are formulated and interpreted.
- Compared to students, teachers generally have a greater number and variety of experiences to draw from to use in communication. Teachers must make conscious efforts to minimize this difference. One important way to accomplish this goal is to draw from the students' experiences.
- Cultural and social factors influence how and what people communicate. Human beings are affected by the environment and the cultural climate in which they were raised. To offset this, teachers should strive for both awareness and objectivity within the communication process.

Enhancing Student Attending Behavior in the Teaching-Learning Situation

Students' abilities to receive and interpret teacher initiated messages are in large part contingent upon their attentiveness to the cogent stimuli within the learning environment. There are several variables that affect attending behavior as follows:

- The teacher should try to maintain the student's focus of attention by minimizing competing distractions through enhancing the manner of instructional delivery by altering voice or body tenor. If this strategy does not appear to mitigate the competition for the student's attention, the teacher must recognize this reality and make further adjustments (auditory to visual) accordingly. This may be done by dramatically altering the lesson (passive to active), its manner of presentation, or the mode of response expected of students (active responding versus passive attending). The more actively involved students are in the learning process, the greater their attention.
- Teachers should be aware of the intensity of their own communication stimuli. Increasing the strength of the stimulus has the effect of drawing the students back to the matter at hand. To maintain its effectiveness, this technique should be used selectively and sparingly. The preferred teaching mode is that of preventing students' distraction through planning lessons that are interesting, thought provoking, and involve students as active participants. Student-oriented approaches are derived from the students' interests, aptitudes, or value systems.
- The teacher can consider increasing the size or amount of the teaching stimulus through the use of easily visible teaching aids. This strategy has an additional benefit of creating a novelty effect by altering the typical presentation.
- Students' attention can be enhanced through providing tangible references wherever possible when presenting abstract concepts. This may take the form of "models" or verbal analogies. This approach enables attention to be strengthened by increasing the number of sensory channels that are brought into the learning situation.
- Teachers should be aware of the level of their involvement in the learning situation. The combined experience of the authors suggests that there exists a direct relationship between the amount of activity a teacher engages in with students and the students' concomitant degree of attention. Greater teacher involvement elicits and maintains greater student attention.

- The teacher should examine the duration and repetition of the stimulus in relation to all students and in particular to the learning disabled adolescent. The learning disabled student may require additional time to process verbal messages or may need to have messages repeated due to auditory receptive deficits, auditory sequential memory deficits, or another language processing disability.

In summary, material that is best attended to is also best understood and remembered. Although this statement seems simple, it entails a significant responsibility for the teacher. Teachers must be aware of what is occurring within the learning environment in a dynamic sense and must be prepared to adjust the environment as a result of feedback received through attending to and modifying accordingly one of three significant factors. These factors are the environment itself (physical), the student, and the teacher. Finally, the teacher must possess the skills and training essential to make such adjustments. Effectiveness as a teacher is congruent with achieving a structured classroom wherein established educational goals are attained through an orchestrated integration of material, setting, and method. The teacher must be able to guide or facilitate the students' learning and thus be an effective manager of the class.

MANAGEMENT OF THE LEARNING ENVIRONMENT: THE CLASSROOM

The degree of learning that occurs is contingent upon an environment that enables both group and individual instruction. Teachers should give consideration to the following variables in "managing" an optimal learning setting.

- Communication is the essence of good teaching. The teacher should understand and practice both verbal and nonverbal communication skills.
- The teacher should continuously monitor student behavior so as to keep alert to the interactions that occur in the classroom in an ongoing manner.
- The focus should remain on "the class" within the instructional process, e.g., asking questions of the class rather than singling out individuals and calling on students in a random manner. Although individualization of instruction has been emphasized throughout this book, the mainstream setting must be looked at as the context in which the learning occurs.

- The teacher should strive for consistency in grading and involve students in class activities related to other aspects of evaluation or measurement of student performance.
- Teachers should model the behaviors expected of their students. Teacher credibility as it relates to student learning is significant.
- The teacher should establish classroom rules, preferably at the beginning of the school year, and consistently adhere to the conditions agreed upon within the learning setting.
- The teacher should make every attempt to present materials in an enthusiastic manner. This entails variations in presentations, good eye contact, carefully prepared lessons, adherence to scheduled educational activities, and adaption of content to the students' spheres of interest.
- Material should be presented in a manner that is appropriately paced with consideration given to the range of cognitive and affective levels of development of the student within a mainstream setting. For the learning disabled adolescent, this suggests use of strategies, materials, and methods analogous to those prescribed in this book.
- Careful consideration should be given to the physical organization of the classroom. Furniture (student seating, learning centers, etc.) should be conducive to the teacher's preferred teaching style and relate to the students' learning style. Effective teaching means maintaining a balance in the teaching-learning equation.
- Teachers should strive to develop a good repertoire of management techniques. Behavioral or academic contracting procedures, communication skills, and time out from reinforcement are but a few of the many options available to teachers.

It is important to remember that effective adolescent management entails candor, openness, and congruence of verbal and nonverbal behavior. Teachers must preserve respect for both themselves and students in the learning transaction.

Teachers need to interact with the students in such a manner as to keep open the channels of communication. One effective method to convey interest and respect for communication by the learning disabled adolescent is to use paraphrasing techniques.

Paraphrasing is a technique in which the sender's ideas and feelings are expressed in the receiver's own words. This conveys to students both an interest and understanding of their communications. Paraphrasing is an effective communication tool to employ with the learning disabled adolescent. It is applicable to any content area and seems to facilitate an effective teaching-learning interaction.

The following techniques should be used in paraphrasing:

- Teachers should preface paraphrased remarks with phrases such as "it seems to me that," "you feel that," etc. This allows the student the opportunity to respond to the statements by affirming their accuracy or clarifying and modifying where appropriate.
- It is important to separate the communicators from their communications.
- Body language should reinforce verbal language. This consistency is important with the learning disabled student who may experience difficulty in reading social signals.
- Teachers should put themselves in senders' shoes and try to understand what they are feeling and what their messages mean.

In summary, the teacher needs to maintain a sensitivity to the problems the learning disabled student may have with inferential learning. Communication skills with such students are best developed through direct instruction and peer group involvement.

Improving Peer Communications

One of the teacher's important roles within the classroom is to facilitate positive and effective peer relationships. Student grouping based on similarities of interest, academic functioning, etc. have a greater probability of goal attainment than do randomly assigned groupings.

Knowledge of the students as both learners and individuals is the key to this effectiveness. One way to get an accurate reading on the student as an individual is to ask the student directly about his or her interests, skills, etc. in nonacademic areas. In the construction of such questionnaires for learning disabled students, the questions should be structured clearly and succinctly, and the overall length of the survey should be as brief as possible. Gillies (1974) provides a questionnaire that gives information about the student to the teacher and/or the student's peers within the class.

PARENTAL CONSULTATION AND EDUCATION: COMMUNICATION GUIDELINES

Teachers must communicate effectively with students' parents as well as with the students themselves. McWhirter and Kahn (1974) recommend a seven-session format to teach parents ways of influencing the values of their children as shown in Exhibit 3-1.

Exhibit 3-1 A Parent Communication Course

Session I. Course Introduction and Communications Patterns
  A. Get acquainted
    a. Learn names
    b. Have each discuss family situation
  B. Introduce course
    a. Describe different types of parents
    b. Have parents describe themselves
  C. Introduce communications patterns
    a. Emphasize acceptance
    b. Describe role playing
Section II. Communication with Children
  A. Introduce active listening
Section III. Sharing Parental Problems with Children
  A. Discuss "owning" the problem (get parent to recognize when they have a problem)
  B. Use confrontation
Section IV. Conflict in Family Relationships
  A. Parents demonstrate present procedures used to deal with conflict
  B. Discuss negative aspects of authoritarian role
  C. Introduce "no-lose" approach to conflict resolution
Session V. Conflict Resolution
  A. Apply "no-lose" method
Session VI. Parental Values
  A. Help parents clarify values
  B. Draw up lists of issues that do and do not involve parent's values
  C. Discuss influencing values
    a. Modeling
    b. Consulting
    c. Accepting
Session VII. Review and Evaluation

Source: Copyright, 1974, American Personnel and Guidance Association. Reprinted with permission.

A vehicle the school is able to employ toward facilitating positive communication with the parents of learning disabled students is that of consultative service. Parental consultation serves many functions within the educational system and the community. Parental consultation:

- enables the school to establish a liaison with parents that will result in greater support for education,
- increases the effectiveness of public services programs,
- is needed because of the plight of the family in our society, and
- enhances student's academic functioning.

The parents of the adolescent must be both recognized and understood if the teacher's communication is to be effective. The effect of the adolescent stage on the parents was described by Ginott (1969) as, "A day comes in any parent's life when there is a sudden realization: My child is a child no longer. This is a unique moment of elation and fear. There is also conflict. As parents, our need is to be needed: as teenagers their need is not to need us."

Parental Consideration in Communication

Many factors in today's society serve to create confusion in the lives of the adolescent's parents. Some of the factors are:

- At the child's state of adolescence, parents themselves find they are faced with a major identity crisis, i.e., they are at an age (slightly over 40) when they are reevaluating their own career decisions. They need support at this time.
- Parents face the difficult task of altering their parenting style; they have less control over their adolescent "child."
- There is a lack of support for nuclear families. Community support has lessened, and the church plays a more minor role. In light of these factors, it would appear that the school should assist students in clarifying values and making decisions through relevant instruction and curriculum. Schools play a major role in the life of an adolescent. Every effort should be made to maximize the positive potential this role affords the school through involving the adolescent's parents as collaborators.

The basic factors in establishing positive contacts with parents include the following:

- The initial meeting should be primarily informative in nature. The teacher should have empirical data to present to the parents.
- Presenting data is important. Empirical data indicates to parents that teachers have invested time and energy in preparing for the meeting and implies that the teacher is professionally competent. Data objectifies a discussion, provides a focus, and provides protection for the educators. There are four types of data: (1) data concerning student behavior and attempts to improve behavior; (2) data concerning student's academic work; (3) data concerning student conferences; and (4) data concerning conferences with colleagues and specialists.
- Teachers should present parents with a well-designed intervention program that includes specifics in responsibilities, time, services, etc.

- Teachers should report positive student behavior. It is important that the communications channel be kept open with the parents. The teacher can encourage the parents to maintain an involvement by indicating positive aspects of the student's behavior.

Home-School Behavior Intervention Program

Ten steps should be used in developing a collaborative home-school behavior intervention program. These are:

1. Reinforce parents for their willingness to attend the conference.
2. Outline the goal of the conference.
3. Describe the problem in objective terms.
4. Indicate what the school has done to alleviate the problem.
5. Display the data collected to indicate that an additional type of intervention is needed.
6. Present the anticipated consequences should the student's behavior remain unchanged.
7. Indicate that the school has exhausted its available resources and suggest that a collaborative home-school program appears most likely to help the student.
8. Outline the proposed program.
9. Negotiate a final agreement.
10. Plan for a followup.

It is essential that both the school and the parents acknowledge that their respective effectiveness with an adolescent is enhanced through a unification of effort since education encompasses significantly more than academics. Youths learn through direct instruction, inference, experience, and simulated and real life situations. Learning disabled adolescents frequently fail to profit as fully as possible on an inferential level due to deficits in their ability to identify cogent clues or information in a given situation. The specialized training of learning disabilities teachers may prove invaluable to parents in assisting them with their adolescent's non-classroom learning. Techniques such as developing effective communicating skills, enhancing modality processing skills, and identifying and attending to significant stimuli within a setting are some examples of suggested types of training. Teachers may also assist students in being more effective communicators with their parents.

Developing Communication Skills with Parents and Students

It is important to understand that communication is occurring within a learning environment at all times and that this communication involves not only the transmission of information within planned activities but the sending and receiving of information that occurs spontaneously as well.

When instructing adolescents, the teacher should plan skill development activities within the group setting so as to capitalize on peer influence upon the behavior of the adolescent.

Suggested Activities for the Mainstream

Peer relationships can be facilitated through enabling adolescents to become better acquainted with their classmates. In each activity, the teacher should explain to the students the reason for the activity, the expectations, and available options. This last point is an important one for the adolescent whose self-esteem is of major concern and who would feel more secure knowing there is an alternative if he or she chose not to participate fully or was unable to participate. The teacher as the facilitator should make every effort to participate with the students.

"Who's who in class" is an activity designed to have students become better acquainted with their peers through the presentation of information relating to the members. In this process, students are asked to list three things about themselves that they would feel comfortable in sharing with the group. The teacher should provide some suggestions to initiate their thought process such as, "I have an Irish Setter," "I love to ski," etc. The teacher collects the lists from the students and mixes them. The class is then divided into two teams. The teacher reads a student list and one team may respond with a guess as to which class member wrote the list. If they are incorrect, the other team has an opportunity to guess. The team that has the most correct guesses wins.

This activity may be varied to best fit the size of the group, the length of time members have worked together, etc. The activity can lead into a discussion of many issues relating to self, image, how others see us, etc. In addition, it can provide some new insights about the group members. Adolescents frequently will be receptive to classroom discussions if the climate is supportive, positive, and conducive, and it is the teacher who creates this setting.

Making the Most of Classroom Discussions

Effective discussion occurs within a controlled setting. However, an occasional outburst of comment or reaction should be allowed. In some cases, small group discussions may be better than class ones.

Benefits of Classroom Discussions

There are many advantages in promoting discussion as an activity within the mainstream setting. These include:

- Students develop the skill and habit of listening. Each person needs to feel a sense of importance and being listened to enhances an individual's self-worth.
- Students learn to express themselves under a safe yet supervised setting where feedback is available.
- Discussion trains students to question and seek answers.
- Discussion reveals how class members are thinking.
- Discussion encourages the development of communications networks within the class.

Besides discussion, other structured activities can be used to encourage students to become better acquainted with each other. One such activity is shown in Exhibit 3-2.

Suggested Resources

There are many excellent resources to assist teachers in developing group activities similar to the one in Exhibit 3-2.

Canfield, J., & Wells, H. *101 Ways to Enhance Self-Concept in the Classroom: A Handbook for Teachers and Parents.* Englewood Cliffs, N.J.: Prentice-Hall, Inc., 1976.

Castillo, G. *Left-Handed Teaching Lessons in Affective Education.* New York: Praeger, 1974.

Johnson, D. *Reaching Out.* Englewood Cliffs, N.J.: Prentice-Hall, Inc., 1972.

Johnson, D., & Johnson, R. *Learning Together and Alone: Cooperation, Competition, and Individualization.* Englewood Cliffs, N.J.: Prentice-Hall, Inc., 1975.

Simon, S., & Clark, J. *More Values Clarification: Strategies for the Classroom.* San Diego: Pennant Press, 1975.

Simon, S., Howe, L., & Kirschenbaum, H. *Values Clarification.* New York: Hart, 1972.

Stanford, G., & Rourk, A. *Human Interactions in Education.* Boston: Allyn & Bacon, Inc., 1974.

Exhibit 3-2 An Activity To Promote Student Interaction

Objective: To provide an opportunity for group members to become better acquainted with each other.
Process:
1. Place each student's name in a box. Ask half of the students in the class to draw a name. The teacher should choose the selecting students based on his knowledge of the individuals in the class. (Selecting alternately seated students would be an objective selection method.)
2. It is important prior to the name selection phase that students be prepared for the activity through a brief discussion of the importance of each other's feelings. This would help to mitigate some of the groaning when certain student's names are drawn, for example.
3. The directions to the students are that each member of the pair matched through the name drawing has five minutes to elicit from the other information that would be helpful in the class setting to know the student. Each dyad should designate one student of the team to begin.
4. This activity is followed up by a large group discussion. Students might also be asked to write their reaction to the activity. The teacher could assist their efforts by providing a structured response format. One suggested approach follows.

Activity Response
1. I felt this activity was _____.
2. What I liked about the activity was _____.
3. What I didn't like was _____.
4. If we do something like this again, I would suggest _____.
5. I really found it interesting that _____.
6. I didn't know that _____.
7. I wish I had _____.
8. I wish you (teacher) had _____.
9. This activity was (helpful) (not helpful) to me because _____.
10. Any other comments you would like to share? _____

One of the prerequisite skills learning disabled students must exhibit in order to function effectively as a group member is the ability to accurately listen to the ideas being communicated by individuals within the group. One activity the teacher may use in assisting students to become better listeners is suggested in the activity "Do You Hear Me?" (Exhibit 3-3).

In addition to students being able to process spoken communications effectively, they must also be able to accurately interpret nonspoken communication in the form of body language. Exhibit 3-4 provides an activity to assist teachers and students toward this goal.

Additional Resources

In addition to the activities presented in Exhibits 3-3 and 3-4, two resources the teachers of the secondary learning disabled student will find

Exhibit 3-3 Listening Skills Activity

Do you hear me?
Objective: To enhance the listening skills of students through structured discussion groups.
Process:
  1. The teacher explains the activity and the objective to the students. In this discussion, the importance of listening to what the other person is saying and the problems caused by poor listening are highlighted. The teacher states that effective listening is a skill and as such can be learned or improved. The activity is designed toward that goal.
  2. The teacher divides the class into groups of three. Within each group, two students are participants, and one is an observer. Designation of roles is best done through a random selection process.
  3. The teacher provides each group with a list of three topics. The group is given five minutes to decide on a topic to discuss. Fifteen minutes are allotted for the discussion.
  4. One member begins the discussion with a statement relating to the topic. Before the other student participant responds he must paraphrase what the other has said. The student being paraphrased must nod that the other was correct. The observer monitors the transactions. At the end of the fifteen-minute discussion period, the observer provides feedback to the participants regarding their perceptions, impressions and observations relative to the process. The teacher can then conclude the activity with a discussion of the application of the activity to the classroom.

---

of great assistance in group activities are the works of Johnson and Johnson (1975) and Stanford and Stanford (1969).

Johnson, D., & Johnson, F. *Joining Together: Group Theory and Group Skills.* Englewood Cliffs, N.J.: Prentice-Hall, Inc., 1975.
Stanford, G., & Stanford, R. *Learning Discussion Skills Through Games.* New York: Citation, 1969.

SMALL GROUP INSTRUCTION

It has been well documented in the literature that students learn most effectively when they are actively involved in their own learning. In order to facilitate student involvement in a small group setting, the teacher should:

- Build in an evaluation process. The group process should also entail specific goal tasks. Teachers need to guard against allowing the group discussion to deteriorate into nothing more than a "gab session."

Exhibit 3-4 Interpreting Body Language

"Reading" Body Language
Objective: To assist students with accurately interpreting nonverbal communications.
Process:
1. The activity should be preceded by a discussion of some basic tenets of effective communicating. This would include addressing the use of words in encoding messages as well as nonverbal modes (for example, tightening of the jaw, averting of the eyes, clenched fists, etc.). The teacher should also discuss the problems frequently associated with misinterpreting other's behaviors.
2. The teacher should present to students a model to use in the description of behavior on a purely empirical level, i.e., stating in nonevaluative, noninterpretive terms what the student is observing. The teacher can begin by presenting a scenario to the students and asking that they state "what is being observed." The teacher or another student feeds back to the student the degree of objectivity they felt their statements reflected. Students can also attempt to objectively describe their behavior as requested by the teacher.
3. It is important that this activity be carefully structured and sequenced by the teacher so that it proceeds in the following sequence: (1) teacher presentation of model; (2) scenario presentation; (3) self-description; (4) dyad activity; and (5) group activity. Adolescent students should be provided with opportunities to practice this skill in a group setting.
4. The students should be encouraged to monitor their use of the skill through notes in a journal. This will provide important data for the teacher to use in guiding the students to further skill development.

- Hold the group accountable for its behavior. The teacher should attempt to ensure that the group goals are realized through keeping the group on task.
- Establish expectations for a group product to culminate from the activity. The teacher must state clearly what is expected in observable and measurable terms.
- Establish clear and consistent expectations for student behavior within the group. Effective groups have definitive operating guidelines, and the members should be monitored for their adherence to these guides.
- Ensure there exists sufficient space within the classroom to allow the different grouping modes to be used effectively. Factors such as space, sound, furniture, etc. should all be considered prior to the implementation of a group activity.

Student Benefits Derived

Small group organization necessitates a modification in the conventional roles assumed by the student and the teacher. Creating effective groups requires commitment and persistence. The small group process, however, results in many positive student outcomes, including:

- Students develop the ability to listen to what others are saying, thus avoiding the possibility of confused or contaminated reception of messages.
- Students develop the ability to share viewpoints.
- Empathy is developed for the other communicator in the process.
- Students learn to both discuss and debate issues.

Small Group Guidelines for Students

In order for the students to derive maximal benefit from small group activities, it is important that instruction and direction be provided to them relative to their roles and behavioral expectations within the group situation.

Some guidelines for the use of the small group process include:

- Conversation must be on the topic.
- Every effort must be made to stick to the task.
- Attention must be concentrated within the student's own group, and movement must be limited so as to minimize interference with other groups.
- Effective group work requires cooperation.
- Each student in the group has the responsibility to listen to each of the other students.

Counseling Techniques for the Mainstream Teacher

One of the most effective vehicles for communicating with the adolescent is the formal structure of counseling. Some suggestions for counseling include:

- Teachers should decide for themselves what constitutes a good opening for the interview. However, it is important that teachers be as noncommittal as possible and avoid adding to the adolescent's self-concern through remarks that highlight the student's problem.
- The teacher should not monopolize the interview and should allow the students an opportunity to express their feelings and/or thoughts.
- The teacher must be a good listener and encourage a student's verbalization through a warm and permissive attitude.

- Teachers should avoid questions as far as possible. Adolescents react with avoidance and defensive behavior when they feel they are being subjected to the third degree.
- The teacher should accept the counselee's statements of the initial interview as factual and should allow the student to talk out the problem he or she is facing by enabling the channels of communication to remain open through an accepting attitude.
- Teachers should adopt a nonjudgmental attitude toward the difficulties in which their clients find themselves. It is important that the student's problems be judged separately from the student as a "person."
- The teacher should use conversational hooks to facilitate continuation of the conversation. Examples of these strategies include paraphrasing, summarizing, or rephrasing the student's comments.
- The teacher should attempt to reflect the verbal content of what the counselee has said.
- Teachers should keep the focus of the interview on the counselee through avoiding any unnecessary reference to themselves, i.e., "If I were you."
- Periods of silence can be used to reach the student. The teacher should consider silence as time the counselee (student) needs to relate what has been discussed to other problems or to gain insight.
- The student should be aware of the confidential nature of the counseling session. The teacher must avoid making any reference to other students or clients and must maintain the confidentiality of the counseling discussions.
- Teachers should be aware of their own limitations as counselors. If teachers feel that the problem(s) are beyond their capabilities as counselors, the most important contribution they can make is to seek referral to outside professionals.
- The teacher should establish the expectations and parameters for the interview with the student, i.e., the amount of time designated for the interview, the rules, etc.
- Students should be allowed to formulate their own plans of action. It is important that the teacher show the students respect and also support their self-respect.

Counseling Objectives

Strang (1949) has defined the goal of counseling as:
    The aim of counseling is self-realization for a social purpose. This involves helping the individual to understand what he can do and what he should do, to strengthen his best qualities, to

handle his difficulties rationally rather than being driven by unconscious forces, to find suitable channels for emotions, and to move toward his more acceptable self. . . . Counseling at its best is the art of helping a person to understand himself, his relations to others, and the world in which he lives. (p. 15. Reprinted with permission.)

Counseling goals should satisfy three criteria: (1) the goal must be desired by the client; (2) the counselor must be willing to help the client achieve this goal; and (3) it must be possible to assess the extent to which the client achieves the goal (Krumboltz & Thoresen, 1969).

PROBLEM-SOLVING STRATEGIES

The group is an effective structure to assist the learning disabled student in developing more efficient problem-solving skills. One of the strategies that lends itself to the teaching of such skills relative to social, cognitive, and psychomotor areas is that of role-playing. A delineation of the advantages of such an approach follows.

Role-Playing

Role-playing is an important problem-solving strategy (Gray, 1974; Wagner, 1968). Role playing:

1. focuses on specific learning behaviors and enables the student to "try out" specific behavioral skills within a safe environment with the availability of built-in feedback mechanisms;
2. provides a concrete response to the student's concerns; in role-playing, the necessity for generalization of the learning from an academic to a real-life situation is minimized;
3. provides immediate reinforcement to the students;
4. provides a multisensory integrated approach; and
5. lends itself to a variety of issues:
   a. It may be used as a strategy to desensitize students by enabling them to experience the stressful situation within a controlled setting and analyze the elements in the situation in an objective manner.
   b. It may be used to teach social skills. This activity should occur within the larger group context where students have the opportunity to receive feedback from their peers. The teacher should

carefully state the ground rules for the group and should monitor the group to ensure its adherence to these rules. For example, the student should have an opportunity to extricate himself from the situation if it becomes too stressful, the adult should summarize the learning that occurred within the group or assist the group in developing such a summary.

Gray (1974) and Wagner (1968) offer additional suggestions.

Systematic Desensitization

Developed by Wolpe and Lazarus (1966), the systematic desensitization technique is based on a three-step procedure:

1. The student is taught how to relax using a relaxation method such as the one developed by Jacobson (1938).
2. The student is asked to develop a hierarchical listing of related events that cause the anxiety.
3. The student is asked to imagine these events within a relaxed state. Since the anxiety normally associated with these images is in opposition to the relaxed state, the anxiety will be reduced.

This approach may be used in assisting students who are experiencing difficulty with speaking in class, test taking, and initiating peer contact.

Contact Desensitization

Ritter (1969) describes contact desensitization as a three-step procedure:
1. the counselor models or demonstrates behaviors that the counselee and counselor have mutually decided are relevant to the problem.
2. The counselor assists the client in repeating the modeled behavior by using behavioral prompts such as placing the client's hands on the counselor's while the counselor touches a feared object or holding the client's arm while walking in a crowded area.
3. The counselor's prompts are gradually faded out with a concomitant fading in of independent behavioral rehearsal by the client (Krumboltz & Thoresen, 1969).

The Use of Contracts with Adolescents

Contracts may be used to assist the students in making the transition from the special class into the mainstream setting. The basic components of a behavior contract are stated by Jones (1980). A contract should include the following six variables:

1. What is the contract's goal? Why has the contract been developed?
2. What specific behaviors must the adolescent perform in order to receive the rewards or incur the punishment?
3. What reinforcers or punishers will be employed?
4. What are the time dimensions?
5. Who will monitor the behavior and how will it be monitored?
6. How often and with whom will the contract be evaluated? (p. 230).

The behavioral contract is a document that specifies relationships between behaviors and consequences. An effective contract should be tailored to include:

- specific statements of responsibilities and privileges
- easily measurable behaviors
- specifically stated privileges which are not dispensed when the responsibilities are discharged
- the criterion stated for which the student may be eligible for a bonus.
- statements of the manner in which student responsibilities are monitored and recorded

STUDENT COUNSELING TECHNIQUES

No matter what the specific form of counseling, there are basic guidelines for effective counseling to which the teacher should adhere. Otto, McNenemy, and Smith (1973) provide 24 counseling techniques as follows:

1. Drop the authoritative teacher role. Be an interested human being.
2. Communicate by transmitting attitudes and feelings. Do this by being real; it is more effective than simply to use words.
3. Arrange the physical setting so as to be close to the pupil. Do not sit behind the desk, but rather share the desk by having the pupil sit at the side.
4. Talk only about ⅓ of the time when the pupil discusses his problem. This gives him the opportunity to do most of the talking and shows that you are interested.
5. Ask questions that cannot be answered with yes or no. Instead of saying "Do you like to read?" say "What do you dislike about reading?"

6. Ask questions using the declarative tone of voice. Otherwise you may sound like an interrogator.
7. Do not interrupt the pupil when he is talking. This communicates that what he has to say is important. However, if he digresses from the subject, focus him back on the subject by saying, "How does this apply to the subject we started talking about?" or "What does this mean to you?"
8. Give the pupil silence in which to think. Realize that there will be periods of silence during the time the pupil is thinking. This may take practice, for in normal conversation silence produces a feeling of awkwardness.
9. Move the focus from intellectual thought to emotional feelings when feelings are being discussed. Ask such questions (as) "How do you feel about that?"
10. Observe and interpret nonverbal clues. Notice when the pupil moves his body or cries or drums his fingers. It is important to understand the relationship between his nonverbal clues and the subject being discussed.
11. Be alert to notice a change in the rate of speech, a change in the volume of speech, or a change in the pitch or tone of the voice. Such changes may indicate that there are emotional feelings connected with the subject being discussed and that the subject needs further exploration.
12. Point out what is currently happening. Say "I notice your eyes are moist. What kind of feelings do you have?"
13. Use brief remarks. Do not confuse the pupil with long complicated questions or comments.
14. Pause before talking. The pupil may wish to make additional remarks—a pause of a few seconds enables him to continue.
15. Don't give lectures on ways to behave. Ask the pupil to suggest alternatives and let him make the decision. Help him to examine the consequences of his alternatives. Information, possibilities and alternatives may be presented, but only for his consideration.
16. Avoid talking about yourself and your experiences. Do not use "I" and avoid personal anecdotes. Focus on the pupil and his problems.
17. Clarify and interpret what the pupil is saying. Use such remarks as "It seems to me that . . ." At other times make a summarizing remark. But make these brief interpretations after the pupil has presented his ideas.

18. Do not be alarmed at remarks made by the pupil. Instead focus on the reason behind what was said or done.
19. Do not reassure the pupil that things will be all right. This will be recognized as superficial. Look for ways to demonstrate change and progress.
20. Do not make false promises. Instead communicate a feeling for the pupil and a desire to see and understand his problem; but do not appear to be overly concerned or to assume his problem.
21. Do not make moralistic judgments. Instead focus on what is behind the pupil's behavior: ask yourself "What is there about this person that causes him to behave in this manner?"
22. Avoid undue flattery and praise. Instead focus on why the student asks for an undue amount of praise. If a pupil constantly asks such questions as "Do you like this dress?" say "Yes, but why do you ask?"
23. Do not reject the pupil through your remarks or nonverbal clues, but instead attempt to accept him. Try not to show impatience; do not threaten or argue; guard against any act that might appear to belittle the student.
24. Refer "more serious" cases. (pp. 419–420. Reprinted with permission.)

When engaging in the counseling of adolescents, it is important that two major factors be kept in mind: (1) keep the discussion general in nature; and (2) keep it pragmatic.

Counseling should stress the positive growth of the individual toward greater self-understanding, self-reliance and self-respect. The goal of counseling is to enable individuals to help themselves.

THE TEACHER'S ROLE

Rogers (1969) defined the teacher's role and responsibility in establishing a relationship with students very aptly:

It is my contention that tomorrow's educator, whether the humblest kindergarten teacher, or the president of a great university, must know, at the deepest personal level, the stance he takes in life. Unless he has true convictions as to how his values are arrived at, what sort of an individual he hopes will emerge from his educational organization, whether he is manipulating

Table 3-2 Generalizations and Principles in Motivating Students

Generalization	Principle
1. When certain objectives are to be achieved, the student's attention must be directed toward those objectives.	1. Focus student attention on desired objectives.
2. Curiosity, interest and achievement are positive motives that may be manipulated readily to focus student behavior toward desired objectives.	2. Encourage the development of positive motives.
3. Meaningful learning sets and advance organizers enhance motivation for learning new material by relating previous abilities and knowledge to the present task.	3. Use learning sets and advance organizers.
4. Setting and attaining goals encourage consistent effort and permit knowledge of progress and feelings of success to operate effectively.	4. Help students to set and attain realistic goals.
5. A warm, businesslike environment promotes continued effort and favorable attitudes toward learning.	5. Create a warm, orderly atmosphere.
6. Rewards are effective with some children in initiating and directing behavior; punishment may suppress undesirable behavior.	6. Provide incentives and punish, if necessary.
7. Extended intense motivation, accompanied by anxiety, disorganizes behavior and impairs learning efficiency.	7. Avoid high stress and disorganization.

Source: Reprinted from *Learning and Human Abilities* by H.J. Klausmier and W. Goodwin by permission of Harper and Row Pub., Inc., © 1966.

---

human robots, or dealing with free individual persons, and what kind of a relationship he is striving to build with these persons, he will have failed not only his profession, but his culture. (pp. 217–218. Reprinted with permission.)

PRINCIPLES FOR MOTIVATING

All counseling efforts are, however, ineffectual if the students themselves do not desire to resolve their problems or if they are unmotivated. Klausmier and Goodwin (1966) have identified seven generalizations and accompanying principles for motivating pupils as shown in Table 3-2.

SUMMARY

Effective instruction is nondivorceable from effective communication. The teacher who succeeds with learning disabled adolescents serves in many roles concomitantly, including inculcator of knowledge, facilitator of positive behavior change, learning climate engineer, and social psychologist.

The common thread permeating each of these roles is that of communication. This chapter has sought to present an overview of the communication process. Methods and strategies have been suggested for use with mainstreamed students in both individual and group situations. Suggestions have also been given for effecting positive, collaborative parent-teacher liaisons.

The goal of effective communicaton is realized through the development of teacher skills in a receiver or sender role in conjunction with a sensitivity to the student as a dynamic variable in this process.

The heterogeneity of processing deficits (learning problems) exhibited by the students categorized as learning disabled suggests that teachers develop a broad repertoire of interventions to be used with the individual student. There do exist, however, basic tenets and strategies of effective communicating that apply to all adolescents. This chapter has sought to provide for the secondary mainstream teachers the ingredients essential for effective communication along with the latitude that allows for the instructor's unique teaching style.

RESOURCE MATERIALS

School/Teacher Opinionaires for Determining a Student's Attitude

Battle, James. *The Culture-Free Self-Esteem Inventories for Children and Adults.* Monterey, California: Publishers Test Service, 1981. (Administration: individual or group. Administer/score in 30 minutes)

The Culture-Free Self-Esteem Inventory is designed to screen to identify individuals who need psychological assistance and/or who may be experiencing depression. Form A (50 items) and Form B (25 items for posttesting). Five subscales are produced from either form. The inventories measure general self-esteem, social/peer-related self-esteem, parents/home-related self-esteem, and a defensiveness or lie scale.

The Culture-Free Self-Esteem Inventory for adults has 30 items and produces four subscales: (1) general self-esteem; (2) social self-esteem; (3) personal self-esteem; and (4) defensiveness, a lie scale. The manual contains directions for administration, research data, keys, frequency distributions, and case histories.

Bentley, Ralph R. and Rempel, Averno M. *The Purdue Teacher Opinionaire*. (Level A) Lafayette, Indiana: Purdue Research Foundation, Purdue University.

This instrument provides school boards, administrators, and teachers with information that can be used to improve the educational programs of their schools. Data are collected by giving teachers an opportunity to express their opinions on items about the school environment in which they work without their individual responses being identifiable.

The instrument is designed to measure important dimensions of teacher morale. No time limit is imposed; however, most teachers complete the instrument in 20–30 minutes.

Bentley, Ralph R. and Starry, Allan R. *The Purdue Teacher Evaluation Scale*. (Level A) Lafayette, Indiana: Purdue Research Foundation, Purdue University.

This scale is designed for student evaluation of their teachers. Some major areas of concentration deal with:

- how students assess the learning environment in the classroom
- how students evaluate teaching methods
- how students feel about the teacher's relationship with them
- how an individual evaluation profile compares with the profiles of other teachers
- where to begin a personal program of self-improvement and development

This instrument is designated to provide a teacher at the junior or senior high school level with evaluative information in a form that will be extremely useful in a program of self-improvement and development. Data are obtained by giving students an opportunity to express their feelings about their teacher and the things he or she does without their individual responses being identifiable. Total administration is about 20 minutes.

Fitts, William H. *Tennessee Self-Concept Scale*. Monterey, California: Publishers Test Service, 1965. (Age range: 12 through adult; Administration: individual or group)

A measurement of overall self-esteem, the Tennessee Self-Concept Scale (TSCS) also provides a number of other useful measurements of self-concept. The profile includes subscales for areas such as identity, self-satisfaction, and perception of physical self, social self, personal self, and moral-ethical self. The TSCS is available in two forms. Form

C is the counseling form and Form C&R is designed for clinical and research purposes. The scoring of Form C deals with fewer variables and is appropriate for self-interpretation and feedback to counselees. Form C&R is more complex in terms of scoring, analysis, and interpretation.

TSCS consists of 100 self-descriptive statements that the subject uses to portray himself or herself. It is self-administered and can be given to persons who are at least 12 years of age and who have a sixth-grade reading level.

Remmers, H. H. (Ed.). *Master Attitude Scales* (Level A) Lafayette, Ind.: Purdue Research Foundation, Purdue University. (Published by University Book Store, 360 State Street, West Lafayette, Indiana.)

One way for the teacher to ascertain a student's attitude toward school and the educational process is through administering a questionnaire or scale.

Each of the scales is available in two equivalent forms, A and B. The scales are separately available as follows. Scales measure attitude toward:

- any school subject
- any vocation
- any institution
- any defined group
- any proposed social action
- any practice
- any homemaking activity
- individual and group morale
- the high school

COMMUNICATIONS SCALE

Woodward, D. M. *Communications Scale for Adolescents.*

This scale is intended to assist you with communicating by identifying how you feel about talking with and to others.

If you feel the statement is like you most of the time, check in that column. If you feel the statement is never like you, check that column. If you feel that the statement describes you some of the time, check that column.

There are no right or wrong answers. Your first answer is usually the best, so try to work as quickly as possible, although there is no time limit.

I feel that:	Always like me	Often like me	Never like me
1. In talking with a new peer, I'm very nervous.	0	1	2
2. I don't mind talking in front of the class.	2	1	0
3. I like to give my point of view in class.	2	1	0
4. When I talk, I feel tight inside.	0	1	2
5. I'm not too nervous when I have to talk in a group.	2	1	0
6. I'm OK with my friends but really nervous in public.	0	1	2
7. I really try to get out of talking in public.	0	1	2
8. When I have to talk in front of a group, I get confused.	0	1	2
9. Once I'm talking in front of a group, I'm OK.	2	1	0
10. Authority figures, like the principal, really make me nervous.	0	1	2
11. I'm not afraid of being called on in class.	2	1	0
12. Talking in class is not a big deal.	2	1	0
13. I'm more comfortable talking in some classes than others.	1	1	1
14. The teacher has an effect on how comfortable I feel talking.	1	1	1
15. What my friends will think really affects what I say.	1	1	1
	15	15	15

SCORING PROCEDURE

The responses indicated with the number two are the preferred answers. Scores that differ five or more points in the "always" or "never" columns from the "often like me" column suggest the student is relatively nonapprehensive in communicating ("always" column) or rather apprehensive communicators as indicated in the "never" column.

SELF-CONCEPT ORGANIZATIONS

Affective Education Development Project, Rm. 323, Philadelphia Board of Education, Twenty-first and Parkway, Philadelphia, Pennsylvania 19103. (Norman Newberg, Director) This project has been developing curricula and providing in-service training in affective education in the Philadelphia area.

Association for Humanistic Psychology, 325 Ninth Street, San Francisco, California 94103. Holds annual national and regional conferences and publishes a monthly newsletter and the *Journal of Humanistic Psychology*.

The Center for Humanistic Education, University of Massachusetts, Amherst, Massachusetts 01002 (Gerald Weinstein, Director) The center offers courses in values clarification, humanistic curriculum development, etc.

Educator Training Center, 2140 West Olympic Boulevard, Los Angeles, California 90006. The center was created by William Glasser to research ideas and develop methods for combating school failure.

Institute for Humanistic Education of the New England Center, Box 575, Amherst, Massachusetts 01002. (Jack Canfield, Director) The institute conducts workshops, offers consulting services, and distributes publications in the area of humanistic education.

Institute for Humanistic Education, 535 St. Paul Place, Baltimore, Maryland 21202. (Barbara Raines, Director) The institute is involved in training teachers to implement humanistic education.

ANNOTATED BIBLIOGRAPHY

Communication and Interpersonal Skills Materials

Alschuler, Alfred, Tabor, Diane, and McIntyre, James. *Achievement Motivation Materials*. Middletown, Connecticut: Education Ventures, Inc.

These materials were adapted for the grade use from those developed by the Achievement Motivation Development Project at Harvard University.

Berlin, Jerome. *Basic Interpersonal Relations*. Instructional Dynamics, Inc., 1971. (grades 7 through 12, adult)

The small group setting of five or six people is the basis for this package of materials by Dr. Jerome Berlin. The program is made up of five session booklets. Each booklet structures on a 1½ hour session for the group, and guides the participants through it step by step. The entire course is actually a series of guided interactions among the group members, allowing them to begin to connect these experiences to basic principles and interpersonal concepts that they can then apply to their relationships with other people.

Combs, Arthur W. *Perceiving, Behaving, and Becoming.* Washington, D.C.: Yearbook of the Association for Supervision and Curriculum Development, 1962.

This book contains a series of articles by leading educational theorists in perception, self-concept, and self-actualization.

Express Yourself: The Art of Communication, Educational Enrichment, 1980. (3 color sound filmstrips/grades 9 through adult)

The main objective of this set is to acquaint young adults with techniques proven effective in: becoming a better listener, organizing one's ideas, "reading" body language. Allows for practice and reinforcement in the expression of ideas and emotions.

Ginott, Haim G. *Teacher and Child.* New York: MacMillan Publishing Co., Inc., 1972.

Ginott offers a model for a language of acceptance and comparison. His suggestions are designed to enhance the quality of life in the classroom.

Hamachek, Donald E. *Encounter with the Self.* New York: Holt, Rinehart and Winston, 1971.

Written for educators, this book is filled with references to case histories, anecdotal materials, and current research.

Hill, Russell A. and staff. *Achievement Competence Training.* Philadelphia, Pennsylvania: Research for Better Schools.

ACT is a comprehensive learning package designed to teach students a variety of strategies for setting and reaching their goals.

Interpersonal Relations in the Group. Human Development Institute, 1978.

The basic reference book for this program, *Effective Group Work* by Alan F. Klein, contains the principles of working with groups and how these principles are applied in many different types of setting. The 384-page hardcover book contains practical suggestions for helping groups solve problems and facilitate growth.

Maltz, Maxwell. *Psycho-Cybernetics.* Englewood Cliffs, N.J.: Prentice-Hall, 1960.

Using real-life examples, the author shows how a person can create a totally new image of himself or herself as a successful and happy person. Maltz offers many useful suggestions in the use of creative imagery.

Padomares, Uvaldo, Ball, Geraldine, and Bessell, Harold. *The Human Development Program*. LaMesa, California: Human Development Training Institute.

This program is designed to facilitate learning in the affective domain, thereby improving motivation and achievement in all areas of education.

Peterson, Audrey J. *Motivation Advance Program*. Achievement Motivation System, Chicago.

This program provides experiences and information to assist young people in expanding their attitudes toward self-acceptance as worthwhile, unique individuals.

Powell, John. *Why Am I Afraid to Tell You Who I Am?* Argus Communications. Paperback, Filmstrip and Character Cards Program. (grades 7 through 12, adult)

Explores 40 games and roles that block self-understanding. Students will quickly realize how many ways there are to mask and distort the truth about themselves.

Rosenthal, Robert and Jacobsen, L. *Pygmalion in the Classroom: Teacher's Expectations and Pupil's Intellectual Development*. New York: Holt, Rinehart and Winston, 1968.

Rosenthal and Jacobsen report their research indicating the need for teachers to "believe in" students' ability to succeed.

Schrank, Jeffrey. *Effective Communication*. Argus Communications, 1977. (grades 7 through adult)

This program is designed to help students become more skillful in the transmission of words, ideas, and feelings. It involves listening skills, nonverbal expression (speech mannerisms and body language), and awareness of feelings. It is a self-instructional four-part series with cassette and duplicating master exercises.

Simon, Sidney B., Howe, Leland W., and Kirschenbaum, Howard. *Values Clarification: A Handbook of Practical Strategies for Teachers and Students*. New York: Hart Publishing Co., 1972.

This book contains 79 classroom exercises designed to help students clarify their values.

Social Consequences Series. Interpretive Education, 1979. (grades 9 through 12 remedial, adult)

A variety of programs designed to help students make intelligent decisions and evaluate their consequences. Hypothetical problem situations are drawn from home, school, and work settings.

Stevens, John P. *Awareness*. Moab, Utah: Real People Press, 1971. (paperback, New York: Bantam Books, 1973)

This book combines theory with over 100 exercises drawn from Gestalt awareness training. The exercises include personal awareness, communication with others, group exercises, and a special section entitled "To the Group Leader or Teacher."

The Business of Communicating. Milliken Publishing, 1980. (grades 9 through 12, adult; duplicating master/transparency book)

A comprehensive overview of communication skills with emphasis on effective written and verbal communication in a teaching aid format.

This Is Me! Developmental Learning Materials. Allen, TX.

This program motivates students to exercise their communication skills, and at the same time provides opportunities for them to appreciate themselves and others more. Students are presented with 64 issues that, when discussed, help them become aware of their emerging preferences and values. The teacher guide offers numerous teaching strategies such as role playing, games, mock interviews, and ideas for creative writing.

Transition. American Guidance Service. Circle Pines, Minn.

Transition explores the needs, goals, expectations, feelings, values, and conflict of middle school students. The program helps to develop self-respect and regard for others by promoting human understanding, empathy and personal responsibility.

You. Frank E. Richards Publishing Co., Phoenix, NY.

You is a hardbound social adjustment textbook written to help young people understand themselves, create a better self-image, and improve their self-control, social skills, and attitudes. *You* is designed so that all members of the class, nonreaders and low level readers as well, can take part.

REFERENCES

Bell, T.M. Let's 'dejuvenilize' secondary education. In J. Chaffee, Jr. and J.P. Clark (Eds.), *New Dimensions for Educating Youth.* Denver: U.S. Department of Health, Education, and Welfare, 1976.

Berger, E., & Winters, B. *Social Studies in the Open Classroom.* New York: Teachers College Press, 1973.

Blance, Cook, & Mark. *Reading in the Open Classroom: An Individualized Approach.* New York: Community Resources Institute, 1971.

Bobcock, S.S., & Schild, E.O. *Simulation Games in Learning.* Beverly Hills, Calif.: Sage, 1968.

Brown, G.I. *Human Teaching for Human Learning.* New York: Viking, 1971.

Canfield, J. T., & Wells, H. C. *100 Ways to Enhance Self-Concept in the Classroom.* Amherst, Mass.: New England Center, 1976.

Castello, Gloria A. *Left-Handed Teacher.* New York: Praeger, 1974.

DeSteforo, J. *Language, the Learner and the School.* New York: John Wiley & Sons, Inc., 1978.

Dollar, B. *Humanizing Classroom Instruction: A Behavioral Approach.* New York: Harper and Row, 1972.

Doughty, P., Pearce, J., & Thornton, G. *Language in Use.* London: Edward Arnold, 1971.

Gillies, J. *My Needs, Your Needs, Our Needs.* New York: Doubleday & Co., Inc., 1974.

Ginott, H.G. *Between Parent and Teenager.* New York: MacMillan Publishing Co., Inc., 1969.

Glasser, W. *Schools Without Failure.* New York: Harper & Row, 1969.

Gordon, T. *Parent Effectiveness Training.* New York: Wyden, 1970.

Gray, R., Graubard, P., & Roseberg, H. "Little Brother is Changing You." *Psychology Today*, March 1974, 42–46.

Howe, L.W., & Howe, M.M. *Personalizing Education: Values Clarification and Beyond.* New York: Hart Publishing Co., Inc., 1975.

Hurt, H.T., Scott, M.D., & McCroskey, J.C. *Communication in the Classroom.* Reading, Mass.: Addison-Wesley Publishing Co., Inc., 1978.

Jacobson, E. *Progressive Relaxation.* Chicago: University of Chicago Press, 1938.

Johnson, D.W., & Johnson, R.T. *Learning Together and Alone: Cooperation, Competition and Individualization.* Englewood Cliffs, N.J.: Prentice-Hall, Inc., 1975.

Johnson, E.W. *Teaching School: Points Mixed Up.* Boston: National Association of Independent Schools, 1979.

Jones, V. *Adolescents with Behavior Problems: Strategies for Teaching, Counseling, and Parent Involvement.* Boston: Allyn and Bacon, Inc., 1980.

Klausmier, H.J., & Goodwin, W. *Learning and Human Abilities.* (2nd ed.) New York: Harper and Row, 1966.

Krumboltz, J., & Thoresen, C. *Behavioral Counseling: Cases and Techniques.* New York: Holt, Rinehart and Winston, Inc., 1969.

McWhirter, J.J., & Kahn, S.E. A parent communication group. *Elementary School Guidance and Counseling*, 1974, *9*, 116–122.

Miles, M. *Learning to Work in Groups.* New York: Bureau of Publications, Teachers College, Columbia University, 1959.

Neill, S.B. Two R's for students: Rights and responsibilities. In J. Chaffee, Jr., & J.P. Clark (Eds.), *New Dimensions for Educating Youth.* Denver: U.S. Department of Health, Education, and Welfare, 1976.

Otto, H.A. *A Guide to Developing Your Potential.* New York: Charles Schribner's Sons, 1967.

Otto, W., McMenemy, R., & Smith, R. *Corrective and Remedial Teaching* (2nd ed.) Boston: Houghton Mifflin Co., 1973.

Postman., N., & Weingartner, C. *Teaching as a Subversive Activity.* New York: Delta, 1969.

Ritter, B. Eliminating excessive fears of the environment through contact desensitization. In J. Krumboltz & F. Thoresen (Eds.), *Behavioral Counseling Cases and Techniques.* New York: Holt, Rinehart and Winston, Inc., 1969.

Rogers, C.R. *Freedom to Learn.* Columbus, Ohio: Charles E. Merrill, 1969.

Schein, E., & Bennis, W. *Personal and Organizational Change Through Group Methods.* New York: John Wiley & Sons, Inc., 1965.

Schrank, J. *Teaching Human Beings.* Boston: Beacon, 1972.

Schultz, W.C. FIRO: *A Three Dimensional Theory of Interpersonal Behavior.* New York: Holt, Rinehart and Winston, Inc., 1958.

Shaftel, F., & Shaftel, G. *Role Playing for Social Values.* Englewood Cliffs, N.J.: Prentice-Hall, Inc., 1966.

Simon, S.B., Howe, L.W., & Kirschenbaum, H. *Values Clarification: A Handbook of Practical Strategies.* New York: Hart, 1972.

Spears, H. Kappans Ponder the Goals of Education. *Phi Delta Kappan,* 1973, *55,* 29–32.

Stanford, G., & Stanford, B. *Learning Discussion Skills Through Games.* New York: Citation, 1969.

Strang, R. *Counseling Techniques in College and Secondary School.* New York: Harper & Brothers, 1949.

Thompson, J. *Using Role Playing in the Classroom.* Bloomington, Indiana: Phi Delta Kappa Educational Foundation, 1978.

Torrance, E. Raul, & Myers, R.E. *Creative Learning and Teaching.* New York: Dodd, Mead, 1972.

Wagner, M. Reinforcement of the expression of anger through role playing. In C. Weinstein & M. Fantini (Eds.), *The Disadvantages: Challenges to Education.* New York: Harper & Row, 1968.

Wolpe, J., & Lazarus, A. *Behavior Therapy Techniques.* New York: Pergamon Press, 1966.

SUGGESTED READINGS

Berger, E., & Winters, B. *Social Studies in the Open Classroom.* New York: Teachers College Press, 1973.

Blance, Cook, & Mark. *Reading in the Open Classroom: An Individualized Approach.* New York: Community Resources Institute, 1971.

Bobcock, S.S., & Schild, E.O. *Simulation Games in Learning.* Beverly Hills, Calif.: Sage, 1968.

Canfield, J.T., & Wells, H.C. *100 Ways to Enhance Self-Concept in the Classroom.* Amherst, Mass: New England Center, 1976.

Castello, Gloria A. *Left-Handed Teaching.* New York: Prager, 1974.

DeSteforo, J. *Language, the Learner and the School.* New York: John Wiley & Sons, Inc., 1978.

Dollar, B. *Humanizing Classroom Instruction: A Behavioral Approach.* New York: Harper and Row, 1972.

Doughty, P., Pearce, J., & Thornton, G. *Language in Use.* London: Edward Arnold, 1971.

Gordon, T. *Parent Effectiveness Training.* New York: Wyden, 1970.

Gray, R., Graubard, P., & Roseberg H. "Little Brother is Changing You." *Psychology Today,* March 1974, 42–46.

Howe, L.W., & Howe, M.M. *Personalizing Education: Values Clarification and Beyond.* New York: Hart Publishing Co., Inc., 1975.

Johnson, D.W., & Johnson, R.T. *Learning Together and Alone: Cooperation, Competition and Individualization.* Englewood Cliffs, N.J.: Prentice-Hall, Inc., 1975.

Johnson, E.W. *Teaching School: Points Mixed Up.* Boston: National Association of Independent Schools, 1979.

Miles, M. *Learning to Work in Groups*. New York: Bureau of Publications, Teachers College, Columbia University, 1959.

Otto, H.A. *A Guide to Developing Your Potential*. New York: Charles Schribner's Sons, 1967.

Postman, N. & Weingartner, C. *Teaching as a Subversive Activity*. New York: Delta, 1969.

Schein, E., & Bennis, W. *Personal and Organizational Change Through Group Methods*. New York: John Wiley & Sons, Inc., 1965.

Schrank, J. *Teaching Human Beings*. Boston: Beacon, 1972.

Shaftel, F., & Shaftel, G. *Role Playing for Social Values*. Englewood Cliffs, N.J.: Prentice-Hall, Inc., 1966.

Simon, S.B., Howe, L.W., & Kirschenbaum, H. *Values Clarification: A Handbook of Practical Strategies*. New York: Hart, 1972.

Stanford, G., & Stanford, B. *Learning Discussion Skills Through Games*. New York: Citation, 1969.

Thompson, J. *Using Role Playing in the Classroom*. Bloomington, Indiana: Phi Delta Kappa Educational Foundation, 1978.

Torrance, E. Raul, & Myers, R.E. *Creative Learning and Teaching*. New York: Dodd, Mead, 1972.

Chapter 4

Math and the Learning Disabled Adolescent

INTRODUCTION

According to Brown (1975):

> Instruction in mathematics for the child labeled learning disabled is an area about which little has been written except that little has been written. Few pages are allotted to it in special education method books, and instructional personnel seem to be on their own when trying to evaluate children or to select methodologies and materials.

A number of works such as those written by Hammill and Bartel (1978) and Mann, Suiter, and McClung (1979) include arithmetic along with several other academic curriculum areas. However, only one or two programs are devoted totally to arithmetic.

A math curriculum on the secondary level is composed of objectives, instruction, and assessment. This chapter addresses each of the three areas and is designed to provide for the secondary math teacher:

- a delineation and discussion of math-related learning problems exhibited by the learning disabled secondary student
- presentation of instructional interventions, materials, and suggestions for curriculum adaptation to enable the mainstream teacher to meet the unique needs of the adolescents with learning disabilities
- diagnostic approaches (formal and informal) to assist the mainstream teacher to pinpoint specific math problems or deficits

THE MATH DISABLED ADOLESCENT

There is still a significant void in the literature pertaining to a learning disability's role in arithmetic difficulties. Although there currently exists a vast reservoir of materials in math education, the practitioner still receives little practical guidance in integrating arithmetic learning and learning disabilities.

Reisman (1972) delineated five processes for the diagnostic teaching of math. They are:

1. identifying students' strengths and weaknesses in arithmetic
2. hypothesizing possible reasons for the observed strengths and weaknesses
3. formulating behavioral objectives
4. creating and trying corrective remedial procedures
5. continued reevaluation of student's achievement (Reprinted with permission.)

In developing an educational plan for learning disabled students, the specific deficits exhibited by the adolescent should be considered.

Arithmetic Deficits Observed Most Commonly in Learning Disabled Students

Johnson and Myklebust (1967) list the problems most often mentioned by writers as:

1. inability to establish a one-to-one correspondence
2. inability to count meaningfully. Although numbers can be said in rote fashion, relationship between the symbol and the quantity is not established.
3. inability to associate the auditory and visual symbols. It is possible to count auditorially but not to identify the numbers visually.
4. inability to learn both the cardinal and ordinal systems of counting
5. inability to visualize clusters of objectives within a larger group; each object in a group must always be counted
6. inability to group the principle of conservation of quantity
7. inability to perform arithmetic operations
8. inability to understand the meaning of the process signs

9. inability to understand the arrangement of the numbers on the page
10. inability to follow and remember the sequences of steps to be used in various mathematical operations
11. inability to understand the principles of measurement
12. inability to read maps and graphs
13. inability to choose the principles for solving problems in arithmetic reasoning (Reprinted with permission.)

Task Analysis

Any attempt to analyze a student's math performance on the secondary level should also take into consideration the curriculum demands and the nature of varied content areas. An approach that allows the teacher to identify progressive behaviors that are encountered at each level and to analyze the behavioral demands present at each level is task analysis. Resnick, Wang, and Kaplan (1973) identify six content processes that must be analyzed separately for each level. They are: decision making, classifying, divergent thinking, synthesizing, conservation, and hypothesizing.

Task analysis should give consideration to the content, relative to cognitive skills and competencies required of the students, as well as the instructional methodology used to present the content. From the latter perspective, the sensory mode of presentation and expected mode of response would need to be addressed.

A Diagnostic Model

Dunlap and House (1976) outline a comprehensive diagnostic plan. The steps they suggest taking are:

1. determination of a terminal task
2. application of task analysis to identify prerequisite skills to the terminal task
3. placement of skills into a hierarchy showing the relationship of each skill to other prerequisite skills and to the terminal task
4. construction of test items to measure each skill in the hierarchy on three levels; enactive, iconic, symbolic. This hierarchy suggests the order of remediating math deficits.

Three-Step Math Remedial Method

a. Work first with concrete materials which can be shown later schematically.

     b. Move to schematic representation when the student is able to work problems on paper.

     c. Use memory (student's internal imagery) wherein the student is able to picture the problem in his mind.

  5. administration of the test

  6. analysis of the child's performance on the test items (Reprinted with permission.)

The nature of the subject matter must be considered when looking at the math-related deficits.

Mathematics is a body of concepts that is organized into a logical, sequential, hierarchical system. The system of mathematics that each learner must master to some degree remains invariate. Handicapped children who exhibit learning difficulties in math are either not achieving the required range of educational objectives in the same manner as their nonhandicapped peers or not at the same rate as the majority of their peers. For these children, consideration must be given to the range of topics expected of the students as well as the instructional methods to be used. This determination is made from a diagnosis of the student's strengths, weaknesses, competencies, and deficits in math.

MATH DIAGNOSTIC TESTS

1. The Schonell Diagnostic Arithmetic Test (Schonell & Schonell, 1957) covers only whole number combinations and tends to be lengthy.

2. *The Buswell-John Diagnostic Chart for Individual Differences: Fundamental Process in Arithmetic* (Buswell and John, 1925) provides for an individual analysis of a pupil's difficulty in the four basic operations with whole numbers. The problems are arranged according to difficulty within each operation. The teacher has a checklist of errors that is used as the student orally explains his or her method of solving the problems. The test is not excessively long and is relatively easy to analyze for sequence of process.

3. *Key Math* (Connolly, Nachtman, and Pritchett, 1971) lends itself more to a grade placement from a set of norms developed with a population of average children, rather than diagnosis.

GROUP ACHIEVEMENT TESTS WITH ARITHMETIC SUBTESTS

There are several group achievement tests published that contain mathematics subtests. Six of the most commonly used tests are:

1. *The California Achievement Test* (California Test Bureau) is useful for grades one through fourteen. The arithmetic section consists of four subsections on reasoning. The fundamental section covers all basic computational areas. Single booklet editions are available for arithmetic. Grades and age equivalents and percentile grade norms are provided.
2. *The Iowa Test of Basic Skills* (Houghton Mifflin) can be used with grades three through nine. A spiral-bound, multilevel, reusable booklet is available. Grade norms and percentile norms allow for testing three times during the school year.
3. *The American School Achievement Tests* (Public School Publishing Company) includes tests for primary, intermediate and advanced levels. There are three sections: numbers, arithmetic computation, and arithmetic problems. Self-marking answer booklets are provided. All batteries are supplied with age and grade norms.
4. *The Metropolitan Achievement Tests* (Harcourt) are useful for grades one through nine. These tests consist of concepts and skills sections for all levels, with problem solving and computation sections for grades three through nine. Stanine scores, grade equivalents, and percentile grade norms are provided.
5. *The Stanford Achievement Tests* (Harcourt) can be used with grades two through nine. Sections on computation and reasoning are provided for all grade levels. Percentile norms by grades and model-age norms are provided.
6. *The SRA Achievement Test* (Science Research Associates) can be used with grades one through nine. Grade equivalent and percentile grade norms for first and second semesters are available.

Teacher-Made Tests

One of the most effective assessments of a student's specific skill proficiency is the use of a teacher-made test. An example of an informal survey-type test is presented in Table 4-1.

The teacher analyzes the student's responses relative to performance errors. Common errors are shown in Table 4-2.

Strauss and Lehtinen (1947) felt that "brain injured" students have little, if any, problem with performing operations for calculations, but the meaning associated with the processes seems to be difficult for them to grasp. Two other prominent authorities in the learning disabled field, Johnson and Myklebust (1967) have delineated two arithmetic disorders in the learning disabled. One type, termed *dyscalculia* describes a child's inabil-

Table 4-1 Teacher-Made Informal Math Survey Test

Operations—6th Grade Level

Addition	200	25			
	50	23		432	125
	305	7	341	745	423
	21	15	167	361	541
Subtraction	965	731	5,054	8,026	90,072
	− 422	− 408	− 4,585	− 6,737	− 42,672
Multiplication	34	66	521	483	640
	× 10	× 43	× 246	× 302	× 257
Division	4)24	12)48	3)966	14)1,085	15)7,926

ity to perform arithmetic calculations, while the other refers to an overriding *language dysfunction* that interferes with a child's arithmetic performance.

In attempting to define the elements essential in an appropriate mathematics instructional program for the older learning disabled student, the teacher must consider a number of factors related to this student group.

Cogent factors inherent in math requirements at the secondary level relate to the sequential nature of mathematics, concomitant reading demands, students' preferred learning styles, and the subject area focus of the secondary curriculum. Each of these factors requires consideration by the teacher in attempting to design an individualized, appropriate math program and are presented for review in the following discussion.

Table 4-2 Common Errors in Math Operations

Addition	Subtraction
errors in combinations	combinations
counting	counting
carrying	regrouping
faulty procedures	faulty procedures

Multiplication	Division
combinations	combinations
counting	counting
remainder difficulties	carrying
faulty procedures	faulty procedures

Sequential Math Hierarchy

The teacher must recognize that any effective math instruction is inherently sequential in the manner of its presentation. The student must be provided the opportunity to learn subordinate concepts prior to being presented with supraordinate concepts (Gagne, 1965). This approach is based on the use of behavioral task analysis. The underlying assumption is that if prior requisite concepts in a task analysis model are mastered, following concepts will be more easily attained. This type of developmental mathematics approach is employed in the programs outlined by Resnick, Wang, and Kaplan (1973).

Reading Demands

An inherent problem for the learning disabled student who exhibits language processing deficits is that, as the mathematics concepts increase in difficulty, there is also a corresponding increase in the difficulty of the related reading level (vocabulary, word problems, etc.). In attempting to pinpoint a student's deficits in math, the teacher should be careful to ferret out the reading demands from the "pure" mathematical demands.

Learning Style

Learning style, the manner in which students approach a math task, is as important as the specific task itself. It is critical in ensuring the success of the interventions employed that specific instruction be provided to the students in "how to learn." The teacher should know, for example, if a student uses a trial-and-error approach to problem solving; if a student uses a purposeful and goal-directed strategy; if he or she learns more efficiently in an environment with background music; or if a student's attention span is limited and therefore short-term study sessions are more effective. Other related factors to be considered here include compensation techniques and specific learning "tricks of the trade" such as oddity learning, serial learning, paired-associate learning, memory training, etc.

Subject Area Focus

The subject area focus in the secondary level curricula emphasizes normative-based achievement. This is clearly seen in the number of mathematics programs that operate on a fixed-frequency basis. That is, a certain number of pages are devoted to a specific concept, for example, the addition of two-digit numbers. The teacher's responsibility is to ensure that the student achieves at a certain correct percentage level before he or she moves on to the next concept. Learning disabled students must be provided the opportunity for mastery learning, an approach advocated by Cawley and Vitello (1972). In this method, the primary guiding principle is a trials-to-criterion or a criterion-based approach in contrast to the more commonly employed percentage-correct method. In a criterion approach, for example, the teacher assumes a student is ready to progress when he or she has attained the performance level of 90 percent correct on at least five consecutive trials in relation to a specific math skill or concept. In planning a program, it must be understood that, in order to master math skills, the student must receive, interpret, and organize important stimuli from the outside world and then relate the stimuli to each other. Both the student's behavior and his or her total response to the environment must be taken into account.

Interfering Behaviors

The adolescent with a learning disability frequently manifests one or more of the following five behaviors.

1. *The student's level of activity* is excessive in relation to task demands. In response, the teacher should attempt to legitimize movement by structuring the lesson so that movement is required. Experiential activities can be built in for the student to apply the concepts taught.
2. The student is easily distractible and is unable to selectively attend to his or her environment. A short attention span may make the student unable to maintain attending behavior to the instructional tasks presented. In response, the teacher should control the verbiage by saying only what is essential and should involve the student in the task through requiring frequent responses from him or her.
3. Students may overreact to a task through frustration, anxiety, or anger. The teacher's response should be to back up a step or two until the student can adequately deal with the material. The student's frustration will be mitigated through a foundation of success experiences with the less difficult material.
4. The student exhibits impulsive behavior and carries out an act prior to thinking it through. In response, the teacher should assist the student in recognizing and realizing the potential consequences of his or her behavior. Role-playing, simulations, and group discussions are suggested.
5. The student appears disorganized and is unable to "get it together." The teacher's response should be to provide the structure and exter-

nal organization that will enable the student to immediately respond to the task while efforts are undertaken to remediate the disorganization problems.

TEACHING OBJECTIVES FOR THE LEARNING DISABLED STUDENT

The teacher who is interested in succeeding with the learning disabled adolescent with mathematics deficits should be aware of the following five underlying instructional principles (objectives):

1. Provide for initial student success. Failure experiences become psychological blocks in future math involvements with adolescents.
2. Attempt consistently to decrease the student's levels of anxiety about mathematical instruction. To reduce anxiety, let students know clearly what will be expected of them and what resources will be made available to them. Allow them to have a voice in the design of their own instructional plans.
3. Provide an environment that allows the students opportunities for questioning and decision making and reinforces students for exhibiting this classroom behavior.
4. Concept mastery must be integrated with memorization to foster meaningful retention and the application of knowledge in new situations.
5. Maintain a high-interest learning environment. This is particularly important with the adolescent who has "turned off" to learning as a result of years of frustration and failure experiences and needs to be catalyzed into an active and receptive student role. Presenting material within a framework of games, hobbies, and other self-stimulating media provides a motivational environment. This instructional format develops the student's ability to deal with new and complex learning in a nonthreatening manner. The strategies involved in some games will often suggest cause-effect relationships corresponding to formal mathematics.

Math Games

Seymore and Snider (1974) offer suggestions for math games, as follows:

1. [Use] math labs for experiments.

    a. Have students copy plan figures, dissect them and rearrange them to form squares. Using these models ask students to find the areas contained in triangles, parallelograms, trapezoids.

    b. Do line designs in a geometry unit.

2. Use think sheets containing logic problems, algebra problems, magic squares and other puzzles.

3. Play "Matho-Bongo." Have the students number bingo-type cards. Make up, beforehand, problems which when solved will equal the numbers on their cards. Problems can be made to stress the unit you are covering.

4. Use "reflection sheets" to give students an opportunity at the end of the week to tell what they did not understand in math for the week. They can write what they liked or disliked about the class. This also provides them with an opportunity to communicate with you on an individual basis. (Reprinted with permission.)

The objectives that serve as an educational focus are derived from the specific math content to be presented to the adolescent.

Math Content

The selection of mathematical content for instruction in the schools is subject to three demand categories: (1) psychological; (2) sociological; and (3) structural.

Psychological demands may be dichotomized into: (1) the holistic or field theories that view the learner as comprehending the entirety or gestalt of learning, usually through sudden inspiration or insight; and (2) the behavioristic, mechanistic theories that view the learner as mastering pieces of mathematical content that collectively produce a whole of learning. The authors posit the latter theoretical perspective, i.e., that the student acquires cognitive skills and competencies in a hierarchical sequence of increasing difficulty and complexity. The beginning stage involves simple association. This is followed by the establishment of relationships and generalizations along a continuum of abstraction.

Teachers who teach math to the learning disabled student must understand the psychology of math. Reisman and Kaufman (1980) provide a model that graphically depicts the psychological structure of math as shown in Figure 4-1.

Sociological demands emphasize students' needs for certain mathematics. This was the major force influencing the design of the modern math curriculum. Questions such as, "What is a number?" "What is an equa-

Figure 4-1 Structure for Understanding the Psychological Nature of
a Mathematics Curriculum

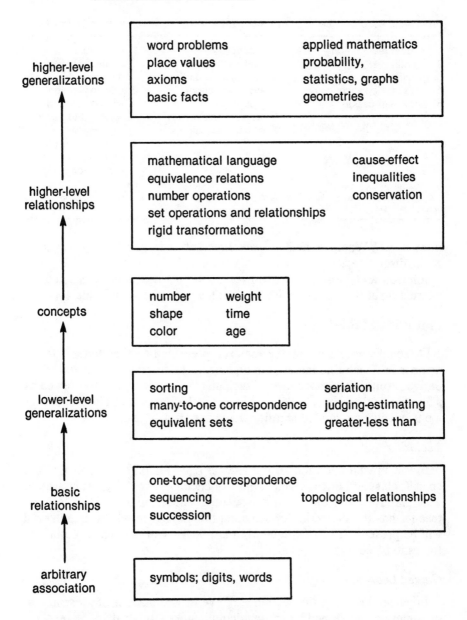

Source: Reprinted from *Teaching Mathematics to Children with Special Needs* by F. Reisman and
S. Kauffman by permission of Charles E. Merrill Publishing Co., © 1980.

Table 4-3 Curriculum Content Areas Included on Cross-Referencing Charts

Pre-School Readiness Level	Introductory Level	Post-Introductory Level
1. number recognition 2. counting 3. grouping 4. relationships vocabulary 5. verbal expression	1. vocabulary 2. relationship, sets 3. operations (addition and subtraction) 4. grouping 5. problem solving 6. verbal expression	1. operations (multiplication and division) 2. rule application 3. written problem solving and expression 4. nonwritten problem solving and expression

Source: Reprinted from *Learning Disabilities (2nd Ed.)* by S.W. Johnson and R. Morasky by permission of Allyn & Bacon, Inc., © 1980.

tion?'' and "What is a field?'' were aimed at understanding the structure of the discipline.

Johnson and Morasky (1980) present the math content suggested for instruction at three functioning student levels as shown in Table 4-3.

Instructional Procedures

Of equal importance to the material presented to the student, is the manner in which this material is organized. Instructional procedures are derived from this organization. Curricular organization can be viewed as a function of the instructional procedures in the classroom. The procedures include lecturing, guided learning, and pure student learning.

Lecturing

In this presentation mode, the teacher exerts maximum control of the specific class activities as well as the sequencing of events in the classroom. This pattern is the one most prevalent in American schools in that the teacher has the discretion of selecting the manner in which the material will be presented. Most frequently the teacher works from an outline of topics to be covered.

Guided Learning

In guided learning, the sequence of events and manner of presentation of content is developed by the curriculum maker rather than the teacher. Programmed learning is an example of this approach.

Pure Student Learning

In this approach, the teacher's role is that of a counselor, i.e., providing initial direction for the student. The curriculum is thus highly flexible with a focus on creativity and individual student freedom. It is important, however, with the learning disabled students that specific instruction be provided to enhance their understanding of concepts and symbols. This suggests the need for the teacher to assume a more directive and instructional role.

DEVELOPING MEANING FOR MATH CONCEPTS AND SYMBOLS

Arithmetic Operations Instruction

Teachers should instruct students to employ various heuristic strategies to solve addition and subtraction problems. For example, using 10 as an intermediate number fact in the problem ($6 + 7 = \square$, students might reason $6 + 4$ is 10 and 3 more is 13 or, using doubles, $6 + 6$ is 12, so $6 + 7$ is 13.

Teachers should provide opportunities for children to develop their own solution processes. Verbal problems help give meaning to the basic math operations and provide for different interpretations of addition and subtraction.

Symbol Representations

A link should be established and maintained between the concepts the students have already acquired and the symbols being introduced. Teachers can provide a variety of experiences for students in the context of verbal problems. These enhance number comprehension via the inherent meaning in the verbal problem approach. Teachers can also structure concrete activities so that frequent links are made between the physical and symbolic representation.

In providing any area of math instruction to the disabled adolescent, it is important to apply the following four guidelines:

1. The teacher must organize the learning task so that the student's attention is focused on the desired stimuli for learning. In remediating specific math deficits, the teacher initially is the prime executor of the task requirements with the student as the observer. Through modeling, verbalization of procedures, and regulation of behavior,

the students will be able to regulate their own behavior when engaging in a similar procedure.

2. The teacher must assist students to notice structurally important features of a situation (such as numbers of objects) rather than more obvious surface features (such as the color of the objects). It must be remembered that learning disabled students' knowledge is often context-bound, i.e., what they learn is related to the specific context in which they learned it.

3. The teacher should help learning disabled students use external memory (things written on paper, for instance) to avoid overloading their mental processes and thereby enhancing organization and recall.

4. The teacher should provide a rich range of math experiences to allow the students to choose those most consistent with their particular pattern of thinking. In order to provide such a range of experiences, a teacher must decide what is relevant and appropriate for instructing the learning disabled adolescent.

TEACHERS' DECISION MAKING

Cooney, Davis, and Henderson (1975) identified the following factors that affect teachers' decisions in selecting content:

a. requirements or regulations from governing bodies such as state departments of education
b. objectives developed by a teacher, department head, etc.
c. the expected use of the content to be taught
d. the student's interest in the content as well as the teacher's interest in teaching it
e. the predicted difficulty of the content
f. authoritative judgments expressed by professional groups or prestigious individuals within the field. Frequently, decisions related to topic selections are passive and based primarily on what appears in textbooks. (Reprinted with permission.)

The teacher's choice of content should be determined by attempting to strike a balance between both cognitive and affective needs of the student, i.e., balancing the need for specific instructional intervention with consideration of a student's self-esteem and the need for his or her continued class participation. The determination of the intervention necessitates that teachers know and understand their students. This knowledge is the key to achieving success with the learning disabled student.

Teacher effectiveness with students has been the study of many research efforts. Good, Grouros, Beckerman, Edmeier, and Schneeberger (1977), for instance, found teacher effectiveness to be strongly associated with the following behavioral clusters:

1. general clarity of instruction
2. task-focused environment
3. nonevaluative (comparatively little use of praise and criticism) interactions
4. higher achievement expectations (more homework, faster pace)
5. relatively few behavioral problems
6. the class taught as a unit (Reprinted with permission.)

Further, teachers were very active and demonstrated alternative approaches for responding to problems. They also emphasized the meaning of mathematical concepts and built systematic review procedures into their instructional plans.

A MATH PRESENTATION MODEL

Once teachers have decided what specific concepts, knowledge, and skills they wish to present, they must then determine the instructional mode. There is no single system for effectively presenting math concepts to learning disabled students. However, four specific aspects of a system should be considered as follows:

1. Students should be adequately prepared for each lesson in order to maximize their involvement and thereby their comprehension. Students must be provided with the necessary experience/information base to be able to deal with the task.
2. The teacher should spend a substantial portion of each lesson actively developing ideas, giving examples, and conveying meaning. Both the teacher and the student should be active in the learning situation.
3. Instructional content should be reviewed in the context of meaning. Application of the concepts taught should be a pervasive factor in the curriculum.
4. A clear feedback system should be used consistently to provide specific information to the students about the quality and nature of their performance.

PROBLEM SOLVING

The first of the National Council of Teachers of Mathematics (NCTM) recommendations for school mathematics of the 1980's (1980) states, "Problem solving must be the focus of school mathematics in the 1980's." This statement not only indicates the importance of instruction in problem solving but also implies that a concerted effort is needed in order to establish problem solving as an integral part of the secondary math curriculum.

Children learn much of their arithmetic at a rote level without understanding how to apply what they know to solve word problems. This finding of the National Assessment of Educational Progress survey of over 70,000 students aged 9, 13, and 17 was reported in *The Arithmetic Teacher* (Carpenter, 1980).

The assessment results clearly indicate that for most children the inability to solve word problems is not a result of their inability to compute. The difficulty experienced by most students in solving word problems is that they simply do not know how to choose the correct operation to deal with the information. They must be able to connect the appropriate arithmetic processes to the situations presented in the stories.

A Place to Start

The everyday language and experience of the student must be the starting point for developing an understanding of the concepts of the operations. In this view, the student is said to understand the arithmetic operations if he or she can recognize the situations that call for these operations as they appear in the real world and can describe these situations with the appropriate language. The goal is for children to generalize for themselves—from many experiences—the language patterns of the operations. The word problems that facilitate this ability should be an ongoing part of the curriculum.

Activities

Unfinished Word Problems

To focus children's attention on the questions in word problems, give students "word problems" in which situations are described but no questions are asked as shown in the following examples:

- Twenty-seven students came to school on Tuesday. Each one put in 15¢ to buy a present for a sick classmate.

- Halley's Comet is seen once about every 77 years. It was last seen in 1910.

Students write a math question based on the situation and then find the solution.

Missing Information

Give students problems that aren't solvable because information is missing. Students must determine what information is missing, supply the information in a reasonable fashion, and then solve the problem. Some examples are:

- Paul has used his allowance to go to the movies on Saturday and to buy a gift for his brother's birthday. He spent $2.00 on the movie and $2.50 on the gift. How much did he have left?
- Sara read 30 pages of the book she checked out of the library. How many more pages does she have left to read?

Diagnosis of Problem-Solving Ability

In attempting to diagnose a student's ability to effectively solve word problems, the teacher should observe the following:

1. Does the student organize a procedure?
2. Is the student able to focus on pertinent elements?
3. Does the student monitor his or her work and check his or her answers?
4. Is the student able to relate the problem elements to each other?
5. Is the student able to determine what is wanted in the problem?
6. Is the student able to select the appropriate computational process?
7. What is the student's approach to the problem? Is it trial and error or is it systematic?
8. Most importantly, is the student able to read the problem and understand the vocabulary?

The Learning Disabled Student and Problem Solving

The teacher who attempts to effectively instruct adolescent learning disabled students in problem solving is posed with several obstacles. These are:

- The learning disabled student group members are not equally familiar with the essential requisite skills or content necessary to effectively solve problems, i.e., a diversity of skill levels and basic skill knowledge exists in learning disabled groups. This means teachers must individualize in presenting lessons to their mainstreamed learning disabled students.
- Learning disabled students have many different problem-solving styles. The manner of presentation and mode of response must be considered.
- Problem solving demands no new skills but requires students to apply and integrate already acquired knowledge. Techniques to facilitate this application are not readily available, and students who have significant basic skill deficits are extremely disadvantaged.
- Learning disabled students vary in the amount of time they require to solve the problems presented as well as in the conditions necessary for effective learning.
- The curricular requirements at the secondary level in the mainstream class mitigate against a criterion-referenced prescriptive plan for individual students.

Problem-solving ability in a student appears to develop slowly over time and is strengthened through actual experience in solving problems. Systematically planned instruction is essential and should be based on a diagnostic foundation.

Polya (1973) suggests four phases in the solution of a problem as: (1) understanding the problem; (2) planning; (3) computational skill; and (4) looking back.

Understanding the Problem

This implies grasping the relationships among the conditions of the problem and perceiving what is given mathematically. In order for the student to understand problems, instruction should include slow-down mechanisms to motivate students to make a concerted effort to understand the problem. For example, the problem could be expressed in some other form (model, equation, etc.) that forces the student to translate the problem. Teachers can also pose problems with missing information. This technique requires the student to "think through" the problem rather than approaching it mechanically.

In addition, teachers can suggest that students make up their own problems and solve them. Pupils must become aware of their own processes in solving problems. Teachers can also assign problems with redundant or contradictory information.

Planning

Teachers should suggest a variety of plans for solving the same problem to indicate to students there is more than one way to solve a problem. In order to ensure the student's persistence in solving the problem, teachers can provide hints or cues to assist students in moving closer to a solution.

Basic Computational Skills Utilization

Teachers can use a sequential delineation of skills in the four operations (addition, subtraction, multiplication, and division) to pinpoint an instructional focus.

Self-Monitoring Behavior: Looking Back

Students should be encouraged to think through the steps taken in solving the problem. Teachers should take students through alternate solution options and compare the processes and steps.

Math Service Delivery Principles

The secondary school system has several options for delivering educational services to the upper level learning disabled student. Whatever options are exercised, however, it is important to recognize the following five points:

1. The program should not isolate learning disabled students from their nonhandicapped peers. This factor is significant with adolescents for whom the peer group is important.
2. The program should be made as invisible as possible among other course offerings. Learning disabled students are very concerned about their images with their peers. Any intervention should be considered with this in mind.
3. The school should be flexible enough to make modifications in curriculum, teaching procedures, and testing methods to meet the needs of learning disabled students.
4. The program should have a reasonable expectancy for achievement. Given an instructionally sound learning environment, students tend to perform in accordance with the expectations placed on them.
5. The program should be realistic and relevant to the students' immediate needs—the need for success, meaningful functional content, etc.

Program Characteristics for the High School Learning Disabled Student

In attempting to design math programs for learning disabled students on the secondary level, the following points should be considered:

- The program should be practical. Problems for everyday living should be stressed.
- Goals should be considered in terms of helping individuals attain independence in society, i.e., giving and receiving the correct change in the market place, paying bills, and balancing a checkbook.
- Students should learn measurement through the use of rulers, scales, and other units of measurement. The initial focus should be on the concrete and practical.
- Students must learn to make judgments about time, distance, and space and to read maps and estimate how long it will take to go from one place to another.
- Students should be taught how to read recipes, to measure liquids and solids, and to measure clothes and surfaces.
- Each new concept should be concretized and presented through direct experience whenever possible.
- Emphasis should be placed on logic and rational thought rather than on rote memorization.

A FIVE-POINT MATH PROGRAM DESIGN

In designing an effective math program for the learning disabled adolescent, the following five points should be considered:

1. The program should have a diagnostic/prescriptive format. The instructional plan for each learner must be based on criterion-referenced test results. Criterion-referenced instruments are defined as collections of items that have been selected to assess the instructional outcomes of specific instructional objectives. In this approach, the use of absolute standards of performance (criteria) replaces standards derived from normative performance in formulating judgments of pupil (or item) adequacy. The same objectives that are used for program planning and instruction should be used to generate assessment items—thus providing a built-in link between the plans, instruction, and evaluation.
2. The program should emphasize concepts and skills. The focus of the curriculum should be on the development of concepts that will have

value to the learner after his or her formal education ends. Application of curricula to the real world should serve as a foundation.

3. The program should be adaptable and should be adjusted to fit the learner's preferred processing mode. A variety of instructional options is necessary since no one set of curriculum materials or instructional procedures is consistently appropriate.
4. The program must be relevant. The content of the curriculum should permit "purposeful" learning experiences for the students. Real-life simulations and examples of concepts presented enable the learning disabled students to more easily generalize from the learning situations to life situations. This is important with the learning disabled student for whom inferential learning is difficult.
5. Social skills should be emphasized. The curriculum should contain activities that teach students how to function successfully both in school and in the larger society. Examples of social skills include cooperation, social responsibility, decision making, establishing goals, etc.

Structure

In discussing the importance of structure, Bruner (1965) states that, "Learning should not only take us someplace; it should allow us later to go further more easily." The capacity to move students progressively forward is contingent upon the students' basic comprehension of the subject matter.

The five points discussed above provide the structure that serves as the foundation for the secondary math curriculum. Structure is a critical factor for the learning disabled adolescent.

PROGRAMS ON READING DISABILITY IN MATH

Comprehension in any academic subject depends upon the students' knowledge and understanding of the vocabulary, as well as the readability of the tests. *The Aukerman Prognostic Test of Reading Disability in Secondary School Math* (1971) measures a student's potential math problems. The test is shown in Exhibit 4-1.

TECHNIQUES TO INCREASE COMPREHENSION IN MATH READING

Aukerman (1972) suggests the following guides to enhance a student's math reading comprehension:

Exhibit 4-1 Aukerman Prognostic Test of Reading Disability in
Secondary School Math

This program will provide a means by which the teacher can identify the student who will experience difficulty with secondary math textbooks. The program is given individually. Each student reads directly from the page in the book, pronouncing the words aloud. One or two minutes are enough. Use one of the three forms for each student.

Directions: Cover the two forms not being used (5x7 inch cards will do).

Ask the student to read from left to right, pronouncing each word in turn, at his normal rate.

Observe his facial expression as he reads. Note hesitation, repetition, regression, uncertainty, gross mispronunciation, and incorrect stress.

Identify the student who is not able to move along smoothly at about one word every two seconds. He will most probably have great difficulty reading the textbook because he lacks proficiency in general vocabulary. He will be at a total loss when faced with the technical vocabulary of mathematics.

Alternative Form A

horizontal	conclusions	numerical	equivalent
vertical	polygon	measurement	perpendicular
geometrical	estimate	equally	segment
intersect	equidistant	diagonal	surface
symbol	corresponding	definition	indicate
negative	represent	diagram	midpoint
operations	properties	coordinates	irrational
conditional	substitution	congruent	formula
rational	inverse	inconsistent	eliminated
solution	approximation	intercept	determine

Alternative Form B

coincide	difference	variation	circumference
graphically	connecting	velocity	computing
infinite	inequality	multiple	parentheses
projection	approximately	conceptual	probability
demonstrated	derivation	illustrated	relationship
assigning	unspecified	principle	expression
absolute	frequency	associated	distribution
assumptions	numerical	cancellation	reciprocal

Alternative Form C

symmetry	replacement	conditional	significant
consecutive	supplementary	alternate	variable
constant	cumulative	fractional	combinations
displacement	deviation	successive	mutually
approximation	exclusive	origin	relationship
proportion	numerical	simultaneous	terminate
transform	parallel	unsolvable	reduce
multiply	corresponds	simplify	characteristics

Source: Reprinted from *Reading in the Secondary School Classroom* by Robert C. Aukerman. Copyright, 1971. Used with the permission of McGraw-Hill Book Company.

1. Have the students restate the problem in their own words.
2. Discuss the vocabulary with the entire group, comparing as many terms as possible with everyday usage. Study all vocabulary in relationship to context—never in isolation.
3. Have the students note the relationships between the parts of the problem. This can often be visualized by means of a graph or chart.
4. Have the students draw a diagram which will evolve from a step-by-step rereading of the problem.
5. Help the students as a group devise an equation which correctly states the problem.
6. Discuss the estimated or probable answer on a basis of "educated guesses." This is a good check on the adequacy of comprehension.
7. Have the students solve the problem and check the answer against the educated estimate. Then double-check it within the equation to see if it satisfies the conditions of the equation. (p. 212. Reprinted with permission.)

SKILL IN READING MATH

A student's comprehension ability depends upon specific skills essential to the reading process. Effective math reading on the secondary level requires two skills: (1) recognition of the importance of definition in mathematics, i.e., a mathematical word cannot have connotations, and its meaning does not depend on the context; (2) proficiency in actually using the text examples.

Regardless of the text and its format, the following suggestions should be considered in the instructional process:

- Underline important words when they are first defined and provide simple, clear definitions that the student copies into a notebook.
- Develop "discovery exercises" with instructions to the student.
- Begin with a review of topics from material previously covered.
- Give the students an occasional reading assignment to supplement the class lectures. Ask the students to summarize in their own words what was covered in the section.
- Divide the class into groups, each of which represents a range of talents and achievement (Kaplan, 1966).
- Use students as instructors. It is well proven that learning is enhanced through educating others.

- Provide group work in helping with problems, writing problems, discussing ideas, and making reports and projects.
- Try using a math lab approach consisting of regular sessions in which individual and group work projects are completed and review is accomplished (Sweet, 1967).
- Involve students in the grading procedures.

Comprehension problems encountered by secondary learning disabled students are frequently the result of the vocabulary of the subject area, which is technical, polysyllabic, and subject-specific.

Math Vocabulary and the Learning Disabled Student

One of the major factors for the math difficulties encountered by the learning disabled adolescent is the secondary level math vocabulary. The vocabulary tends to fall into one of three categories:

1. words (terms) that are specific and unique to math, such as technical terms;
2. words that occur in everyday usage but that also have a special meaning in math, such as, product, power, etc.; and
3. words that are not unique to math but may be difficult for the learning disabled student to decode or comprehend.

Teachers can use several intervention/remedial strategies in dealing with students' math vocabulary problems. The teacher can use the student's previous experience and knowledge by relating the new vocabulary to what the student already knows. Class discussions relating terms to words in common use will aid both comprehension and retention. For example, relating the term *binary* to the common term *bicycle* will aid the child in remembering it means *two*.

Vocabulary can also be taught through a structural analysis approach, i.e., a study of the parts of the word such as prefixes and roots.

Math Term	Related Common Usage Term	Origin
triangle	tricycle	Latin tri, "three"
binomial	nominate (to name)	Latin nomen, "name"

The teacher can also teach vocabulary by developing the student's ability to use contextual analysis. The student derives the meaning of unknown or unfamiliar terms through understanding the context in which the terms are used.

COMPUTATIONAL SKILLS INVOLVING WHOLE NUMBERS, DECIMALS, FRACTIONS, AND PERCENT

The teacher should attempt to relate or utilize real-life experiences when instructing the learning disabled adolescent. Even basic computational skills may be practiced through real-life activities.

The following list provides some suggestions for activities to teach computational skills:

- Obtain an order form from a fast-food restaurant, along with the available items and their prices. Have the students take orders and compute the bills. Encourage them to estimate each total amount before actually computing it.
- Have students look through the newspapers for sales advertisements in which the regular price and sale price are given, but not the discount. Have students find the percent of discount.
- Have students collect baseball batting averages and place in order to be used with the percent instruction.
- Have students write down their weight and use the facts below to find the weight of different parts of their bodies.

Percent of total body weight	Part of Body
18	Bone
39	Muscle
23	Fat tissue
57	Water

- Obtain road maps from the state highway department. Have students select a place to visit and then compute the distance and the driving time.
- Have students obtain car rental rates from various companies. Compare the results in class.

Federal publications on consumer topics can be used to develop other activities. For a list of these publications write to Consumer Information, Public Documents Distribution Center, Pueblo, Col. 81009. *Sylvia Porter's Money Book* (Softbound version 1975, 1976 published by Avon Books) is another good resource.

In addition to the application of concepts and skills to real-life situations, there are several other strategies secondary math teachers should use in teaching the learning disabled student.

Instructional Strategy Guide

The number and diversity of specific math deficits exhibited by the secondary student are such that the teacher must have a vast repertoire of skills and interventions to employ in effectively instructing this heterogenous group of learners.

Suggestions will be provided to remediate specific deficits such as retention problems, distractibility, difficulty in formulating concepts, and so on.

Retention Problems

If a student has retention problems, the teacher should emphasize patterns that will strengthen the student's associative ability.

Distractibility

If a student is distractible, the teacher should eliminate irrelevant stimuli from the instructional material used with the student. Teachers should keep worksheets simple and clean, eliminating unnecessary data.

Difficulty in Attending

For students who have difficulties in attending to the salient aspects of a situation, teachers should highlight what is significant by using color, underlining, and intensity of focus. Repetition should be built in.

Difficulty Formulating Concepts

If a student has problems in formulating concepts, the teacher can introduce new concepts, by using familiar categories to ensure there is meaning for the student.

Difficulty Forming Generalizations

If a student has trouble forming generalizations, the teacher can direct the transfer of a student's learning through pointing out relevant relationships.

Difficulty Drawing Conclusions

For students who have difficulty drawing conclusions, teachers should use a "fading-out" instructional approach. This means that initially the student is provided with a complete example. Gradually, less and less information is given the student in solving a problem, determining a process to employ, etc. Students should be better able to come to conclusions based on their experiences within this structured and sequential delivery system.

Difficulty in Solving Higher Order Problems

Due to deficient basic operations skills, some students may have difficulties in solving higher order problems. The teacher can allow the student to use a pocket calculator. However, the instructional objective must be clear.

Deficient Organizational Skills

For students with deficient organizational skills, the teacher must provide the structure the students themselves are unable to bring to the instructional task. There are countless ways in which this may be accomplished. Examples might include assisting the student in keeping a notebook of due dates; organizing notes taken in class into a functional mode; encouraging skill development in budgeting time; providing study guides and lecture outlines; and developing step-by-step LAPs.

Difficulty Establishing Math Relationships

If a student has difficulty establishing math relationships, the teacher can initially highlight relevant variables and reinforce the student's attention to a relevant dimension.

Difficulty Making Judgments

The teacher should attempt to maintain an environment of instructional consistency if students have trouble making judgments. Learning disabled students are better able to judge situations or respond to stimuli if they have a reliable base to draw from. The teacher should encourage a student to respond to similar stimuli in a consistent manner and should reinforce this behavior when it is observed within the classroom.

Difficulty Abstracting

If students have difficulty in abstracting, the teacher should begin on a concrete level. From this base, the teacher should provide sequenced experiences comprised of increased abstraction.

Difficulty Learning Math Symbols

For students who have difficulties in learning math symbol systems, teachers should use concrete examples to enable students to "see" the concept.

Poor Motivation

If a student has poor motivation, the teacher should present material through the student's interest base. For example, baseball averages can be used to teach percentages, and horse racing can be used to teach probability.

Visual Perception Problems

To aid students with visual perception problems, teachers can screen out extraneous stimuli, emphasize salient task elements, and enhance deficient visual processing by adding auditory stimuli, i.e., tape explanations of problems in a step-by-step format. Teachers can also use highlighting media aids such as overhead projectors or programmed instruction.

General Sensory Limitations

For students with other sensory limitations, teachers should also use a multisensory approach. For example, students with auditory processing problems could be aided by the use of visual or tactile stimuli.

Psychomotor Difficulties

Teachers should eliminate or minimize writing as a task requirement wherever possible for students with psychomotor problems. Teachers could provide sheets of examples rather than asking students to copy from board or book. The requirements for note taking in class should be kept to a minimum or outlines should be provided for students.

Difficulty with Basic Math Relationships

If a student has trouble learning basic math relationships, the teacher should begin instruction at a point where the student is familiar with prerequisite concepts. This familiarity can be used to develop word-object associations.

Difficulty with Mathematical Terms

If students have trouble understanding the language of mathematics, the teacher should be sure to use consistent vocabulary. Other sections of this chapter provide additional suggestions for enhancing a student's comprehension in math reading.

Difficulty Coping with Complexity

To aid students who have trouble coping with complexity, teachers should present structured intentional learning tasks. Tasks should be directed toward a clear and objective learning goal. The teacher should minimize the opportunity for incidental learning to occur within the initial instructional phase.

Math Anxiety

To aid students with math anxiety, teachers must establish a base of success experiences for the student. Instruction should begin at the point where the student demonstrates subject mastery. The teacher should limit the quantity of performance required of the student, i.e., numbers of examples, pages of text, etc. Material should be presented at an appropriate level of complexity and abstractness, and feedback should be provided on a frequent basis. Reinforcement should be given for exhibited success.

Limited Persistence to Task

For students with limited persistence, the teacher can provide a feedback schedule at fixed intervals, i.e., initially reinforce students for work completed on a frequent basis (short-term, limited response required, etc.). As students experience success and receive teacher reinforcement for their performance, the time span for reinforcement and the amount of performance required can be gradually increased.

Difficulty Asking for Assistance

Some students may have difficulty in asking the teacher for assistance. Teachers should consider using some of the small group techniques suggested in Chapter 3. Student team problem solving could be useful.

Deficits in Short-Term Memory

For students who have trouble with short-term memory, teachers can use verbal rehearsal such as labeling. Ellis (1970) provides examples of this strategy. Teachers can also reinforce attention to relevant stimuli by highlighting relevant or significant dimensions.

Language Deficiency

In order to enhance the learning of students with language deficiencies, teachers should control the verbiage in the presentation of content and use short, simple sentences. Teachers should highlight relationship prepositions through concrete examples and use prompting. Modeling experiences should be provided whenever possible.

Math Anxiety

Adolescents on the secondary level confront math with an anxiety that is the product of several years of failure-related math instruction. The traditionally accepted method of presenting math is responsible for creating three sources of math anxiety for the learning disabled adolescent as follows:

1. Traditionally, the emphasis has been on the right answer. With learning disabled students, the process must be emphasized as well as the product. The teacher should attempt to find out how the student arrived at the answer given as well as to reward him or her for any creative thought brought to the problem. (Refer to the Buswell-John test description.)
2. Learning is isolated. The focus on each student doing his or her "own" work limits exploration and exchange of ideas. The teacher should consider having students work out problems in small groups.
3. Students are under time pressure. The emphasis on timed tests, flash cards, etc. handicaps the learning disabled adolescent who requires time to process the information and who needs a relaxed, self-paced response period. The teacher should stress quality rather than quantity.

Methods To Teach the Metric System

In addressing the instruction of the metric system (a requirement of some school systems), teachers of the secondary learning disabled student should be cognizant of the need to concretize the task and relate it to the reality of the adolescent. Specific suggestions toward this goal include:

- Students could write sample questions that could be used on a state driving test to evaluate a driver's knowledge of metric terms related to driving.
- Students can select a topic and report on how it will be affected by the switch to the metric system (cooking, sports, clothing, etc.).
- The teacher can select items in the classroom for students to measure and have students record their estimate before taking the actual measure.
- Students could take a school survey and use the information to construct a bar or line graph.

Resources for teaching metrics include the National Bureau of Standards; U.S. Department of Commerce; the Metric Information Office, Washington, D.C. 20234; and the American National Metric Council, 1625 Massachusetts Avenue, Washington, D.C. 20036.

In order to add variety and interest to the basic instructional base, the teacher should use games and activities to enhance the teaching-learning process.

SUMMARY

Mainstream teachers who seek effectiveness of instruction with the secondary learning disabled student must be aware of the nature of the subject of mathematics and the problems encountered by learning disabled students. Teachers also must possess a broad repertoire of interventions to employ in dealing with the specific disabilities manifested by the students.

This chapter has presented guidelines and specific instructional strategies that the mainstream teacher can use to teach the learning disabled adolescent within the regular classroom setting. Application to real-life experiences and the interests of the adolescent were stressed as significant to the teacher's effectiveness.

Approaches presented have integrated the student, the teacher, and the task and have dealt with diagnostic measures, materials selection, and instructional delivery systems.

The materials suggested are pragmatic and life-role related and may be used by the teacher to supplement the basic curriculum used in the school setting.

In summary, this chapter has provided the secondary mainstream teacher with the information essential to effectively instruct the learning disabled adolescent within the regular classroom setting.

ANNOTATED BIBLIOGRAPHY

Ideas and Activities

Do-a-Number. Port Washington, N.Y.: Skye Marketing Corp. (grade level: intermediate to junior high)

This game requires mental manipulation of numbers to achieve a specific figure. Players are called upon to exercise all four basic math operations.

Rand, K. and Firor, J. *Handy Math*. Creative Publications. Palo Alto, CA. (grade level: intermediate to junior high)

A set of three booklets that promote practical application of math skills. Each booklet is composed of 56 activity sheets, perforated for removal and duplication and each page focuses on a specific topic and its math-related components: sports (bowling scores, passing percentages, running rates); travel; purchasing (discounts, sales tax).

There are detailed tables of contents as well as brief page notes that indicate the topic, the major skill area and the specific subskills being reinforced.

Notes to the teacher explain the philosophy of the series and offer hints and suggestions for extending activity ideas.

Ideas from the Arithmetic Teacher. Reston, Va.: National Council of Teachers of Mathematics.

This 142-page book of math activity sheets, based on ideas from the *Arithmetic Teacher,* can save teachers the chore of clipping and collecting.

The book is organized into sections on computation, fractions, problem solving, geometry, and measurement. Each page has an activity sheet on one side and teacher material (objectives, grade levels, directions and follow-up activities) on the reverse.

The activities, which include games and puzzles, are innovative and challenging. Students must concentrate and follow carefully to successfully complete most tasks.

Multiplication and Division Games and Ideas. Paoli, Penn.: Instructo/McGraw-Hill Book Co. (grade level: intermediate)

This paperback teacher-resource book provides a wide variety of multiplication and division activities that give students practice with basic facts. The activities in the 124-page book are organized according to specific mathematical objectives, with at least three activities to each.

Sample tests for determining skills, as well as profile forms for recording student's test results, are provided.

Olio, J. *Four-on-Four Math**
The puzzle solver is given four digits and a goal figure—for example, 6, 2, 9, 4 and (48)—and must apply basic math operations to the digits to achieve the goal figure. Students create four-on-four puzzles by following these directions:

1. Choose two digits and an operation. Example: 6 ÷ 2 yielding an initial subtotal of (3). (Students should select combinations that yield whole numbers.)

2. Choose a third digit and an operation applying these to the initial subtotal: (3) + 9 = (12).

3. Choose a third digit and an operation, applying these to the second subtotal: (12) × 4 = (48). The result of this step is the goal figure.

4. Write out the previous three steps as one complete equation. This is the solution to the puzzle: 6 − 2 = (3) + 9 = (12) × 4 = (48).

5. Scramble the four digits and present the puzzle in this form: 9, 6, 4, 2 (48).

Students may solve puzzles simply for the challenge, or they may choose to work against the clock or in competition with others, either individually or in teams (in which case students will need to work out specific game rules).

The puzzle maker's eagerness to stump their friends and the puzzle solvers' determination not to be stumped may camouflage the math practice that's going on, a side effect that shouldn't trouble anyone.

Resources for the Practitioner

Cawley, J.F., & Vitello, S.J. Model for arithmetical programming for handicapped children. *Exceptional Child*, 1972, *39*, 101–110.
The assumption behind this model is that an instructional system for special education "should provide a successful amalgamation of teacher competency, curriculum and materials, and an emphasis on process rather than product" (p. 101).

Fountain Valley Teacher Support System in Mathematics (FVTSS). Huntington Beach, Calif.: Richard L. Zweig Associates, Inc., 1974.
This program provides a direct link between a learner's performance on a series of diagnostic math tests and the materials that a teacher could use to teach the skills the learner needs.

The FVTSS in math contains a series of criterion-referenced diagnostic tests that cover 785 behaviorally stated math objectives suitable for

---

*Idea by: Jerry Olio, Chico, California. *Learning*, 530 University Ave., Palo Alto, CA 94301. Reprinted by permission of Pitman Learning, Inc. © 1981, p. 26.

grades K–8. The objectives cover 9 distinct math strands: (1) numbers and operations; (2) geometry; (3) measurement; (4) application of math; (5) statistics and probability; (6) sets; (7) functions and graphs; (8) logical thinking; and (9) problem solving. The major basal tests and audio-visual supplements have each been analyzed in terms of the 785 objectives and cross-referenced with page numbers in the texts back to each item on the tests. The end result is a direct link between the test and the instructional options.

Herber, H. *Teaching Reading in Content Areas*. Prentice-Hall, Inc. Englewood Cliffs, N.J., 1978.

This book is organized by instructional and cognitive-level considerations rather than by content areas. Applications of the concepts and techniques are imbedded within the entire text. Herber focuses on "reasoning" and provides numerous and varied examples of written exercises designed to show how the organization and structure of such exercises can promote more thoughtful responses about the content area. Herber's chapter on technical vocabulary and language development is one of the more useful for math instruction.

Instructional Aids in Mathematics: Thirty-Fourth Yearbook, Reston, Va.: National Council of Teachers of Mathematics, 1973.

This book is intended to give teachers reliable, organized information regarding the possible range from which they can acquire and use instructional aids in mathematics; to provide teachers with a basis for evaluating the quality and utility of instructional aids; and to present suggestions for making effective use of instructional aids. The scope and content of this handbook make it a valuable reference book.

Learning: The Magazine for Creative Teaching, Palo Alto, Calif. (March, 1975) casts current professional thinking into understandable language.

National Council of Teachers of Mathematics (NCTM), Reston, Va.

Written materials, regional workshops and an annual convention are sponsored. A descriptive publications brochure is available from the Council on request, and two of their yearbooks are highlighted below to show the relevance of their products to special education.

Sternberg, L. *Pattern Recognition Skills Inventory (PRSI)*. North Brook, Ill.: Hubbard Scientific Co., 1976.

The PRSI is arranged in four equivalent sets, with each set consisting of 24 pattern tests. One set (random selection) is presented to the student. As the teacher presents each task, he or she instructs the student to: (1) view the model pattern sequence; (2) view the four-choice array of pattern sequences; and (3) make a choice from this array. The student's responses indicate the student's: (1) pattern task performance;

(2) stimulus dimension performance; and (3) pattern performance. The author has related these performance areas to basic instructional implications in math. This program can also be used to develop pattern recognition skills.

The objective is to relate a specific behavior (pattern recognition) and relate it to conceptual areas (math).

It was designed for use by teachers and requires no reading on the part of the student.

The Slow Learner in Mathematics: Thirty-Fifth Yearbook, Reston, Va.: National Council of Teachers of Mathematics, 1972.

Three major strands recur throughout the book: (1) enhancement of the learner's self-image; (2) learner involvement; and (3) both skills and problem-solving abilities. Many positive instructional techniques are recommended for creating a favorable learning environment. Simple but useful suggestions for individual child-oriented assessment procedures are presented. Promising programs and practices actually used with students experiencing or presenting learning problems are described. The book presents content, techniques, and suggested materials. In addition, content sample lessons across levels are provided.

Math Competency Skills Materials

Arithmetic Skill Test for Daily Living. Special Service Supply, 1970.

This series presents practical math in a newspaper magazine format. Included in each of the three books of this series are word problems related to newspaper type ads found on various pages throughout the book. The students must check ad prices to answer each problem. Topics of different ads relate to the food store, the clothing store, recreation, the department store, and the hardware store.

Banking, Budgeting and Employment. Phoenix, N.Y.: Frank E. Richards Company, Inc.

This book employs a basic approach to simplifying terminology relative to banking operations, budgeting money, and employment. Included in the book are examples of forms on which to practice. It also contains vocabulary lists, maze puzzles, workshop questionnaires, and story problems.

Banking Series. Kalamazoo, Mich.: Interpretive Education, 1973 (five color sound filmstrips and workbooks; grades 7–9; remedial 10–adult)

This is a low vocabulary, high-interest program that explores the important area of bank functions as applied to practical implementations. Some topics covered include filling out and using checks, using bank forms, and how to open a savings account.

Basic Mathematics Filmstrip Series. Baltimore: Hampden Publications, 1980. (ten color sound filmstrips; booklets; grades 6–9; remedial 10–adult; high interest-low reading level)

This multi-sensory approach is designed to heighten students' perceptual and cognitive skills. Students learn to listen, look, and correlate instruction with written exercises provided in their Student Response Booklets. Topics are creatively dealt with through the combined talents of educators, writers, and artists. The program is thoroughly field-tested for effectiveness.

Blair, M.E. *To Buy or Not to Buy.* New York: Random House, Inc.

No one can afford not to be a conscious consumer. This learning unit allows students the opportunity to become aware of consumer issues. Within the classroom, students investigate the buying skills involved in purchasing different types of products. Through the investigation of specific purchases, students are led to an indepth study of key consumer issues: advertising, labeling, product safety, contracts and fine print, and product and service complaints. The complete unit includes cassettes and records.

Bolster, L.C., Woodown, H.D., & Gipson, J.H. *Consumer and Career Mathematics.* Glenview, Ill.: Foresman and Company.

This text contains 18 chapters that deal with such topics as basic math skills, income, banking, credit, transportation, housing, taxes, insurance and investments, and purchasing and budgeting.

Cawley, J.F. *Project Math.* Storrs, Conn.: University of Connecticut, 1976.

This program is a result of research and demonstration efforts of a comprehensive curriculum that has been developed for the teaching of exceptional students from preschool through high school. This type of teaching system is comprised of lesson guides for the teaching of skills and concepts in the areas of numbers and operations, sets and operations, patterns, fractions, geometry, and measurement. It provides a comprehensive parallel system for fostering verbal problem-solving skills and a series of laboratory experiences for the application of various arithmetic concepts to applied social settings.

This program provides the teacher with multiple options in instructing and meeting the math needs of exceptional students. There are various ways for the student to demonstrate competence. Symbolic work, rotely performed is rejected. Creative use of pictorial aids and various manipulations are encouraged throughout the program. Students are also encouraged to use math skills as a vehicle to higher cognitive processes.

Teachers are encouraged to individualize their presentations. The diagnostic-prescriptive tools and materials are included to accentuate the most effective use of the curriculum with each student.

Clues to Math. Tulsa, Okla.: Education Progress Corporation, 1978.

This is an audio-tutorial program for use with students who are studying decimals, percents, and metrics. Three student magazines present stories with number-related concepts. All stories are read or heard on audio tapes. Each magazine is accompanied by eight audio tapes, which provide instruction, as well as four additional tapes that provide an opportunity for further practice. Diagnostic and evaluative tests are also included in the program.

Consumer, Applied, and Business Math. Iowa City, Ia.: Westinghouse Learning Corp., 1980. (plan kit/grades 6–adult)

Designed to expand your student's math abilities, this program uses high interest topics, emphasizing the math skills they will need in everyday situations. Student activities keyed to 111 performance objectives guide the learner in a fascinating application of the theoretical to the real. Topics include: wages and budgets; buying and selling; charge accounts; taxes; etc.

Diagnosing Abilities in Math Test. Johnstown, Pa.: Mafex Test Booklets, 1980. (remedial 7–adult)

This instrument tests basic math facts and diagnoses trouble spots for placing students in individualized math programs. The first section tests instant recall of basic math facts essential for successful performance in testing situations. This 30-minute timed test often reveals simple errors that can be easily corrected. After completion of the basic facts test, students are given the three-hour diagnostic test covering whole numbers, fractions, and decimals. The diagnostic test will pinpoint specific problem areas and permit analysis of the types of errors because students show each step of their work. An answer key is provided.

Equations: The Game of Creative Mathematics. (grades 6–12; remedial adults) Equations Game (WF040). Orange City, Fla.: Rancourt & Co., 1981–82.

This popular game provides creative opportunity to practice arithmetic operations in a variety of number bases (decimal, binary, etc.). Like chess, the game can be as simple or as complex as the players make it, depending on their understanding of the mathematical ideas involved. A five-game kit comes with a teacher's manual. Games can be used with two to four players.

Hudson, M.W., & Weaver, A.A. *Getting Ready for Pay Day.* Phoenix, N.Y.: Frank E. Richards Company, Inc.

This three-part series explores various aspects of checking accounts, savings accounts, and planning ahead. The graphics are poor, but the information is necessary. The material is for the EMR secondary student, but also could be a supplement to a course for the high school learning disabled student.

Individual Corrective Math. Shreveport, La.: Educational Research, Inc., 1976. (12 audio cassettes, student workbook; grades 5–6; remedial 7– adult)

This program is ideal for students preparing to take the GED tests. Topics include base ten, place value, sets, number patterns, and mathematical sentences. This program provides thorough concept training in fundamental addition, subtraction, multiplication, and division.

It Figures Series. Lyons Falls, N.Y.: Educational Images, 1977 (eight color sound filmstrips; grades 6–9; remedial 10–12)

This program was designed for determining skill levels of students in arithmetic; reviewing and reinforcing computational competency; and prescribing and supervising remedial practice as needed by individual students. Students complete and grade their own tests and this helps them realize whether and where they need assistance. Performance on diagnostic tests can be used to guide students to special practice units and achievement tests that build skills in areas of weakness.

Jacobs, R.F. *Basic Skills in Mathematics.* New York: Harcourt Brace Jovanovich, Inc.

This is a program in fundamental operations, designed to help students master basic skills that are necessary for successful life experiences. It consists of four units: whole numbers, fractions, decimals, and percents. Concepts of measurement are included with special emphasis given to the use of metric units. This program is suitable for individualized programs or in a group-paced mode. Involvement of students is encouraged. The reading level is generally low, with special attention given to short words and sentences.

Kahn, C.H., & Hanna, J.B. *Pacemaker Practical Arithmetic Series; Working Makes Sense; Money Makes Sense; Using Dollars and Sense.* Belmont, Calif.: Fearon Pitman.

Does money, working and using money make sense to you? The Pacemaker Practical Arithmetic Series explores questions about money in the world of work. It is a simplified series geared for the moderate learning disabled student who lacks knowledge and experience about working, saving, and spending. It would be an excellent supplement to a course that enrolls adolescents seeking employment.

Landy, M.L. *Let's Go Shopping*. Phoenix, N.Y.: Frank E. Richards Company, Inc.

This program presents interesting concepts that are necessary in our consumer-oriented society. This program discusses the perils and confusion in today's market place but, unfortunately, merely scratches the surface. This program has an antiquated format and uses distorted consumer information.

Lay, R.A. *Measuring the Metric Way*. Phoenix, N.Y.: Frank E. Richards Company, Inc.

This program is designed to introduce students to the metric system. It includes such topics as measuring length, distance, speed, weight, liquid, and temperature the metric way. These topics are the most common and essential for consumer survival in the coming metric world. Except for a chart at the end of the book, there is little mention of English to metric conversions. There are two reasons for this: (1) English to metric is too confusing to mention in a book of this sort; and (2) when the metric system has been instituted, there will be no need for conversion since everything will be metric.

Mathematics Review. Multi-Media Productions, 1976. (six color sound filmstrips; grades 6–9; remedial 10–12)

This series covers the basic mathematical operations in an effective manner for those of limited background in that all operations are related to practical, everyday events. This approach provides the student with the practical knowledge he or she needs to deal with problems most commonly confronted in life.

Sound filmstrips with guides deal with the following topics:

- addition and subtraction
- division and multiplication
- decimals and fractions
- areas and measurement
- ratio and proportion
- interest and percent

Mathematics and You. Kalamazoo, Mich.: Interpretive Education, 1977. (workbooks, hands-on materials; grades 7–11; remedial 12–adult)

This low-cost practical mathematics program helps the student use and understand the function of mathematics in everyday life. This hands-on kit includes 20 student workbooks that are joined with text and activities. It is an excellent low-cost supplementary program for math.

Math Living Skills. Johnstown, Pa.: Mafex Associates, 1979. (cassette/workbooks; remedial grades 7–adult)

These workbooks/cassette programs combine high interest with sound teaching principles. Material is presented in a semiprogrammed approach of small, logical steps followed by self-checking exercises. Self-tests provide immediate reinforcement and preview achievement tests that evaluate competencies. Each set includes ten student workbooks, cassette, achievement tests, and teacher's guide.

Math Test Taking. St. Louis, Mo.: McDonald Duplicating Master, 1979. (transparency book; grades 6–8; remedial 9–12)

This workbook strengthens basic mathematics skills and reduces students' text anxiety. It is similar in format to questions on standardized achievement tests and includes hints for maximizing test scores.

Mooney, T.J. *The Getting Along Series of Skills.* Phoenix, N.Y.: Frank E. Richards Company, Inc.

This three-part series emphasizes various skills (math, reading, spelling, and work study). The major theme is how to find and keep a job in the community. It is an excellent idea, but the material is dated. Jobs exist, but not in this context. Also, this series is too wordy and, consequently, presents potential problems of overloading.

Real-Life Math. Hubbard, 1977. (grades 7–9; remedial 10–12)

A multimedia program that teaches arithmetic skills through practical situations. Material and role playing activities set up a simulated world in which students deal with immediate challenges. Progressing at his or her own rate, each student has the opportunity to independently and correctly achieve specific objectives. Examples of objectives include opening a checking and savings account at a bank, and writing and sending a check to pay a bill.

Survival Mathematics. Barron's, 1979. (grades 7–9; remedial 10–adult)

This is a math book for students who hate math! Geared to high school students who lack motivation in mathematics, this book introduces practical math concepts that will come in handy on the job and in everyday life. Numerous practice exercises help students develop the necessary skills for satisfactory performance on basic competency tests.

Wiltsil, D.H. *Skills for Everyday Living.* Motivation Development Inc. (text-workbook in consumer education)

The main purpose of this program is to help students become more effective in handling situations, particularly new situations. Students will learn how to find information and then how to follow instructions in applying this information. Students will think for themselves and work out solutions to various problems.

Many projects require that students understand decimal fractions and percents. Application of skills is always stressed.

Topics include using a restaurant menu, sales tax chart, and sales slips; using a calendar and maps; using a phone book; the post office; comparative shopping; social security; finding a job; work permits and job applications; savings and checking accounts; phone bills; using a bus schedule; time and time zones; recipes; grocery ads; credit cards; buying a new or used car; living within your income; and paying taxes.

Wool, J.D. *The Bank Book*. Phoenix, N.Y.: Frank E. Richards Company, Inc.

The publication explores the various services of the bank. By comparison to other publications, the program is factual and easy to follow. If a student is exposed to these types of exercises he will be able to transfer and apply this information in his daily experiences.

Wool, J.D. *Using Money Series*. Phoenix, N.Y.: Frank E. Richards Company, Inc.

This four-part series covers counting money, making money, buying power, and earning, spending and saving. This series attempts to prepare students to be responsible, contributing adults. Emphasis is on good money management. An excellent idea, but this series is more appropriate as a supplement to a community survival course. Could be used in the classroom and then transfer the class into the community. The goal is a practical, daily, application of classroom application.

Wool, J. & Baker, R.J. *Useful Arithmetic*. Phoenix, N.Y.: Frank E. Richards Company, Inc.

This is a two part series discussing practical, relevant topics that are and will be of major concern to individuals entering the world of work. Topics such as grocery bills, savings bonds, checking sales slips, transportation costs, electric bills, and price comparing are all included. The format could be a little more realistic and prices need to be updated, but the information is essential.

BIBLIOGRAPHY

Aaron, Ira E. Reading in mathematics. *Journal of Reading*, 1965, *VIII*(6), 391–401.

Ashlock, R.B. *Error patterns in computations: A semi-programmed approach*. Columbus, Ohio: Charles E. Merrill Publishing Co., 1972.

*Boston Public Schools. *Curriculum guide mathematics—Elementary #2*.Boston: Boston Public Schools, 1973.

Brainerd, C.J. The origins of number concepts. *Scientific American*. March, 1973.

---

*Starred entries are sources for collections of specific behavioral objectives and evaluation items in the subject area of mathematics.

Burns, M., & Richardson, K. Making sense out of word problems. *Learning Magazine*, 1981, *9*(6).

Call, R.J., & Wiggin, Neal A. Reading and mathematics. *Mathematics Teacher*, 1966, *59*, 149–157.

Carpenter, G.P. Solving verbal problems: results and implications from the National Assessment. *The Arithmetic Teacher*, Summer 1980, 8–12.

Cawley, J.F. Teaching arithmetic to mentally handicapped children. *Focus on Exceptional Children*, 1975, *2*(4).

Cawley, J.S., Goodstein, H.A., Fitzmaurice, A.M., Lepore, A., Sedlack, R., & Althaus, V. *Project Math. Level I*. Tulsa, Okla.: Educational Progress, a division of Educational Development Corporation, 1976.

Cohn, R. Arithmetic and learning disabilities. In H. Myklebust (Ed.), *Progress in learning disabilities* (Vol. 2). New York: Grune & Stratton, 1971.

Coleman, F., et al. *The effects of a sequential computational skills math program on an underachieving 4th grade class*. Vermont, (ED 102 787).

Copeland, R.W. *How children learn mathematics*. New York: MacMillan Publishing Co., Inc., 1974.

*Department of Education. *Student-centered learning system—mathematics*. Quincy, Mass.: Quincy Public Schools, 1973.

Duncan, E.R., Capps, L.R., Dolciani, M., Quast, W.G., and Zweig, M. *Modern school mathematics—Structure and use*. Boston: Houghton Mifflin Co., 1972.

*Duncan, E., et al. *A behavioral objectives guide for individualizing modern school mathematics structure and use*. Boston: Houghton Mifflin Co., 1974.

Eagle, E. The relationship of certain reading abilities to success in mathematics. *Mathematics Teacher*, 1948, *41*, 175–179.

Earp, N.W. Observations on teaching reading in mathematics. *Journal of Reading*, 1970, *13*(7), 529–532.

Eisner, H. The challenge of the slow pupil, *The Mathematics Teacher*, 1939, *32*, 9–15.

*Evaluation and Assessment Unit. *Basic Cognitive Skill Objective Banks*. Santa Fe: New Mexico State Department of Education, January, 1967.

Fremont, H. Diagnosis: An active approach. *The Mathematics Teacher*, 1975, *68*, 323–326.

Fountain Valley teacher support system in mathematics. Huntington Beach, Calif.: Richard L. Zweig Associates, Inc., 1974.

Systems management guide to individualized mathematics system. Lexington, Mass.: Ginn & Co.

Goodstein, H.A. Assessment and programming in mathematics for the handicapped. *Focus on Exceptional Children*. 1975, *7*(7), 1–12.

*Herbert Hoover Junior High School. *Project R-3 mathematics component*. San Jose: San Jose Unified School District, 1967.

*Instructional Objectives Exchange. *Mathematics: Data relationships; numbers and their operations; geometry; symbolism and notations; figure and objective characteristics*. Los Angeles: Instructional Objectives Exchange, 1972.

Jurgensen, D., & Brown, King. Geometry. In *Modern school mathematics*. Boston: Houghton Mifflin Co., 1974.

Keys, R. *Is there life after high school?* Boston: Little, Brown & Co., 1976.

Maertens, R., & Dunlap, W. *Meeting individual needs in elementary mathematics*. Hinsdale, Ill.: The Dryden Press, 1973.

Moore, N.A. *A survey of the usage of arithmetic in the daily life of adults*. Unpublished dissertation, Institute of Education, University of Birmingham, 1957.

Glass, E. *A guide for mathematics curriculum development, K–12*. Hartford, Conn.: Bureau of Elementary and Secondary Education, State Department of Education, 1974.

*Massachusetts Department of Education. Reference guide performance statements. In *Core evaluation manual*. Bedford, Mass.: Institute for Educational Service, 1974.

*Merlin Elementary School. *A systems approach to individualized instruction*. Merlin, Oregon: Merlin Public Schools.

*Mesa Public Schools. *Behavioral objectives*. Mesa, Arizona: Mesa Public Schools.

*Michigan Department of Education. *Minimal performance objectives for mathematics education in Michigan*. Lansing, Mich.: Michigan Department of Education, 1973.

Muelder, Richard H. Reading in a mathematics class. In *Fusing reading skills and content*. Newark, Del.: International Reading Association, 1969.

Osborn, W.J. Ten reasons why pupils fail in mathematics. *The Mathematics Teacher*, 1925, *18*, 234–238.

*Phillips, E.R., & Karne, H.B. Validating learning hierarchy for sequencing math; tasks in elementary math. *Journal of Research in Mathematical Education*. 1973, *4*, 141–151.

Piaget, J. *The child's conception of number*. New York: Jeffrey Norton Publishing Co., 1965.

Project League. *Skill check lists*. (Working Draft). Chelmsford: Merrimack Education Center.

*Project Primes. *Resource guide*. Harrisburg, Pennsylvania: Pennsylvania Department of Education, 1971.

Resnick, L., Wang, M, and Kaplan, J. Task analysis in curriculum design: A hierarchically sequenced introductory mathematics curriculum. *Journal of Applied Behavior Analysis*, 1973, *6*(4), 679–710.

Rudman, B. Causes for failure in senior high school mathematics and suggested remedial treatment. *The Mathematics Teacher*, 1934, *27*, 409–411.

Sharma, H.C. *Mathematics in primary grades*. Newton, Mass.: Educational Development Center, 1974.

*Shaw, B.R., & Hiehle, P.M.W. *Teacher's Manual: Individualized computational skills program*. Boston: Houghton Mifflin Co., 1972.

Sobel, M.A. Providing for the slow learner in the junior high school. *The Mathematics Teacher*, 1959, *52*, 347–353.

Sternberg, L., & Mauser, A.J. The LD child and mathematics. *Academic Therapy*, 1975, *10*, 481–488.

*Texas Education Agency. *Essential mathematics objectives*. Austin, Texas: Texas Education Agency, 1975.

Wiebe, A.J. *Foundations of mathematics*. New York: Holt, Rinehart & Winston, Inc., 1963.

Whitcraft, L.H. Remedial work in high school mathematics. *The Mathematics Teacher*, 1930, *23*, 36–51.

Williams, E., & Shuard, H. *Elementary Mathematics Today: A Resource for Teachers*. Reading, Mass.: Addison Wesley Publishing Co., Inc., 1970.

*Wisconsin Mathematics Advisory Committee. *An exemplary mathematics program and a hierarchy of student behavioral objectives*. Wisconsin: Department of Public Instruction.

REFERENCES

Aukerman, R.C. *Reading in the secondary school classroom*. New York: McGraw-Hill Book Company, 1972.

Bartel, N. Problems in arithmetic achievement. In D. Hammill and N. Bartel (Eds.), *Teaching children with learning and behavioral problems*. Boston: Allyn & Bacon, Inc., 1975.

Brown, U. Learning about mathematics instruction. *Journal of Learning Disabilities*. 1975, *8*, 476–485.

Bruner, J. *The process of education*. Cambridge: Harvard University Press, 1965.

Buswell, G.T., & John L. *Diagnostic Chart for Individual Difficulties: Fundamental Processes in Arithmetic*. Indianapolis: Bobbs-Merrill, 1925.

Cawley, J.F., Goodstein, H.A., Fitzmaurice, A.M., Lepore, A., Sedlack, R., & Althaus, V. *Project Math: A program of the mainstream series*. Wallingford, Conn.: Educational Sciences, Inc., 1975.

Cawley, J.F., Fitzmaurice, A.M., Goodstein, H.A., Lepore, A.V., Sedlak, R., & Althaus, V. *Project Math, Level I*. Tulsa, Okla.: Educational Progress, a Division of Educational Development Corporation, 1976.

Cawley, John, & Vitello, S. Model for arithmetical programming for handicapped children, *Exceptional Children*, 1972, 101–110.

Connolly, A.M., Nachtman, W., & Pritchett, E.M. *Key math*. Circle Pines, Minn.: American Guidance Service, 1971.

Cooney, T.J., Davis, E.J., & Henderson, K.B. *Dynamics of Teaching Secondary School Mathematics*. Boston: Houghton Mifflin Co., 1975.

Dunlap, W., & House, A. Why can't Johnny compute? *Journal of Learning Disabilities*, 1976, *9*, 210–214.

Ellis, N.R. Memory processes in retardates and normals. In N.R. Ellis (Ed.) *International review in mental retardation* (Vol. 4). New York: Academic Press, 1970.

Gagne, R. *The conditions of learning*. New York: Holt, Rinehart & Winston, Inc., 1965.

Good, T., Grouros, D., Beckerman, T., Edmeier, H., Flatt, L., & Schneeberger, S. *Teacher's manual: Missouri mathematics effectiveness project* (Technical Report No. 132). Columbia, Mo.: Center for Research in Social Behavior, University of Missouri-Columbia, 1977.

Hammill, D., & Bartel, N. *Teaching children with learning and behavior problems: A resource book for preschool, elementary and special education teachers*. Boston: Allyn & Bacon, Inc., 1978.

Henderson, K.B. Concepts. In *The teaching of secondary school mathematics* (33rd Yearbook, NCTM). Washington, D.C.: National Council of Teachers of Mathematics, 1970.

Johnson, S.W., & Morasky, R. *Learning disabilities* (2nd ed.). Boston: Allyn & Bacon, Inc., 1980.

Johnson, D., & Myklebust, H. *Learning disabilities: Educational principles and practices*. New York: Grune & Stratton, 1967.

Kaplan, J. Classroom management. *The Mathematics Teacher*. 1966, *LXI*, 8.

Mann, P., Suiter, P., & McClung, R. *Handbook in diagnostic teaching* (2nd ed.). Boston: Allyn & Bacon, Inc., 1979.

National Council of Teachers of Mathematics. *A history of mathematics education in the United States and Canada* (32nd Yearbook). Washington, D.C.: National Council of Teachers of Mathematics, 1970.

National Council of Teachers of Mathematics. *An agenda for action: Recommendation for school mathematics of the 1980's.* Reston, Va.: National Council for Teachers of Mathematics, 1980.

Polya, G. *How to solve it.* (2nd ed.). New York: Doubleday & Co., Inc., 1973.

Reisman, F.R. *A guide to the diagnostic teaching of arithmetic.* Columbus, Ohio: Charles E. Merrill Publishing Co., 1972.

Reisman, F., & Kauffman, S. *Teaching mathematics to children with special needs.* Columbus, Ohio: Charles E. Merrill Publishing Co., 1980.

Resnick, L., Wang, M., & Kaplan, J. Task analysis in curriculum design: A hierarchically sequenced introductory mathematics curriculum. *Journal of Applied Behavior Analysis,* 1973, *6*(4), 679–710.

Schonell, F.J., & Schonell, F.E. *Diagnosis and remedial teaching in arithmetic.* London: Oliver & Boyd, 1957.

Seymore, D., & Snider. *Line designs.* Palo Alto, Calif.: Creative Publications, 1974.

Strauss, A., & Lehtinen, L. *Psychopathology and education of the brain-injured child.* New York: Grune & Stratton, 1947.

Sweet. Organizing a mathematics laboratory. *The Mathematics Teacher,* 1967, *LX*(2), 117–120.

Torrance, E.P. *Encouraging creativity in the classroom.* Dubuque, Iowa: William C. Brown Company Publishers, 1970.

Chapter 5

Social Studies

INTRODUCTION

The goal of social studies education should be to motivate students and enable them to function as informed and effective members of a modern democratic political system.

The achievement of this goal depends not only on the curriculum, classroom teaching, and learning, but also involves the entire school system. Several professional education societies (Association for Supervision and Curriculum Development (ASCD), the National Council for Social Studies, International Reading Association, teachers of math, art, speech, and health education, among others) have issued a statement entitled *Organizations for the Essentials of Education* (International Reading Association, 1971) that they have endorsed collectively. They argue that society must reaffirm the value of a balanced education resting upon the interdependence of skills and subject matter content of all the essential studies in the school curriculum.

The document states:

> Educators agree that the overreaching goal of education is to develop informed, thinking citizens capable of participating in both domestic and world affairs. The development of such citizens depends not only upon education for citizenship, but also upon other essentials of education shared by all subjects.

This chapter reflects the same view. Effective social studies instruction for the learning disabled adolescent must be integrated, individualized, meaningful, and student-centered. This chapter provides guiding principles, objectives, activities, methods, and resources to assist teachers in reaching these goals.

SECONDARY LEVEL SOCIAL STUDIES OBJECTIVES

These goals are defined from the perspective of projecting skills and competencies students will need in order to function effectively in the current role as students as well as those skills necessary to function effectively within community and societal roles.

Concomitant with the specific social studies content presented, considerations in instruction should focus on study skills; student utilization of the media; ability to interpret historical/societal visual material, related graphics, and problem-solving skills.

In order for the learning disabled student to assimilate social studies content and, moreover, to be able to apply this learning to new situations, the following delineation of competencies is articulated in observable behavior.

The following section provides proposed curricular goals for all students on the secondary level.

Reading and Study Skills

Proposed goals for reading and study skills are:

1. Students will demonstrate skill in defining social studies terminology appropriate to each course.
2. When given appropriate printed material, students will: (a) identify the main points of the material read; (b) identify major themes of the material; and (c) draw valid conclusions based upon an analysis of the materials presented.
3. Students will demonstrate skill in the use of a variety of media: (a) use of the card catalog and retrieval of special material; and (b) use of references appropriate to social studies.
4. Students will demonstrate efficient note-taking skills.
5. Students will demonstrate an ability to follow both written and oral directions.

Visual Skills

In the area of visual skills, the following objectives should be required:

1. After viewing video material (filmstrip, film), students will be able to identify the main point of the presentation.
2. Given pictures of historic events, students will identify, in written or oral form, a description of the related perspective in the picture.

3. Given still pictures that show an event, social situation, or problem, students will be able to draw some valid conclusions about the event and be able to express those conclusions in written or oral form.

Graphs, Tables, Charts, and Maps

The objectives for the use of graphs, tables, charts, and maps are as follows:

1. Given relevant data, students will be able to translate data into the proper graphics of a map, table, graph, or chart.
2. Given charts, maps, tables, or graphs, students will be able to compare the information obtained from such data.
3. Given a graphic, students will be able to draw inferences, identify trends, interpret information, indicate relationships, and draw conclusions about the data presented.

Critical Thinking Skills

In the area of critical thinking skills, the proposed objectives are as follows:

1. Given social studies problems or situations, students will be able to identify the problem or issue in written or oral form.
2. Given problems or issues, students will be able to analyze the problem accurately.
3. Following the gathering of data relating to a problem or issue, students will be able to present, in written or oral form, a summary of the pertinent data.

Conflict Resolution

Proposed objectives for the area of conflict resolution are as follows:

1. Given a conflict situation, students will be able to suggest some ways of resolving the conflict as related to a contemporary or historical event.
2. Given a conflict situation, students will be able to identify the specific parts of the situation that make it a conflict in society.

PROGRAM EFFECTIVENESS WITH THE LEARNING DISABLED STUDENT

An effective social studies program with learning disabled students should include the following five suggestions:

1. The learning experiences should be related to the students' own experiences so that they perceive them as meaningful. Students' interest and attention are increased in direct relation to the meaningfulness of the instructional material presented.
2. The learning experiences should provide for a "feedback loop," i.e., reflection, discussion, and interpretation of the experience. Learning disabled students need to receive frequent and objective feedback in order to maintain their involvement in the learning activity.
3. Cumulative reinforcement without boring repetition is essential for the learning disabled student.
4. Learning disabled students require active learning experiences with student involvement in the design, implementation, and evaluation of the experiences. Adolescents must feel they have some input into their instructional plans.
5. Conceptual, abstract, or theoretical learning must be applied in real-life situations. Learning disabled students frequently have difficulty generalizing and applying from the academic realm into the world of reality. Teachers can enhance these students' abilities to apply concepts by providing concrete examples and activities.

SOCIAL STUDIES CURRICULUM IN THE SECONDARY SCHOOL

In the area of social studies, educators must recognize the importance of academic disciplines as organizing principles and the preeminence of history as an organizing discipline.

Some suggestions offered by Spillane and Regnier (1981) are:

- A social studies curriculum stressing only current events rather than knowledge of the past does not prepare students adequately to make adult decisions. [The perspective of the present in the context of the past assists students to formulate accurate judgments.]
- Students cannot comment intelligently on contemporary problems unless they have a clear understanding of the events and

ideas of the past and of different ways in which these events can be analyzed. [Students should be shown the many and varied interpretations of a particular social situation—effects on a culture; political system designs; roles played by society members; etc.]

- Social studies curricula organized around current events can prepare students only for the present. They do not prepare students for the future. [The adage "history repeats itself" suggests that, in order to prevent a repetition of the errors of the past, we must first know the errors.]
- Social studies curricula should be organized around the academic disciplines that make up the "social studies," e.g., history, geography, economics, sociology, anthropology. [The curriculum should include a study of culture from varied perspectives—how society is held together, how it functions, the roles of society's members, etc.]
- History should be the major discipline of the social studies, especially in the early school years. [In order for people to know where they are going, they must know where they've been. Students should be taught to use this viewpoint.]
- Students should learn the differences among the goals and methods of different academic disciplines—including the disciplines that make up the social studies as well as the connections among them. [Instruction, particularly for learning disabled adolescents, should emphasize process as well as product. Instruction should go beyond the presentation of facts; should involve the students; and should be dynamic in presentation and meaningful in design.] (p. 731. Reprinted with permission.)

A SOCIAL STUDIES MODEL

Given the variety of social study subjects, it is difficult to suggest a model that appropriately "fits" the unique nature of each of the areas. There are, however, five common elements that a curriculum should contain as follows:

1. The first step is to identify the elements of abstract knowledge to be taught, i.e., what concepts will be presented and in what sequence. This task has been addressed for the most part by curriculum specialists who, in texts and surveys, have published what they consider

the most important knowledge in their field. It is the teacher's responsibility to present this knowledge in an effective manner. The proper method is paramount to success, particularly with the learning disabled student.

2. Next, specific cognitive objectives that relate to the students' thought processes should be established. This process involves deciding what specific elements a student should learn, given the specific cognitive functioning level on which that student is functioning. The teacher must ascertain entry cognitive levels through a pretest.

3. The teacher must then select appropriate knowledge, contexts, and/or communications useful to achieve the objectives. Using both behavioral and sensory processing task analysis, the teacher should fit the subject content with the approach that will most effectively produce the desired results for the given student and/or the given group.

4. The teacher must aid students to associate the different kinds of knowledge in order to reach the specified goal. Teachers should strive to enable students to see the interrelationships among the concepts and facts within the social studies disciplines. The student's thinking must be noncompartmentalized.

5. Finally, the teacher must determine whether the specific knowledge has been developed by giving a posttest or using some other form of evaluation such as a model, a play, a report, etc.

CLASSROOM DISCUSSION

One effective classroom strategy with the adolescent is the classroom discussion. Discussion gives the students common opportunities to engage in challenging inquiry and clarification of content. The following four suggestions can be used to enhance the effectiveness of classroom discussions:

1. Teachers should actively solicit students' opinions by asking for generalizations or interpretations of information presented. This requires the student to actively engage in the discussion rather than responding automatically or superficially.

2. The teacher should direct the discussion through building upon the previous day's work, eliminating irrelevant comments, and focusing on identifiable goals and tasks. Keeping the focus of the discussion on target serves to maintain the student's interest in the topic.

3. Teachers should create an open classroom climate wherein questions and divergent thinking are respectfully examined. Effective discus-

sion requires that students express their true feelings and opinions and feel secure in doing so. The teacher should reinforce this behavior when it is exhibited in the classroom.

4. Teachers must provide supportive and specific feedback to students to encourage and reinforce active student participation. Feedback is effective when it is specific, objective, and addresses a behavior that is within the student's capacity to change.

Learning disabled students who have difficulty with written expression are often able to demonstrate their knowledge through the discussion mode. The teacher should make every effort to ensure that the learning disabled student has an opportunity to participate in the discussion and benefit from the experiences. It is important that the teacher analyze the discussion process.

Analyzing the Classroom Discussion: A Guide

The teacher should critically assess the caliber and content of classroom discussions. Specific questions that provide a guide to evaluate whether the discussion is meeting the intended objectives are suggested as follows:

1. What kinds of questions are asked or raised? Are they factual or value questions?
2. What additional questions arise? Do these questions contribute toward clarifying major questions or do they relate to peripheral issues?
3. What happens to unusual ideas raised in the discussion?
4. What factors appear to cause specific questions and ideas to be dropped from further consideration?
5. What type of questions and what kind of evidence are proposed to test the hypotheses that are raised in the classroom?
6. Is a question that is considered important by a number of students or by the teacher carried to a satisfactory conclusion?
7. Does one member of the group dominate the conversation?
8. Is there a noticeable difference in the conversations from one group to another? What can be done to facilitate those groups that seem to lack participation from their members or "get stuck" in the process?
9. Is there relatively equal participation by the group members?
10. Does the teacher assume the role of group leader or is this role taken up by various members at different times?

In order for the teacher to elicit the student participation and involvement that leads to effective classroom discussion, the manner in which the student's responses are sought is critical. The types of questions asked and the frequency of questions should be geared to the cognitive level of the particular students involved and should be tailored to the nature of the content under discussion. A reference that will assist teachers is Bloom's taxonomy (1956). Bloom's taxonomy consists of cognitive categories, together with illustrative objectives and test items for each.

Bloom's Seven Forms of Thinking

Asking student's questions that relate to the seven specific forms of thinking enables the students to engage in the specific behavior as follows:

1. Memory questions ask students to recall or recognize ideas presented to them previously in reading or listening. Students are simply required to restate or represent information as stated.

   For example, the students have read a current events newspaper on present day Africa. The memory question would be, "What are the main problems facing Africa today?"

2. Translation questions present students with an idea and then ask them to restate the same idea in a different form. The student does not have to reason out the idea but simply restate it in a literal way.

   For example, the student has read a paragraph in the textbook. The translation question is "Now tell me in your own words what you read."

3. Interpretation questions ask students to compare certain ideas or to use a functional idea that they studied previously to solve problems new to them. Usually the answer is quite objective and may be in a short answer or discussion form.

   For example, if the students have learned to use the *Reader's Guide to Periodical Literature,* the interpretation question would be "Choose a topic of current interest and use the *Reader's Guide* to find five good sources of information."

4. Application questions require that students demonstrate that they can use an idea in a new situation not when they are told to do so but when the problem calls for it. In other words, application requires the transfer of training.

   For example, students have had instruction in defining a problem, organizing ideas, writing footnotes, preparing a bibliography, etc. The application question would be "Choose one of the most pressing social problems facing our nation today and write a term paper on the problem."

5. Analysis questions ask the student to solve a problem with a conscious observance of the rules for good thinking of the type called for by the problem.

   For example, the students have studied a group of ten informal fallacies. An analysis question would be, "React to the thinking in this case: A survey showed that most wealthy men were Republicans. A Democrat commented that the survey proved that most Republicans were wealthy."

6. Synthesis questions ask the student to create something. Such questions never have only one correct response.

   For example, students are studying the Roaring Twenties. A sample synthesis question is "Compose a collage that depicts the historic spirit of the Roaring Twenties."

7. Evaluation questions require students to make value judgments. Students must state if something is right or wrong, good or bad, etc. and indicate what considerations led them to make the judgment.

   For example, students have studied the colonial period of U.S. history. An evaluation question would be "Did the colonists do right in throwing tea overboard at the Boston Tea Party? Tell why."

Guidelines for Using the Taxonomy of Questioning in Social Studies

The following list provides five guidelines for using the taxonomy of questioning in social studies:

1. It is important that the questions asked in an examination be congruent with the type of thinking that was required of the student in the instruction. Analysis questions should be based on instruction that required students to engage in an analysis of the subject matter being presented.

2. The teacher has the responsibility to facilitate a student's ability to respond to the specific type of question by creating the appropriate classroom climate. For example, questions that require students to think divergently or freely express ideas are effective if the teacher has created a supportive and democratic setting that first encourages and later reinforces the student for his or her free expression of ideas.

3. The manner in which the questions are worded is important. The teacher should avoid providing the student with contextual clues or stating the question in a manner that mitigates against the student successfully answering the question because it is stated in a nebulous way.

4. The type of question category used should be congruent with the level of cognitive development of the specific student being questioned. It must be remembered that the categories of questions are both sequential and cumulative in the following order: memory, translation, interpretation, application, analysis, synthesis, and evaluation.
5. The application category promotes transfer of training through having students practice using ideas in new situations. This is particularly important for the learning disabled student whose comprehension is enhanced through opportunities to try out the new skills learned.

SOCIAL STUDIES INSTRUCTIONAL OBJECTIVES

A review of current thought on the goals of a social studies program indicates that there is no universally accepted model. However, there is considerable agreement on the following three points:

1. One goal of social studies instruction is to develop a cognitive structure of knowledge in the learner.
2. Students should be taught scientific modes of thought.
3. Goals should be defined in terms of social policy, social action, and value commitments.

It is important that the goals should be stated in terms of observable student outcomes. Mager (1962) has stated the significance of objectives as follows:

> He (the teacher) must first decide upon the goals he intends to reach at the end of his course or program. He must then select procedures, content, and methods which are relevant to the objective, cause the student to interact with appropriate subject matter in accordance with principles of learning, and finally measure or evaluate the student's performance according to the objectives or goals originally selected . . . If we are interested in preparing instructional programs which will help us reach our objectives, we must first be sure objectives are clearly and unequivocally stated.

Selection of Content: Some Criteria

In attempting to select content for social studies instruction for learning disabled students, consideration should be given to objectives, current significance, student interest and ability, and the facilitation of particular skills.

The University of Minnesota's Project Social Studies Curriculum Center (1968) has developed a useful list of curricula questions:

1. Does a topic lend itself to teaching important concepts in the social sciences, particularly those which cut across fields and which are important analytical tools in examining new data?
2. Is the topic of significance in the modern world? Is it, for example, related to a persisting societal problem, particularly one involving a major value-conflict in our society? Is it related to a significant trend in the modern world? . . .
3. Is the topic of particular interest and concern and so significant to pupils at certain grade levels because it gives pupils either an opportunity to examine their own values or provides them with help in coping with personal problems of direct concern to them?
4. Does the topic lend itself well to the development of one or more of the attitudinal behaviors identified as goals by the staff?
5. Does the topic facilitate the development of specific skills identified as goals of the program, particularly skills related to methods of inquiry?
6. Is the topic suited to the maturity level and abilities of pupils at each grade level? . . . Since the difficulty of topics at each grade level is related to the previous experiences of pupils at that level, can some experiences needed as background for this topic be included at earlier grade levels?
7. Can the topic be related to the interests of pupils at that level? . . .
8. Does the topic fit together with other topics at a grade level to form some kind of coherent theme of study so that pupils will find it easier to organize information into meaningful structures than they would if the topics remained isolated in their minds?

The University of Minnesota Project staff states that curriculum developers should consider multiple factors in making decisions:

These decisions will vary over time as factors such as society, knowledge in the social sciences, knowledge about learning and motivation, and goals change. Since tactics and materials must be chosen to achieve multiple goals with different kinds of students, choices may not fit into neat, elegant modes . . . (p. 126).

THE SOCIAL STUDIES TEXTBOOK

The social studies curriculum in the secondary classroom is designed to produce informed citizens capable of making appropriate and effective choices based on the weighing of alternatives. One of the most important teaching tools available to the teacher is the text designated for use in the secondary classroom.

Students must understand clearly the manner in which the social studies textbook is organized. There are four alternatives possible from the nature of the material content as follows:

1. Chronological organization is used to present historical facts and information along a time line divided into periods such as "Colonialism," for example.
2. In topical organization, material is presented in a framework of topics, i.e., "The Justice System."
3. In theoretical organization, social studies theory is presented in abstract segments.
4. Regional organization is most common and obvious in geography textbooks.

Irrespective of the particular organizational format employed, students' success within the social studies area is contingent upon their attainment of certain basic skills.

ESSENTIAL SKILLS FOR STUDENTS' SOCIAL STUDIES
   SUCCESS

Elements essential to adequate comprehension in social studies are:

- reading for the main idea
- comprehension of vocabulary
- drawing conclusions
- interpretation of charts, maps, and graphs
- distinguishing between fact and opinion
- locating, reading, collecting, and organizing data for reports

UNDERSTANDING GRAPHS, CHARTS, AND TABLES

The following five-step guide is suggested to be used by the student in dealing with math data presented in a graphic form of a chart or table:

1. The first step is for students to read the title. The teacher should ask students what is being compared with what and they should respond in their own words.
2. Next, students should read the figures and labels on the graph and explain what they stand for.
3. Students should read the titles on each axis.
4. Students should then study the graph carefully in order to compare the items represented with accuracy.
5. Finally, students should be able to draw conclusions from the graph or chart through being able to answer the following questions:
   a. What does the graph or chart as a whole represent?
   b. What are the items being compared?
   c. What interpretations can be drawn from the comparisons?
   d. What are the resulting conclusions drawn from a to c?

Refer to appropriate suggested sections in this book for specific recommendations in developing these skills in students. There are, however, basic strategies that teachers may employ to enhance the effective presentation of social studies material within a mainstream class.

STRATEGIES FOR TEACHING SOCIAL STUDIES

Implicit in the teaching of social studies is instruction in social behavior. The following are some suggestions:

- Teachers can use the "committee" as a teaching vehicle. It is important in establishing committees to include instructions for rotating the leadership and to suit the assigned tasks to the particular group members. Remember the most potent teachers for an adolescent are his or her peers. Cooperation is also facilitated when groups of students work together on common tasks.
- Music can be used to teach social conditions. Music is both a teaching tool as well as a form of entertainment and thus tends to hold the student's interest in the instruction. Music has been called the universal language. It is a vehicle that reaches across time and cultures bringing to the surface the commonalities among men. Students often "see" in music that which they are blind to in the written word.

- Teachers can use panel discussions or debates to stimulate the slow learner or the turned-off adolescent. Teachers should select stimulating subjects that are somewhat controversial or student based. It is essential that students feel they have some opportunity to make decisions regarding their educational program content.
- Teachers should consider construction projects in lieu of tests or to demonstrate concepts. This facilitates diversity in task as well as providing for options in specific student requirements. Students who have aptitudes in areas other than academics (carpentry, painting, drawing, etc.) have an opportunity to gain in self-esteem and in self-worth for their specific talents.
- Teachers can use additional media (books, movies, slides, etc.) to amplify the basic curriculum material and to provide students with a realistic picture of life during other times and in other places. In teaching a unit on Hawaii, a teacher can have students see the play or the film *South Pacific* or read portions of James Michener's book *Hawaii*.
- A total immersion approach can be useful when teaching geography or cultures of the world. For example, the teacher can obtain records of the music of a given land, slides or films of the cities, pictures of the costumes worn, or samples of the country's national dishes. This serves to provide the student with a comprehensive perspective through varied foci. This approach also lends itself to a committee type format wherein students interested in pursuing a particular topic or issue band together in a common task.
- A social studies newspaper could be established. The teacher can have students write articles for a newspaper as if they were alive during a different period of time. Committees can be assigned to prepare various sections of the newspaper. Students with specific nonacademic talents (art, caricature, photography, etc.) have an opportunity to express these abilities.
- Teachers can help make national, state, and local elections exciting. The class can hold debates, study slogans, invite speakers, or use the newspaper to check for facts and for editorializing in the news columns.
- A class or individual legacy can be left to the school. Committees can make scrapbooks of current events or of topics they are studying. The completed books should be titled "Current events of ____, compiled by class 4-211." Paintings, poems, and montages may all be included.
- Teachers can list occupations students are interested in and divide the class into committees to study related occupations. Interviewing

is one of the best techniques for studying occupations and assists the students in developing self-assurance.

Suggested Activities in the Social Studies

Service Projects

One of the most effective ways to teach students empathy and understanding for other groups within the social structure is by involving them with a group or an institution that advocates a human or environmental concern. Students will learn that they (in spite of their learning disability) have skills and contributions that are both helpful to others and appreciated by them.

With student participation, the teacher can plan a service project and assist students in taking stock of their interests and talents. From this discussion two or three workable ideas can be generated. Some examples are:

- Students could run a benefit tag sale.
- They could visit a convalescent hospital for the elderly.
- Students could plan and give a party for disadvantaged elementary school children.
- In a student participative mode, the teacher can designate responsibilities to the group members, i.e., contacting the agency, purchasing materials, arranging for publicity, etc.
- In running the service project, the teacher should emphasize quality of work and full participation.
- This basic plan should be augmented with whatever the students' talents and interests allow, i.e., an article written for the school newspaper, a photographic journal of the event, or a collage.
- The teacher can use this project to discuss with the students how they felt while engaged in the project and, where possible, relate roles, responsibilities, and positions to the classroom as a social system and as a "community."
- The teacher can evaluate this project by including a comparison of student classroom social behaviors exhibited prior to the project with those manifested at the end of the project; by asking students to write in a journal their impressions of the project; or by asking them to symbolically illustrate what they feel as individuals they gained from the experiences.

Community Relationships

The objective is for students to understand the concept of "neighbor-hood" and its related connotations through direct experiential activities. The steps in this activity are:

1. The teacher uses a city map as a geographical reference base for the activity and has students target different sections within the city boundaries as areas for them to explore.
2. The teacher arranges for student groups to make a site visit to the area they have expressed an interest in pursuing. Prior to the actual visit, the teacher should prepare an observation guide that will serve as a tool to help students selectively focus their attention. This guide would state that students should note the type of home and dwelling (single family, multiple, apartment); note the types of businesses (any seeming overrepresentation of one business type or underrepresentation); note the relative age of the community (a new development); the condition of the community in general; and any other observations the students feel are important.
3. The teacher should have the student groups report back to the class. Students should be allowed to present their reports as they feel will best represent their impressions and the data they collected. Options might include drawings of the community; scale models; photographs, etc.
4. The teacher should create discussion groups.

Teaching Government Relationships

The objective is for the student to describe how state government works. The process involves the following steps:

- The teacher can arrange for a visit to the state capitol and prepare a list of questions to guide students' experiences. Following the field trip, the teacher should discuss with students what information they collected and what they found most interesting or most unexpected.
- The teacher can review the state constitution and create a simulation of what students feel might have been the climate of the time when the constitution was written. Political condition, economic, social, and moral factors should be included.
- The teacher can identify major roles played within the state system of government such as governor, lieutenant governor, aides, etc. The teacher can assign students a role and have them research the responsibilities inherent in the role and also describe how the assigned role

fits into the state organizational system. Students can also write a play to act out the results of their study.

- Students can research state symbols such as the state seal and state flower.
- Students can compare various state maps for size, location, and features.
- Students can follow the development and evolution of a piece of legislation through the state legislative process. The teacher can have student groups investigate the three branches of the state government and teach each other about the branch they've researched.
- Students can compare and contrast the state constitution with the U.S. Constitution. The teacher could create student study/discussion groups around such topics as, "Why do you feel any noted differences exist? What are the benefits or disadvantages to the citizens?"

Using the Newspaper as a Text Book Supplement to Social Studies

The newspaper is a valuable tool in bringing social studies concepts alive. It also effectively serves to bring together local, state, national, and world news.

The objectives for using the newspaper are that students will be able to relate the present to the past through the newspaper and that students will demonstrate the enhanced social studies related skills of locating information, interpreting maps and cartoons, and analyzing information.

Teachers should provide instruction to students on the various sections and features of the newspaper as follows:

- The teacher can obtain copies of several newspapers and compare the front page makeup of several papers. Students can be asked to note which stories are featured, what pictures are used, and where stories are placed on the page.
- Each student should follow an event from day to day and keep a file of clippings on the topic. The student should also compare the type of coverage provided about the event by different newspapers.
- The teacher can assign students graphics (political cartoons, charts, etc.) for study and have them interpret the graphics and show their connection with the news.
- Politics can be effectively taught through the newspaper. Students could compare the political coverage given to both events and parties. The teacher can ask students if they feel there is any observable bias in the manner in which the news is being reported.

- Students can read an editorial and express the editor's views in their own words. They can write their views on the function of the editorial column.
- Students can select a comic strip they enjoy and analyze the "message" within the comic strip. Is it designed merely to make people laugh or to present a political view or a commentary?
- Students can visit the local library's archives of old newspapers and compare present reporting styles with those of the past. To what do they attribute any changes noted?

SOCIAL STUDIES RESOURCES

Programs and Materials

The Law: Where You Stand and What You Need to Know. Lyons Falls, N.Y.: Educational Images. 1976 (12 audio cassettes; grades 10 through 12)
   Program content includes sequences recorded in a "live" high school law course. These are supplemented by mini cases that challenge students to use their new knowledge. The "Law Brief" is a printed set of notes summarizing the audio presentations for student review and reinforcement. Also provided are quizzes on major topics and overall achievement tests. The last two taped segments guide students in conducting a mock trial in their classroom.

Foundations in History. Chatsworth, Calif.: Opportunities for Learning, 1979–1980 (four work-texts; remedial 7 through adult)
   A series of work-texts covering U.S. history from exploration and colonization to the present, with special updates to relate past events with modern conditions. Numerous illustrations, maps, and timelines are combined with lively factual text. Chapters are short and concise and written at a fourth grade level.

Introduction to the Use of Globe, Maps, Atlas. Wichita, Kan.: Library Filmstrip Center, 1975 (color sound filmstrip; grades 7 through 12)
   This filmstrip is designed to show students how to use globes, maps, and atlases. It explains legends, symbols, space, direction, scale, latitude, and other important information found on a globe, map, or atlas. This filmstrip has the approval of outstanding cartographers.

How to Read a Map. Kalamazoo, Mich.: Interpretive Education, 1977 (color sound filmstrip; grades 7 through 10, remedial 11 through adult)
   This filmstrip illustrates the legend and index of a map and how to use them. It shows how to interpret the scale in miles on a map and

when to use and how to read maps of the entire country as well as sectional, state, and city maps.

How to Read a Map: A Personal Reading Module. Indian Rocks Beach, Fla.: Aquarius, Inc. Relevant Productions, 1975 (audio cassette—book module; grades 7 through 10; remedial 11 through adult)

Using a problem-solving approach, this module teaches the effective use and interpretation of map skills. The complete module contains 30 copies of a high-interest, easy reading (3.7 reading level) illustrated map reading text; a read-along cassette; 30 four-page skill development booklets; and a teacher's manual.

Shaver, James P. (Ed.) *Building Rationales for Citizenship Education.* Washington, D.C.: National Council for the Social Studies, 1977.

This bulletin is intended to involve teacher educators, teachers, and supervisors in reexamining the assumptions underlying curricular and teaching decisions and their implications for citizenship education. Assumptions about slow learners and citizenship are examined.

Skills in Citizen Action. Skokie, Ill.: National Textbook Co.

This program is directed to high school teachers and administrators interested in more systematic curriculum in community involvement. The one-year English/social studies program focuses on the development of citizen skills. The approach is a synthesis of contributions from disparate movements such as action learning, values clarification, law-related education, and humanistic education.

Map Reading Skills. Kalamazoo, Mich.: Interpretive Education, 1977 (filmstrip; grades 7 through 10; remedial 11 through adult)

This filmstrip illustrates the legend index of a map and how to use it. It shows how to interpret the scale in miles on a map and when to use and how to read maps of the entire country as well as sectional, state, and city maps.

Map and Globe Skills. Dansville, N.Y.: Instructor, 1976 (grades 4 through 9; remedial 10 through adult)

This is a coordinated, easy-to-use set of study/practice materials for every phase of map reading instruction. It encourages map reading through practice materials addressing distance scale, map symbols, political division, etc.

U.S. Government: How It Functions. Portland, Ore.: National Book Company, 1973 (grades 11 through adult)

This book provides a comprehensive description and exploration of principal government functions and procedures and answers almost 200 commonly asked questions that are sketchily answered by standard textbooks. It includes things every citizen should know and lessons.

American Law: Where It Comes From, What It Means. Stanford, Calif.: Multi-Media Productions, 1978 (grades 7 through adult)

Part One traces lawmaking from prehistoric times to the present. Part Two lays out the creation, amendment, and interpretation of laws on federal, state, and local levels, citing cases and examples.

Organizations

Citizenship Development Program. The Mershon Center, The Ohio State University, 199 West 10th Avenue, Columbus, Ohio 43201.

This program seeks to promote citizen competencies with basic citizenship skills such as decision making. A handbook of citizenship competencies has been produced in conjunction with the Basic Citizenship Competencies Project.

National Council for the Social Studies (NCSS), 3615 Wisconsin Avenue, N.W., Washington, D.C. 20016.

NCSS strives to promote citizenship education through its efforts to improve social studies education. NCSS publishes a newsletter, the journal *Social Education* and numerous bulletins, reports, and guidelines salient to citizenship education.

Social Studies Development Center (SSDC), Indiana University, 513 North Park, Bloomingdale, Ind. 47405.

SSDC has produced commercially available curriculum products in geography, American government, and world history.

Social Science Education Consortium, Inc. (SSEC), 855 Broadway, Boulder, Col. 80302.

SSEC gathers, organizes, and disseminates information pertinent to social science education. It provides consulting and workshop services to school districts on various topics as well as serving as the Social Studies/Social Science Education Clearinghouse for the Educational Resources Information Center (ERIC). SSEC also publishes numerous source books in social studies and social science education, including curriculum guides, annotated bibliographies, and resource lists. A full catalog of materials is available upon request.

REFERENCES

Bloom, B.S., et al. (Eds.). *Taxonomy of educational objectives: Cognitive domain*. New York: David McKay Company, 1956.

Mager, R.F. *Preparing instructional objectives*. San Francisco: Fearon Publishers, 1962.

Organizations for the essentials of education. Newark, Del.: The International Reading Association, 1971.

Spillane, R., & Regnier, P. Revitalizing the academic curriculum: The case of the social studies. *Phi Delta Kappan,* 1981, *62*(10), 731.

West, E. Preparation and evaluation of social studies curriculum for grades K–14 (Project No. HS-045) Final report. Minneapolis, Minn.: University of Minnesota, 1968.

Chapter 6

Occupational Education: Interfacing Career and Vocational Programs with Academics for the Learning Disabled Student

INTRODUCTION

The preparation of students to function effectively in the workplace is a major responsibility of the educational system. This is vital for learning disabled adolescents whose disabilities indicate the need for a comprehensive and integrative program of academic instruction with occupational training through a combination of career preparation with vocational pursuits.

In the preparation of this book, it seemed impossible to discuss subject matter content without considering the objectives, intent, and purpose of the material being presented to the students, i.e., putting the matter into context. A term used frequently in the recent literature on education is the *total child*. The student in his or her totality must be considered in the educational process.

The ratio of academics to work-skill training and the amount of counseling and testing necessary to produce a meaningful preparatory program can only be determined in relation to the individual student. Age, current educational status (grade and functioning level), interests, and the support systems available must each be considered in the development of a program.

This chapter will examine vocational and career programs, present suggested guidelines and recommendations for the implementation of such programs, and offer resources to aid in the planning and implementation of these programs for learning disabled students in the public school system. For specific and additional information relating to this area refer to Woodward's (1981) *Mainstreaming the Learning Disabled Adolescent*.

VOCATIONAL EDUCATION

Many issues must be considered when vocational programs for learning disabled students are being developed. It is important to understand that the conceptualization of the role of vocational education results from the existent value system of the predominant culture. As Green (1973) has noted, we tend to ask children "What do you want to be when you grow up?" The job a person performs, thus, becomes a part of his or her identity. Furthermore, people are often characterized by their occupations. Students' preferences are influenced by the status ascribed to certain occupations and are limited by their knowledge of the available job options.

More recently in American education, the emphasis has been on career education, defined by Hoyt (1976) as, "The totality of experiences through which one learns about and prepares to engage in work as part of her or his way of existing" (p. 4).

Although both vocational and career education have as their goal the gainful employment of students in work experiences, the major difference between career education and vocational education is that the former is reflective of a philosophy.

The societal objectives of career education should be to help all individuals acquire marketable skills that enable them to engage in work that is beneficial to them as well as to society.

DEVELOPING VOCATIONAL OPPORTUNITIES FOR
LEARNING DISABLED ADOLESCENTS

Dan Andrews of the Connecticut State Department of Education (1976) has suggested that:

> Education for learning disabled youngsters can be described as a "lump of coal." While we recognize the beauty and fascination of the more traditional gemstones, we must also be aware that these same gemstones have no capability for the generation of any energy, and as opposed to the "lump of coal," are far less valuable from a utilitarian viewpoint. If we view the "lump of coal" as being capable of transmitting energy, as well as being multifaceted, then we, as special educators, must provide the ignition and direction of that energy. (p. 2)

Most special educators agree that, when and wherever it is feasible, persons identified as being "exceptional" should be provided with the opportunity for both career exploration and vocational/occupational preparation.

Given this assumption, the question is, "why isn't this being done to the extent that it should be?" The most immediate response would be that available funds are lacking. The vocational facet of the broad educational need is more expensive than many other types of instructional efforts. When the unique needs of the exceptional person require a greater specificity in terms of responding to the individual needs of the student, the cost of this instruction increases significantly.

Although there are many vocational programs for the retarded and for the physically handicapped, there are relatively few programs specifically designed to meet the career/occupational/vocational needs of learning disabled youngsters.

While the reasons for this lack are numerous, the authors suggest the following explanations:

- The academic skills or lack of them are common to most learning disabled youngsters, and this commonality provides a basis for a larger educational response.
- By its very nature and the nature of learning disabled students themselves, vocational instruction must be individualistic. In order to plan an integrated vocational learning activity for learning disabled youngsters, educators must provide for training in a variety of vocational choices, seek and encourage the development of students' capabilities, analyze the job or task, and determine students' relation to these factors.
- Due to the historically recent definition and identification of learning disabilities, vocational instruction for these students is relatively less sophisticated than the techniques available for the mentally retarded and physically handicapped.

In developing a career/vocational plan, the following six issues should be considered:

1. The ability and interests of the youngster must be determined. The approach should be to discover what the child *can* do and to introduce as many opportunities of a prevocational nature as possible. The lack of exposure and awareness to a variety of occupations and experiences can be a severe limitation on the youngster's vocational options.
2. The availability of on-the-job placement is vital to establish a concrete consequence for the training effort.
3. Facilities and materials must be available for the training.

4. The availability of funding would appear to be the most basic need for the development of a program. Most school systems or facilities that deal with exceptional persons are aware of the various categorical funding programs and the services available through them. Some relatively untapped funding sources are not immediately directed to education. As an example, the Comprehensive Employment and Training Act (CETA) has as its objective the reentry or entry of unemployed and disadvantaged adults. While it would be difficult to provide funding for in-school youths under this Act, it would be possible to provide vocational training for people who would, in turn, instruct exceptional students. Needless to say, curriculum and equipment needs would be identified and provided for use in the training of the presently unemployed prospective special vocational instructor. Although sketchy, this is an example of how a funding source with a specific purpose can be used to meet several related needs.
5. The availability of teachers is another important factor. While there are many persons being trained to meet special classroom needs of learning disabled youngsters, the majority of these trained teachers do not have an adequate vocational background. The reverse situation applies with regard to vocational instructors. The solution to this particular teacher shortage would be met most immediately by providing tradespeople with the special instructional skills required.
6. It must be recognized that vocational education, while having the potential for therapeutic use, should have as its objective the development of abilities that not only provide for the concrete application of academic skills and concepts, but also provide a means for self-sufficiency in adulthood.

TYPES OF VOCATIONAL PROGRAMS

Vocational programs can be divided into five types as follows:

1. In *work experience,* the emphasis is to guide the students toward a general employment orientation through the use of simulated work experiences.
2. The *work-study* approach uses on-campus and off-campus work stations.
3. *On-the-job training* is based on the concept that specific skills may be directly taught at the job site.
4. In the *off-campus work station,* an industry or business in the community provides a work location in its facility.

5. *Cooperative programs* entail a cooperative agreement between an institution (residential) and a cooperating school for services.

These five programs take into consideration community and school resources as well as the individual student's needs and characteristics.

Whatever the specific program option entered into, the goal should be directly concerned with developing work skills. The objectives of the program should relate to a functional and current application of content presented.

Bail and Hamilton (1967) stated that the success of any secondary work preparatory program (career or vocational) is dependent on seven essential ingredients:

1. use of community leaders with competencies in vocational training
2. use of community facilities when appropriate and relevant
3. counseling from various state agencies concerned with vocational training
4. concern for practical application of the academic and vocational training
5. indepth preplanning of programs and facilities [This facilitates the maximal integration of program and site.]
6. adequate equipment and facilities to facilitate continuity between the program and career goals
7. teachers trained to recognize the needs of the youth and the community. (Reprinted with permission.)

The imperative is to build an integrated program consisting of the following elements: academic and vocational assessment, career exploration, programming and instruction, working, and program evaluation.

The program should attempt to first consider the students' interests, needs, levels of performance, and motivation through a process of formal testing and informal interviewing. This information may then be used to shape the program to the individual students.

VOCATIONAL EDUCATION AND LEARNING DISABLED STUDENTS

Educationally handicapped students have been considered for acceptance into vocational programs through legislation mandates.

The Vocational Education Amendment of 1976 (Public Law 94-482), for example, requires that each state spend at least 20% of their federal vocational dollars for disadvantaged individuals with 10% of these moneys to be used to serve handicapped individuals.

DEFINITION

The Vocational Act of 1963 (Public Law 88-201) defines Vocational Education as:

> Vocational education means vocational or technical training or retraining which is given in schools or classes (including field or laboratory work and remedial or related academic and technical instruction incident thereto) under public supervision and control or under contract with a state board or local educational agency and is conducted as part of a program designed to prepare individuals for gainful employment as semiskilled or skilled workers or technicians or subprofessionals in recognized occupations and in new and emerging occupations or to prepare individuals for enrollment in advanced technical programs, but excluding any program to prepare individuals for employment in occupations which the Commissioner determines, and specifies by regulation, to be generally considered professional or which requires a baccalaureate or higher degree . . . (Sec. 108)

Although the definition of vocational education as stated was developed with the "regular" student as a reference, it was not long before the handicapped students were addressed.

The Vocational Education Amendments of 1968 mandated vocational education for students with special needs. Vocational education differs from general education only in the areas of preparation and focus. Employment is the criterion for success in a vocational program while, with general education, the criterion is successful functioning in many life roles.

When considering the specific design of a vocational education program, it is essential that a basic concept be used as a foundation, i.e., that individuals are more alike than different. All vocational programs should contain certain common essentials regardless of the particular nuances of each program design. These elements are career exploration, vocational assessment, on-the-job training, vocational training, and vocational counseling.

Brolin (1976) identified six vocational competencies for special students as follows:

1. Knowing about and exploring occupational possibilities. Students should be aware of the options available for them in both extent and specificity.
2. Selecting and planning appropriate occupational choices. Students should be guided in decision making which addresses the nature of their specific disability.
3. Exhibiting the necessary work habits required in the competitive labor market. Work related behavioral skills must be taught along with technical or concept material.
4. Developing the necessary manual skills and physical tolerances required in the competitive labor market. Effective training programs are those which consider psychomotor (physical) requirements in addition to cognitive and affective aspects.
5. Obtaining a specific and saleable entry level occupational skill. The program should target achievable, marketable goals.
6. Seeking, securing, and maintaining jobs appropriate to level of abilities, interests, and needs. The program should assist students with finding jobs and thereafter maintaining the job. (Reprinted with permission.)

There is obvious governmental support for the effective integration of special needs students. Public Law 94-142 (The Education for All Handicapped Children Act of 1975) has many implications for vocational education of handicapped students. For example, all students, irrespective of any disability, are entitled to receive a vocational education. The tools used in evaluating a student's vocational potential must be tailored for the particular student being evaluated. Schools are encouraged to become involved with the community in a collaborative relationship in serving the student.

THE ROLE OF THE SPECIAL EDUCATOR IN THE VOCATIONAL PROGRAM

Special educators play a critical role in the development of these vocational competencies, and it is important that their responsibilities be clearly articulated. Younie and Clark (1969) identified related responsibilities for specialists as:

1. Evaluating occupational readiness. This is accomplished through formal and informal measurement tools in addition to observation.

2. Correlating classroom experience with work experience. The specialist may relate academics with training in areas of vocabulary, math skills, economics, etc.
3. Planning, securing and supervising on-the-job training situations. Providing feedback to the students on their actual work performance enables them to better adjust and adapt to the demands of work.
4. Counseling pupils and parents on social, personal and vocational problems. The understanding the specialist brings to the situation through knowledge of the student's special needs is significant.
5. Securing or assisting in securing job placements. Determining an appropriate "match" between student and job enhances the potential for success.
6. Serving as a liaison person between the school and state vocational rehabilitation agency. Again the specialist through awareness of school demands and market conditions via the vocational rehabilitation agencies provides a critical link.
7. Maintaining school and work evaluation records. Documentation of skill and knowledge along with behavioral growth is important.
8. Interpreting the work-study program to school personnel. The contributions of the specialist at the planning and placement team meetings convened to evaluate the efficacy of the program with regard to a particular student are significant. (pp. 186–194. Reprinted with permission.)

The authors believe that the special educator has the four roles of service coordinator, catalyzing agent, resource person, and instructor as follows:

1. As service coordinator, the educator is concerned with securing necessary services for the individual student. This includes whatever related services (counseling, transportation, etc.) are necessary to ensure that the student is able to profit from the educational experience.
2. As a catalyzing agent the professional serves in uniting the student with the vocational program. This is accomplished through providing the student with feedback and assisting with the interpretation and evaluation of educational experiences. The essential for success here involves a sound and trusting relationship between the student and the teacher.

3. The educator serves as a resource to parents and community members who should be aware of the student as a total entity.
4. As an instructor, the specialist provides instruction in areas not available in the regular curriculum. This may include reinforcement or review of technically related vocational vocabulary; specific measurement skills; job interviewing; or the development of specific work-related skills. It is incumbent upon the specialist to be aware of the demands that will be made of the student in the workplace and attempt to provide the cognitive, affective, or psychomotor skills necessary for the student to succeed in that setting. The provision of such services may be a combination of direct service or referral. Many learning disabled adolescents have experienced anxiety and failure in their attempts to generalize their learning to new situations or to deal with change. Every effort must be made to ensure that these adolescents are fully prepared and equipped to deal with the new challenge of the world of work.

Dan Andrews of the State of Connecticut, Department of Vocational Education (1976), has suggested that vocational instruction be presented in the form of a Learning Activity Packet. Using task analysis, individualized learning modules may be developed to enhance the basic vocational instructional presentation.

In developing the modules, the teacher would analyze both the job and the student. Job analysis would consist of describing the job; listing major tasks; writing an instructional goal and course outline; detailing each task; and specifying learning objectives. For the student, the teacher would identify general characteristics, i.e., interests, attitudes, motivation, etc. and determine the student's special needs.

CAREER EDUCATION

Career education may be broken down into three distinct phases that should be presented in sequential order as follows: career awareness, career exploration, and career preparation.

The following descriptions highlight major points in each of the phases as follows:

1. In the career awareness phase, the emphasis is on familiarizing students with the wide variety of career opportunities available to them and the overlapping nature of the opportunities. The objective is to nurture a career perspective that is noncompartmentalized.

2. Career exploration can occur at a job station within the school, at a local business or agency that employs individuals with similar training, or through discussions with professional individuals with training and practice in the selected career areas. The objective is for the student to gain a reality based understanding of what specific careers entail. Frequently, choices are based on perceptions gained from the views or values of parents or peers.
3. Career preparation includes the technical competency specifically associated with the career as well as the underlying academic and informational base associated with and essential for effective career performance. The primary aim of the preparation is to enable students to assume a responsible career position in the community.

In the development of these programs, reference material that outlines the nature of the specific careers and its prerequisites is available. This material may be found in the *Dictionary of Occupational Titles* (1965), *The Dictionary of Occupational Titles Supplement* (1968) and the *Supplement to the Occupational Outlook Handbook* (1974–1975).

The concept of career education was conceived by Dr. Sidney Marland, Commissioner of Education in 1971. Marland (1971) described career education as essentially encompassing three main ideas. These are:

1. Career education was perceived as being for all students— including the handicapped, i.e., the school's responsibility extended to each and all students who were the school's responsibility.
2. Career education begins in kindergarten and goes beyond grade 12 and into adulthood. This statement suggests that preparing students for meaningful roles as producers in our society is an ongoing responsibility and should be implemented with consideration to the student's developmental and individual needs.
3. Career education would give the student a start in earning a living. This statement implies that the product of the career program is a very real one and as such content presented should be targeted toward a functional application goal. There is often confusion in the utilization of the terms "career" and "vocational." (pp. 22–25. Reprinted with permission.)

Kolstoe (1976) defined "career" as the totality of work a person does in a lifetime; he defined "vocation" as the primary work role a person has at any given point in time. He went on to define education as "all those activities and experiences through which one learns" and career education as "all activities and experiences through which one learns about work" (p. 199).

Career education thus implies a dynamic and developmental approach which should be ongoing throughout a student's education.

CAREER EDUCATION OBJECTIVES BY GRADE LEVEL

Suggested guidelines for a school's career program by grade are provided as follows:

1. The initial stage is career awareness and should be implemented from kindergarten through grade six. In this stage, the school attempts to introduce the student to the concept of a "life's work" and what it means to function in the marketplace.
2. The career orientation phase should occur in grades seven through eight. Here the emphasis is on a guiding process incorporating students' inherent strengths and weaknesses and searching out careers for possible consideration through examining career choice demands, criteria, etc.
3. The career preparation phase should be implemented from grades 11 through 12. The assumption is that the student has some sense of identification with at least a career cluster, i.e., related jobs and the task now becomes one of preparing the student for the "job."
4. Career Refinement—Post School. This aspect of career education may take on many different forms. The range of possibilities extends from formal education (college) to on-the-job training. Former commissioner of education, Sidney Marland (1972) reported that for every ten students in high school, two receive vocational training and three go to college (although one drops out). This means that over one-half of all high school students (1,500,000) need more attractive options as they prepare for various careers.

More current statistics, however, present a more optimistic view of the accomplishments of the American educational process. The 1980–81 Annual Report of the American Federation of Teachers (1981) reported the following statistics:

1. In 1950, less than 50% of U.S. students graduated from high school. In 1975, the figure was 74%; in 1977, 80%—and it is still climbing.
2. In 1950, 10% of black students graduated from high school; in 1977, the rate was 76%.

3. In 1910, the average 25-year-old American had completed 8.1 years of schooling. In 1950, he or she had completed 9.3 years; in 1975, 12.3 years.
4. In 1960, only 60% of students enrolled in public schools were actually attending classes. Thanks to dropout prevention programs, 92% of students currently enrolled are attending classes.
5. In 1900, 11.3% of the U.S. population were illiterate. In 1970, according to the Education Commission of the States, only 1.2% were illiterate.
6. There are more 15- to 18-year-olds enrolled in school in the U.S. than in any other country in the world. The U.S. public school system is one of the few major education systems in the world attempting to provide a free, universal public education for all who want it.
7. Reading scores on both comprehension and vocabulary in the first three grades of schooling have increased steadily over the past decade.
8. Reading scores of 14-year-olds in the U.S. are higher than those of students in the Netherlands, Sweden, or the United Kingdom. U.S. students are doing better in science than those in Britain, the Netherlands, or Italy (pp. 5–20).

An analysis of these statistics would suggest that public schools are educating a greater percentage of American children today, keeping them in school longer, and achieving gains. This author suggests that the current task of education is relating those years in school and the instruction received more closely to contemporary realities.

Effective career/vocational education is integrated in design and in delivery. It takes into consideration the student as a person, a significant variable in the educational process. It considers the interface of many disciplines in providing a comprehensive and meaningful program. Counselors, vocational instructors, academic teachers—all are important.

CAREER/VOCATIONAL EDUCATION MODEL

A sequential level model developed by Keller (1972) recommends six principle components of a career/vocational program essential to ensure an integrated curriculum as follows:

1. Society and work—knowledge about the institutions and dynamics in society that generate, define and lend meaning to jobs, i.e., attempting to enable the student to view specific

occupations within the context of society and devoid of the "rose-colored tint."
2. Occupational knowledge—information on broad occupational groups, related jobs, and individual jobs. Students frequently are unaware of the options which exist for them within a particular interest area. This knowledge should provide them with a perspective of the latitude a specific area of pursuit affords them.
3. Self-knowledge—information needed to make accurate and relevant self-assessments in relation to career choice. Knowledge of self-attributes, interests, aptitudes, etc. is critical information as it relates to career demands and expectancies for performance.
4. Career planning—utilizing information on world of work and self-knowledge in decision making. The need to integrate the objective concrete work related information with knowledge of self is the process which differentiates effective from ineffective career programs.
5. Basic technology—school reorganizes curricula around basic skills useful in occupations. The American educational system has a responsibility to provide students with meaningful, useful and congruent education. Educational practice should reflect educational philosophy.
6. Specific occupational training—direct training for entry level skills and attitudes. The last step should be included in the consideration of any career model. This is, the actual academic and experiential skill provision, i.e., giving the student that which he needs to "get in the door."

Another model that has the student as its nucleus was proposed by Bailey and Stadt (1973) as shown in Table 6-1.

In this model, the suggested introduction of elements within the domain of career education is posited by grade level in addition to the child's developmental behavior. The integration, for example, of career awareness with the instruction of concepts of self is proposed for presentation in grades K through 3. At that same grade level, with awareness, is the focus on information processing skills. The model presents the interface of career and behavior in relation to grade level and skill hierarchy.

Both models propose that career development should be viewed as sequential in nature; that effectiveness is contingent upon knowledge of the individual; that delivery of services must be integrated; that content

Table 6-1 Developmental Curriculum Model for Career Education

Domains of Career Development Behavior	A. Awareness	B. Accommodation	C. Orientation	D. Exploration & Preparation
(Grade Levels)	K–3	4–6	7–8	9–12
1. Concepts of self	A1	B1	C1	D1
2. Occupational, educational and economic concepts and skills	A2	B2	C2	D2
3. Sense of agency	A3	B3	C3	D3
4. Information processing skills	A4	B4	C4	D4
5. Interpersonal relationships	A5	B5	C5	D5
6. Work attitudes and values	A6	B6	C6	D6

Source: Reprinted from *Career Education: New Approaches to Human Development* by L.J. Bailey and R.W. Stadt by permission of McKnight Publishing Co., © 1973.

must be functional; and that preparation and application must be viewed as part of one continuum.

CAREER PROGRAM IMPLEMENTATION

In attempting to implement a career program that effects these views Hayes, Hopson, and Daws (1971) recommend the following issues be considered:

1. Treat the work experience as an educational experience and not a final answer to their [students] career goals and needs. [In a world of dynamic change, students should be prepared to be alert to these changes and adapt accordingly.]
2. Students should ideally be given a variety of work experiences so they can become acquainted with alternative career directions. [There are some 5,000 occupations listed in the *Dictionary of Occupational Titles,* but students' career choices are often made on the basis of knowledge of a handful.]
3. Safeguard any experiences against violation of various legal restraints. [Teachers must be aware of the legal regulations regarding training of students; for example, wages, health, or safety regulations.]
4. Cooperation of business, industry, community agencies, and other interested groups is essential. It was recommended that the employer:
   a. Provide experiences of the least and most attractive features of the position.
   b. Offer varieties of experiences during a single day. [This will enable the student to acquire a perspective of the parameters of the position.]
   c. Insure the youth against injury.
   d. Designate an experienced understanding adult to assist the youth. [One of the most effective learning vehicles is that of modeling.]
   e. Parents should be part of the placement and assessment process. [Adolescents are seeking independence, competence, and a sense of power. Parents must be brought into this process so that they can contribute support and information and better serve as an additional resource to their adolescent children.] (Reprinted with permission.)

CURRICULUM AND INSTRUCTION

Learning disabled adolescents who are considered for admission into a vocational or career preparatory program should exhibit a level of cognitive and emotional readiness and maturity that suggests they have the potential for profiting from the program. Some factors to be considered include an ability to work somewhat independently, an ability to accept direction, and an expressed interest in participating in the program. Given the range of differing disabilities that a learning disabled adolescent population exhibits, it is impossible to design a program that has equal applicability for all students. There are, however, certain parameters within which a career preparation program should be designed in order to effectively meet the needs of the handicapped learner.

Guidelines for a Career Preparation Program for Learning Disabled Adolescents

There are few models available to assist the teacher in the development of a model appropriate for the learning disabled student in that the literature relative to career preparation for the learning disabled is limited (Brolin & Brolin, 1979; Brutten, 1966; Colella, 1973; Irvine, 1975; Kameny, 1967; Schweich, 1975; Sunberg, 1970; Washburn, 1975; Williamson, 1974–75).

The following five guidelines are recommended for use in developing a career preparation program as follows:

1. The students should be provided with a unified program of occupational and academic instruction. For example, concurrent with exploration of an occupation in a shop setting, the academic instruction should focus on vocabulary related to the occupation, the reading and mathematics skills needed to succeed in the occupation, and classroom-type instruction for the occupation itself (duties, working conditions, required knowledge, etc.). Methods of presentation should be adapted to the student's preferred sensory modalities. Modifications of the curriculum (as suggested throughout this text) should be made. The expected mode of response from the student should allow for options that give consideration to the student's specific disability. Compensation techniques should be taught wherever possible.
2. The program should be adapted to "fit" the student's needs rather than attempting to fit the student into the program. The student's entry level of cognitive development should be considered along with his or her level of social-emotional maturity and psychomotor devel-

opment. If discrepancies exist within any of these areas, adjustments should be made accordingly.

3. Attention should be given to the development of vocational and personal goals that are realistic in light of the student's potential. Setting expectations beyond the capacity of the student's potential is as damaging to a student's self-esteem and motivation as is stating expectations that delimit the actual potential of the student. It is important that students be provided experiences from which they have an opportunity to derive their own conclusions. As Galileo stated, "You cannot teach a man anything, you can only help him discover it within himself."

4. The teacher should emphasize a positive attitude toward work in related instruction as well as in the actual work experiences. To reiterate a point made elsewhere in this book, the modeling effect of the teacher has a significant effect on what students learn.

5. The teacher should ensure student success via a carefully designed program based on formal and informal assessments of the student's entering level of skills, competencies, and behavior; teacher observation; interest and aptitude testing, etc. Learning disabled students are often poor test takers and may not give the assessor a reliable view of their potential.

Clearly stated short-term goals enable the students to comprehend teacher expectations and receive performance feedback on a frequent basis. Frequent and specific feedback to students is strongly advocated by this author. Equally important, the teacher should check out the student's assumptions about her or his role as a learner through interviews, formal questionnaires, or simply by asking the student.

CHARACTERISTICS OF AN EFFECTIVE CAREER GUIDANCE PROGRAM

Effectiveness assumes an interface between the elements involved in the career process—the teachers, the community, the student's family; the workplace, and most importantly, the student herself or himself. Walz, Smith, and Benjamin (1974) provide six characteristics of an effective career guidance program as follows:

1. An effective program takes into account the changing nature of both individuals and the environment as well as the concurrent need for flexible and adaptable human beings. It is

important to recognize that career decisions include a variety and sequence of roles individuals take during a lifetime. [Students should not develop an attitude and expectation that "getting a job" means the end of their role as a learner. The counselor should attempt to have the adolescent view the job not as a terminal goal but as just another step along the road of life experiences.]

2. The focus of an effective program should be on the individual student and his or her developing needs. [The counseling agent must recognize and facilitate the students' recognition of the realities of changes in interests and needs as a function of maturity and to prepare students to cope with these perceived shifts as normal events.]

3. The program should include building on performance objectives adapted to local needs and creating learning experiences which take into account individual learning styles and career maturity levels.

4. The program should allow for a variety of delivery systems, i.e., classroom based instruction; exploratory experience activities; simulations; peer counseling; independent or self-directed study. [Each learning disabled student should be viewed as unique and, as such, a program should be tailored to meet his or her specifications.]

5. Faculty skills, talents and expertise should be identified, utilized and coordinated. The program to be maximally effective should be coordinated to ensure facilitation, avoid duplication and provide consistency.

6. Provision should be given to ways in which existing career education curriculum, resources and materials can be adapted to the local situation. This involves community orientation and involvement in the design as well as the implementation of the program. [Without consideration of the "buyer," i.e., the potential employer of the students, teachers can only be partially responsive to meeting the needs of the students they serve.] (pp. 26–29. Reprinted with permission.)

PREPARATION OF YOUTHS FOR THE WORLD OF WORK

Preparing students to enter occupations is the ultimate goal of career and vocational programs. In the United States, *work* historically has been both a central value and a basic institution. The efforts of secondary schools to prepare students for the world of work present a mixed picture with considerable variance at the local level. However, regardless of the particular curricular model employed locally, the instructional program should consider the following four factors:

1. The high school diploma is vital in obtaining jobs. Students should be made to understand that without it their options are significantly limited or perhaps almost nonexistent.
2. Secondary schools, employers, and employment services have had limited success in placing youths in jobs. Students need assistance, advocates, and guidance in securing jobs. Left on their own, students frequently fail to take advantage of available options.
3. The schools often fail to accommodate the large percentage of students already working. Consideration should be given to flexible programming for students, and attempts should be made to encourage and support those students constructively involved in a work situation.
4. The school is a workplace, and students should be helped to see the connection between what they are now doing and activities they will be engaged in at some future time.

Recommendations

To aid youths in obtaining jobs, the National Panel on High School and Adolescent Education (1976) recommends the following guidelines:

1. Educational and other societal institutions should be urged to actively support the provision of work opportunities for all youths who want them. It is important to "hook" students into work when they are interested and receptive. Frequently, work experiences may spark an interest in academics. The advantages to an adolescent of having a job include:
   a. The student's sense of independence and self-esteem is enhanced and the adolescent's economic dependence upon parents is reduced.
   b. The student is provided varied nonacademic out-of-school learning experiences that help to develop an adolescent's work-related skills (discipline, job knowledge, etc.).
2. The Panel advocates the use of fiscal and monetary policies to reduce general unemployment and for the young in particular. Such action could concentrate on maintaining and enlarging the demand for manpower and facilitating informed movement of persons within and between small labor markets. Statistics on crimes committed by

youthful offenders indicate an increase in incidence during summer periods and at times of greater unemployment. The enticement for youths to engage in unlawful acts is greater with the increase of unstructured, unproductive free time. Society must recognize the need to behave from a preventative posture and a facilitative mode in assisting its youth.

3. The many structural barriers (unemployment insurance and other payroll taxes, workmen's compensation payments, etc.) to the employment of youth should be removed. A careful review of these barriers should be undertaken in the light of contemporary society, and they should be revised and updated accordingly. Policy, procedures, and philosophy should be congruent entities.

4. Youthful employment should not be left to chance. The Panel emphatically recommends that a local job market information center be set up in each community or group of communities, preferably manned by a combination of adolescents and technically qualified adults. In addition, counseling conducted within the schools and instruction could use the newspaper "want ads" as a tool. Assistance in the form of filling out applications, making phone contacts, and role-playing interviews should be considered.

5. Attention should be given to the creation of a job placement mechanism for youths. Studies should be undertaken to determine the means that have proven most effective in assisting students to secure employment. Pilot programs should be developed that attempt alternative mechanisms.

6. The focus should shift from individual employability to job availability. In planning, educators must look at the economics of supply and demand. Preparing students for a flooded job market in a specific area is creating defeat. Broader preparation with greater options must be considered.

7. Work-study and cooperative education programs should be supported and expanded wherever possible. This is particularly important for the learning disabled student whose feelings of success in an academic environment have been limited. Frequently, the work experience provides the student with a more positive sense of self-worth that may then generalize into the academic setting. The secondary school should reassess its role in the preparation of youths for work to determine where and how it can contribute most effectively. In light of existing data regarding the school's role, the following suggestions are offered:

   a. Occupational and career counseling should be provided to all secondary students.

b. The satisfaction of those who work in the school (students and faculty) should be maximized by reducing environmental rigidity and increasing autonomy.

c. Close and active links with employers should be established. Teachers must practice what they preach. If teachers talk with adolescents about a future with options, harmony, collaboration, etc., they must provide that model for students now!

8. Each vocational training program in a high school or community college should be operated under and with an advisory board of business, industry, and union representatives, as well as teachers and students.

In his televised address (1981) to the nation, President Reagan said, "Education is the principle responsibility of local school systems, teachers, parents, citizen boards and state governments."

SUMMARY

America is in a phase of significant change both economically and philosophically in relation to the education of children and youths. Questions regarding the efficacy of a career or vocational program will include, "Who will be unemployed? What can be done within the educational process to minimize those in the ranks of the unemployed? How can this goal be accomplished? What is the school's responsibility? Where does it end?"

The answers to these questions will be strongly influenced by our images of public education, how we value its product and contributions and where it falls among our priorities.

It is essential to remember the educationally handicapped as we seek to find answers to the questions presented. The education of each child should be a matter of interest to the individual, the municipality, the state, and the nation.

An effective career/vocational program is one that combines the individual, the educational system, the family, the municipality, the state, and finally the nation in a partnership. The preparation of our country's future citizens is a matter of responsibility for all of us today. As President Kennedy stated, "Our children are our most precious resource."

RESOURCES

Career and Vocationally Related Tests

Crites, J.O. *Career Maturity Inventory*. Monterey, Calif.: Publisher's Test Service, McGraw-Hill Book Co., 1978. (grades six through twelve and adults; administration: individual or group)

Five variable attitudes toward career decision-making are measured: decisiveness, involvement, independence, orientation, and compromise. An overall measure of career choice attitudes is undertaken through a counseling form of 50 items. A Competence Test contains five statements that measure competence that is important in career decision making: self-appraisal, occupational information, goal selection, planning, and problem solving.

The Inventory enables counselors to work with individuals or groups in career planning. It defines operationally the attitudinal and competence dimensions of a comprehensive career development model.

Cutler, A., Ferry, F., Kauk, R., & Robinett, R. *Career Exploration Series*. Monterey, Calif.: Publisher's Test Service, McGraw-Hill Book Co., 1979, 1981. (grade range 9–adult; administration: individual or group)

The Career Exploration Series (CES) comprises 6 separate inventories designed to determine a student's interests and attitudes as they relate to employment in the areas of agriculture (A6-0); business (B12-0); industry (IND-0); mathematics, science, and health (SCI-0); consumer, economics, and related professions (CER-0); and design, art, and communications (DAC-0).

The CES format offers students the opportunity to match their educational aspirations, desired job activities, and job interests and skills to job titles within a particular occupational field. The 60 primary job titles were selected from those careers thought to be the most in demand in the coming decade.

Cutler, A., Ferry, F., Kauk, R., & Robinett, R. *JOB-O*. Monterey, Calif.: Publisher's Test Service, McGraw-Hill Book Co. (grade range: seven–adult; administration: individual or group)

This test is a self-administered career exploration instrument that has been used by over 3 million students. In a survey of 20,000 of those students, 97% indicated that the directions and questions were easy to read and to follow, and 93% indicated satisfaction with JOB-O results.

Assessment takes into account nine variables related to educational aspirations, occupational interests, and interpersonal and physical characteristics of occupations. JOB-O is tied to current labor statistics, trends, and predictions. Information on the 120 job titles selected for JOB-O is updated every two years to include the latest national job trends as presented in the *Occupational Outlook Handbook*.

Jackson, D.N. *Jackson Vocational Interest Survey*. Monterey, Calif.: McGraw-Hill Book Co., 1977. (grade range: seven through adult)

This survey (JVIS) is an educational and career planning instrument that elicits individual preferences in terms of vocational roles and vocational styles. *Roles* refer to homogeneous sets of activities relevant to occupations and *styles* refer to preferences for certain kinds of work environments. The JVIS yields scores for 34 Basic Interest Scales directly related to particular occupations. The survey is easily administered in one class period and is easily scored in a brief period (approximately 10 minutes). It places an equal emphasis on the interests of men and women.

Jastak, J.F. & Jastak, S. *Wide Range Interest and Opinion Test.* Monterey, Calif.: Publisher's Test Service, McGraw-Hill Book Co., 1979. (age range: five through adult)

Designed to determine interests and attitudes of individuals, the WRIOT does not require reading or language understanding. It consists of pictures of people engaged in many varieties of activity with which the individual is able to identity directly. The results of the WRIOT are analyzed in terms of consistent personal characteristics.

WRIOT yields scores for 18 interest clusters and 8 attitude clusters. The interest clusters include art, sales, management, office work, mechanics, machine operation, and athletics. The attitude clusters include sedentariness, risk, ambition, and sex stereotyping.

WRIOT can be used with almost all individuals. It aids in career education, planning, and counseling and shows the strength of positive and negative preferences.

Jones, L.K. *Occ-U-Sort.* Monterey, Calif.: Publisher's Test Service, McGraw-Hill Book Co., 1981. (grade range: seven and above; administration: individual or group)

Occ-U-Sort has been recently revised. It aids individuals in making occupational choices through stimulating their thinking about motives and self-perceptions, broadens awareness of occupations, and encourages consideration of nontraditional occupations. The program consists of a set of 60 cards each of which has the name of an occupation, the *Dictionary of Occupational Titles* (DOT) Code, the General Educational Development (GED) education level specified in the DOT and a description of the occupation.

Oliver, J.E. *Career Guidance Inventory in Trades, Services and Technologies.* Monterey, Calif.: Publisher's Test Service, McGraw-Hill Book Co., 1972. (grades nine and above; administration: individual or group)

A special interest inventory designed for students who are not planning on four or more years of college, this inventory aids counselors to help students or adults plan career objectives. It is simple to use and provides immediate scores.

ANNOTATED BIBLIOGRAPHY

Materials for the Student

This section includes materials the student may use either under the supervision of the teacher, with guidance, or in some instances independently.

Beakely, C. (Ed.). *Occupations*. Syracuse, N.Y.: New Readers Press.
This book contains information about job qualifications, pay, and advancement, taken largely from the *Occupational Outlook Handbook*. Information is organized into occupations in these areas: service, service occupations in government, paraprofessional, clerical, hotel and restaurant, driving, and skilled manual occupations. The reading grade level is three to four.

Choosing Careers. RMI Media Productions, 1975. (grades 7–12; 5 color sound filmstrips)
This series examines five basic concepts that will assist students in making the most of their individual talents, aptitudes, and interests. The important decision of choosing a job, career or profession is given careful consideration. Preparation by experienced high school and vocational teachers.

Cook, I.D. *Occupational Notebook Program*. Champaign, Ill.: Research Press.
This program deals with the basics of the world of work. The student becomes aware of the need for skills in various areas, including deciding on a line of work, filling out applications, interviewing, keeping a job, finances, travel, and becoming a pleasant and productive worker. The book is 48 pages and comes with a 64-page teacher's guide.

Finding Your Job Career Briefs. Minneapolis, Minn.: Finney Publishing Co.
Detailed job descriptions are available for several occupations.

Freed, A. *TA for Teens*. Rolling Hills, Calif.: Jalmar Press, 1976. (junior and senior high)
Dr. Alogn Freed uses the concept of Transactional Analysis to explain ups and downs with parents, friends, teachers, and peers. *TA for Teens* deals with the topics of drugs, sex, runaways, and home hassles.

Getting Together: Problems You Face. Englewood Cliffs, N.J.: Scholastic. (senior high)
Getting Together examines peer group pressures—boy-girl relationships, identity crises, family conflicts, etc. Open-ended plays allow students to probe and resolve their own problems.

Howard, R.D. *Unemployed Uglies.* Phoenix, N.Y.; Frank Richards Publishing Co.

This book provides instruction emphasizing what not to do on the job, and it includes a teacher instruction book with 20 cartoons and jingles.

Job Attitudes: Trouble at Work. American Guidance Associates.

This kit explores typical on-the-job conflicts as crackling dialogue and on-location photography portrays tension between workers. Includes four color filmstrips, two cassettes, and one teacher's guide. American Guidance Associates.

Job Survival Skills. Kalamazoo, Mich.: Interpretive Education, 1979. (one color sound filmstrip; grades 8–12; remedial adult)

Job Survival Skills offers practical suggestions for adjusting to a new job. Hints on pacing a work load, understanding job responsibilities, getting along with coworkers and budgeting money are covered.

Part-Time Jobs. Kalamazoo, Mich.: Interpretive Education, 1978. (one color sound filmstrip; grades 7–12)

This filmstrip suggests some good part-time jobs for young people and tells how to go about getting them. It illustrates what to find out before accepting a job, as well as the responsibilities involved in various part-time jobs.

Peace, Harmony, Awareness. Hingham, Mass.: Teaching Resources. (all levels)

This 12-part audio program teaches relaxation and helps increase self-confidence. Children are taught to identify and to deal positively with criticism, stress, and anger. The program can be used with either individuals or groups.

The Coping With Series. Circle Pines, Minn.: American Guidance Service, Inc., 1973. (junior and senior high)

This series is written for today's teenagers as a contribution to the development of sound values during the growing years. There are 23 books written for young people of all backgrounds at a level suitable to the beginning and middle teens. The topics discussed provide valuable insight into problems they encounter at home, at school, in unfamiliar situations, and in facing both the present and future.

Turner, R.H. *The Newspaper You Read.* Chicago, Ill.: Follett Publishing Co.

This workbook covers such topics as how to find information in a newspaper, jobs in the printing and newspaper industries, suburban life, reckless driving, and analyzing news stories. The teacher's guide covers this six-book series. It is suitable for reading levels 4–6.

You and the World of Work. Audio Visual Narrative Arts, 1975. (four color sound filmstrips; grades 7–12)

Students are asked to consider which is most important to them: prestige, money, adventure, security or personal satisfaction. The program outlines various practical techniques for first time job seekers such as preparing a resume, job interviewing. Another section focuses on developing the skills necessary to keep the job.

Your Job Interview. Circle Pines, Minn.: American Guidance Association.

Designed to guide young job seekers through their first interviews, it demonstrates why interviews are a vital step toward getting a job. The kit contains two color filmstrips, two cassettes, and one teaching guide.

Vocational Education

Beyond High School. Pleasantville, N.Y.: Sunburst Communications, 1977. (grades 7–12)

This program provides noncollege-bound students with the tools for making realistic and intelligent choices of careers and career training. It teaches students practical strategies for first choosing and then preparing for an occupation and examines methods for matching capabilities and occupations. The program acquaints students with ways of focusing on career choice, informs them of specialized training available, and advises them of sources of additional information and assistance.

Career Education Clusters. Oak Lawn, Ill.: Westinghouse Learning Corporation, 1973. (grades 7–adult)

This program is essential for every school developing comprehensive career education courses. This innovative series explores the 15 career fields or clusters defined by USOE. The program was photographed on location and uses a dramatization format that students will find especially involving. By matching their interests and aptitudes to one or more of the broad career fields, students soon become active and realistic designers of their own futures.

Career Exploration Kit. Chatsworth, Calif.: Career Aids, Inc., 1977. (grades 7–12 remedial adult)

These activities, which approximate actual working situations, guide the student to discover a career that is both creative and productive. Through group projects, students explore many careers and also develop cooperation, communication, and decision-making ability. Individual projects encourage the student to define career objectives and explore special interests or talents.

Career Lab. Oak Lawn, Ill.: Westinghouse Learning Corp., 1975. (grades 7–12, adult)

This program provides self-instructional activities designed to give students real experience in various aspects of the working world. Nine activity units can be used in various sequential arrangements: your personality; your interests; your needs; work—what it's all about; trying out jobs, job interviews and forms; positive attitudes; your work experience; and your plans.

Gillet, P. *Career Education for Children with Learning Disabilities.* Novato, Calif.: Academic Therapy Publications.

Starting with the career-awareness phase at the elementary level, the author outlines a complete career education program, all the way up to the hands-on work experience at the high school level. Also included are directions for writing IEP s and a comprehensive list of materials applicable for instruction in career education for learning disabled students.

How to Fill Out a Job Application. Kalamazoo, Mich.: Interpretive Education, 1979. (grades 8–12)

This workbook provides the learner with exercises to fill out a job application and awareness of his or her equal employment opportunities.

Job Awareness Inventory. Johnstown, Pa.: Mafex Associates, 1980. (grades 9–10; remedial 11–adult)

The inventory includes a pretest and posttest of 100 questions each.

Job Interview (Step by Step Procedures). Kalamazoo, Mich.: Interpretive Education, 1979. (grades 8–12)

This step-by-step program help students prepare for a job interview, participate in an interview, and accept the outcome of the interview.

Steady Job Game. Johnstown, Pa.: Mafex Associates, 1974. (grades 7–10, remedial 11–adult)

This instructional and fun vocational orientation game is designed for students with learning problems. It reinforces positive job attitudes and behavior essential to employability. Players advance to a steady job for positive behavior and attitudes and are held back for unacceptable job performance.

Washburn, W. *Vocational Mainstreaming: A Manual for Teachers of Learning Disabled Students.* Novato, Calif.: Academic Therapy Publications.

This manual covers each step of prevocational entry skill training: ways to coordinate appropriate placement in vocational classes; specific teaching methods for assisting learning disabled students in regular vocational classes; and ways parents can assist the educational process.

The Appendix to the manual contains a summary of federal regulations, lists of vocational tests and surveys, and a summary of the features of an effective mainstreaming program. Information on postsecondary vocational training for job placement is also included.

Washburn, W. *Vocational Skills Competency Checklist.* Novato, Calif.: Academic Therapy Publications.

This four-page checklist gives the special education teacher a quick reference on a student's vocational interests, job experience, current work abilities, and learning modes. Using this checklist of prevocational skills, special education and vocational teachers can determine if the learning disabled student is adequately prepared to enter regular vocational training classes. Part of the checklist is completed by the student. The remaining information can be procured from parents and IEP records.

REFERENCES

Andrews, D. *Consideration in developing vocational opportunities for learning disabled secondary students.* Unpublished paper, Connecticut Vocational Department, 1976.

Annual Report of the American Federation of Teachers. *American Teacher,* Summer 1981, *66,* 5–20.

Bail, J.P., & Hamilton, W.H. A study of the innovative aspects of emerging off-farm agricultural programs at the secondary levels and the articulation of such programs with technical college curriculum in agriculture. Ithaca, N.Y.: State University of New York, 1967. (ERIC Document Reproduction Service No. ED 012 792)

Bailey, L.J., & Stadt, R.W. *Career Education: New Approaches to Human Development.* Bloomington, Ill.: McKnight Publishing Company, 1973.

Brolin, D. *Vocational preparation of retarded citizens.* Columbus, Ohio: Charles E. Merrill Publishing Co., 1976.

Brolin, D., & Brolin, J. Vocational education for special students. In D. Cullinan & M. Epstein (Eds.), *Special Education for Adolescents.* Columbus, Ohio: Charles E. Merrill Publishing Co., 1979.

Brutten, M. Vocational education for the brain injured adolescent and young adult at the Vanguard School. In *International Approach to Learning Disabilities of Children and Youth.* Tulsa, Okla.: Proceedings of the Third Annual Conference of the ACLD, 1966.

Colella, H.V. Career development center: A modified high school for the handicapped. In *Teaching Exceptional Children,* 1973, *5,* 110–118.

Education for All Handicapped Children Act of 1975, P L 94-142.

Green, T.F. Career education and the pathologies of work. In L. McClure & C. Buan (Eds.), *Essays on Career Education.* Portland, Oregon: Northwest Regional Laboratory, 1973.

Hayes, J., Hopson, B., & Daws, P.P. *Career guidance: The role of the school in vocational development.* London, England: Heinemann Education Books, 1971.

Hoyt, K.B. An introduction to career education. (DHEW Publication No. (OE) 75-005-04.) A policy paper of the U.S. Office of Education, 1976.

Irvine, P. *Exploratory occupational education for learning disabled adolescents.* Paper presented at Learning Disabilities in the Secondary School, a symposium sponsored by the Montgomery County Intermediate Unit, Norristown, Pa., March 1975.

Keller, L.J. Career development—an integrated curriculum approach, K–12. In K. Goldhammer & R. Taylor (Eds.), *Career Education: Perspective and Promise.* Columbus, Ohio: Charles E. Merrill Publishing Co., 1972.

Kostoe, O.P. *Teaching educable mentally retarded children* (2nd ed.) New York: Holt, Rinehart & Winston, Inc., 1976.

Marland, S.P. Career Education. *Today's Education,* 1971, *60,* 22–25.

Marland, S.P. Career education: Every student headed for a goal. *American Vocational Journal,* 1972, *47*(3), 34–36.

National Panel on High School and Adolescent Education. U.S. Office of Education (OE 76-00004); U.S. Office of Educational Publications, 1976, 142.

Sunberg, N. Vocational rehabilitation cooperation in school. In L. Cenderson (Ed.), *Helping the Adolescent with the Hidden Handicap.* Los Angeles: California Association for Neurologically Handicapped Children, 1970.

U.S. Department of Labor. *Dictionary of occupational titles* (Vols. I and II). Washington, D.C.: U.S. Government Printing Office, 1965.

U.S. Department of Labor. *Supplement to the dictionary of occupational titles.* Washington, D.C.: U.S. Government Printing Office, 1968.

U.S. Department of Labor. *Supplement to the occupational outlook handbook.* Washington, D.C.: U.S. Government Printing Office, 1974.

U.S. Office of Education. National panel on high school and adolescent education (OE 76-00004). Washington, D.C.: U.S. Office of Educational Publications, 1976.

Vocational Act of 1963, P L 88-201.

Vocational Education Amendment Act of 1976, P L 94-482.

Vocational Education Amendments of 1968, P L 90-576.

Walz, G., Smith, R., & Benjamin, L. (Eds.), *A Comprehensive View of Career Development.* American Personnel and Guidance Association Press, 1974.

Washburn, W.Y. Where to go in voc-ed for secondary LD students. *Academic Therapy,* 1975, *11,* 31–35.

Williamson, A.P. Career Education: implications for secondary LD students. *Academic Therapy,* 1974–75, *10,* 193–200.

Woodward, D.M. *Mainstreaming the learning disabled adolescent.* Rockville, Md.: Aspen Systems Corporation, 1981.

Younie, W., & Clark, G. Personnel training needs for cooperative secondary school programs for mentally retarded. *Education and Training of the Mentally Retarded,* 1969, *4*(4), 186–194.

SUGGESTED READINGS

Humphrey, J., McEntire, B., & Saski, J. *Administrative strategies for secondary special education programs.* Austin, Texas: Texas Education Agency, 1978.

Kameny, A. Prevocational retraining: A behavioral task-centered approach. In *Management of the Child with Learning Disabilities.* New York: Proceedings of the Fourth Annual Conference of the ACLD, 1967.

Marsh, G., Gearheart, C. & Gearheart, B. *The learning disabled adolescents—Program alternatives in the secondary school.* The C.V. Mosby Company, St. Louis, Missouri, 1978.

Organizations for the essentials of education. Newark, Del.: The International Reading Association, 1971.

Saski, J. *Competencies for teachers of the handicapped adolescent.* Unpublished manuscript. Austin, Texas: The University of Texas at Austin, 1977.

Schweich, P.D. The development of choices—an educational approach to employment. *Academic Therapy,* 1975, *10,* 277–283.

Part II

Enhancing Teachers' Competencies and Skills: Application of Instructional Methodologies and Strategies

In this section of the text, the application of strategies and methodology within the secondary school learning context are addressed. Specifically, these strategies are designed to improve reading comprehension across content areas. Poor and disabled readers typically require more instructional structure and organization by the teacher. Such structure is necessary if these students are to meet the major requirement of the secondary curriculum—reading comprehension.

Upon completion of this section, the reader should:

- understand the importance of reasoning skills in reading comprehension for adolescent students,
- understand the critical differences between reading comprehension and reading/thinking skills,
- possess pragmatic, hands-on approaches that are designed to expedite and enhance the learning achievement of the learning disabled adolescent, and
- realize the significance of directive teaching as it relates to the secondary school curriculum.

In summary, the reader should have a more complete understanding of the components of reading comprehension and possess a full catalog of instructional strategies for classroom use with the poor or disabled reader.

Chapter 7

Introduction to the Components of Reading

This chapter defines and explains the major components essential to success in teaching reading comprehension in the content area. These components include vocabulary meaning; reasoning and thinking skills; organizational patterns; and readability levels.

These components are viewed as important for various reasons. Vocabulary meaning is a prerequisite to conceptualization and reasoning in the reading process. The reasoning/thinking skills are critical if a student is to move beyond the knowledge level of cognition and deal with the abstract concepts presented in secondary level texts. Organizational patterns, which are viewed here as the structure of paragraphs, provide a tool by which the reader can move effectively to determine the author's message. Finally, the student must be able to properly evaluate content level texts and teacher-made materials to maximize instruction.

Chapter 8 illustrates how these components may be combined with direct instruction to develop study guides to increase understanding of content area reading material for the poor or disabled reader.

SIGNIFICANCE OF VOCABULARY DEVELOPMENT IN READING IN THE CONTENT AREA

Each subject has its unique language, a specific set of words with distinctive meanings and connotations related to the particular field of study. Comprehension is impeded unless a student can deal with the vocabulary of the subject. Herber (1978) states, "If students hold limited meaning of words, they also will hold limited understanding of concepts, hence limited understanding of the subject" (p. 130).

The view that vocabulary meaning is essential to understanding in reading is shared by many experts in the field of teaching. Harris and Sipay

(1980) state "a minimum essential for comprehension in reading is an understanding of the words used by the author" (p. 448). The development of a reading vocabulary that is both extensive and accurate is a necessary phase of good comprehension.

Goodman (1970) defines word meaning as, "the ability of the child to sort out his experiences and concepts in relation to words and phrases in the context of what he is reading" (p. 16). This is an especially appropriate definition when addressing vocabulary meaning in the content area since it emphasizes both concept and reasoning development.

Definition

In this book, vocabulary development is viewed as a unitary process in which conceptualization and reasoning are emphasized. The development of word meaning is a prerequisite to the reading/thinking process.

Vocabulary development is defined as introducing meaning to, or broadening the meaning of words, terms, and phrases in reading. Instructional experiences that relate the student's past experiences and present life to the definitions of words adds relevancy to the words.

Vocabulary development is teaching meaning to words so that the words become relevant to a student's life—the words become part of the student's knowledge bank. If words are not relevant they become part of vague memories. A student may say, "I remember Miss Kennedy talking about that in science last year," but that is all he or she remembers. The meaning was not forgotten; it was never learned.

To further clarify the definition of vocabulary development, the example of two tenth grade disabled readers is provided. Reader A lives in a large city, and reader B lives on an island that is ten miles long and five miles wide. Both readers are using a science text that defines soil erosion as a slow natural process that changes the contour of the earth's surface by the action of glaciers, water, winds, and waves. The urban reader, reader A, who has never been to a seashore and has only observed wind and water on city streets, ignores the information about wind, water, and waves and focuses on glaciers. He recalls that over a million years ago, Ice Age glaciers were high masses of ice that formed mountains. Consequently, the urban reader concludes that soil erosion is related to glacier movement and is something that happened millions of years ago.

On the other hand, the island reader (reader B) cannot recall or may not have studied about glaciers but has spent a great deal of his or her life observing and dealing with water, waves, and wind. Reader B ignores the word *glacier* and concludes that soil erosion means sand being washed away from beaches by violent sea storms.

By relating past experiences with information in the reading, both readers have developed a specific meaning for the term *soil erosion*. However, neither of these specific meanings will aid the students in further understanding how different types of soil erosion relate to different methods of soil conservation, which is the information presented in the next section of their text.

Imagine the urban reader trying to understand the necessity of preserving mountains through soil conservation. In his or her mind, mountains were formed millions of years ago and have not changed. Mountains do not erode; mountains are forever.

Imagine the confusion of the island reader trying to understand how the use of corn as a cover crop in strip cropping will keep the sand on the beaches when he or she knows that corn cannot grow in the sand.

For the term *soil erosion* to become a relevant tool or prerequisite information for understanding the relationship of concepts presented in the next section of the science text, these students must be offered instructional experiences that demonstrate that soil erosion takes place in various ways, is caused by several factors, and affects their everyday lives.

The meaning of soil erosion will become more relevant to the urban reader if he is first made aware of how his direct experiences relate to the term *soil erosion*. An example of this would be having him realize that he has observed and experienced soil erosion at the ballpark when the rain washed away homeplate or at the sandlot when the wind whipped the sand around so hard that he could not play stickball.

The island reader can be directed to realize that soil erosion occurs not only on the beach but also on his or her front lawn during a rainstorm when small streams of water trickle through the lawn leaving small paths of dirt where grass once grew or, on the land banks, when heavy winds and rains cause mudslides on the back roads.

Vocabulary introduction, defining words, is not sufficient information for the poor or disabled reader to form accurate concepts. Prior knowledge or prior experiences must be linked with the new definition before the word becomes a useful tool.

The urban and island readers are not alone in forming misconceptions due to the introduction of vocabulary words by definition only. Most secondary students have not had the experience necessary to manage all the meanings and connotations of a word, nor have they had sufficient instructional experiences in applying the meaning of words in one subject area to meanings of words in other subject areas. Consequently, even those students who have a broader understanding of words often select the first meaning that comes to mind. This behavior is especially true of the poor or disabled reader.

Factors that Hinder the Development of Vocabulary Meaning

Several factors such as low general intelligence, physical handicapping conditions, auditory processing weaknesses, and sociocultural aspects influence vocabulary development. The lack of mastery of basic skills in reading and inadequate instruction in word meaning also contribute to poor vocabulary development. The following is a list of three reading behaviors that are most commonly found to hinder vocabulary development.

1. The student recognizes the combination of symbols as a word and can pronounce the word but has no understanding of what the word means.
2. The student cannot recognize or mispronounces the word in print but would know the meaning of the word if presented orally.
3. The student cannot recognize the word and does not know the meaning.

If students have problems in the first category, they need extensive instruction in vocabulary development. This behavior can indicate lack of intellectual stimulation and insufficient practice in the use of words.

Studies have indicated that all too many teachers are "mentioners" (Durkin, 1978–79). Instead of offering the student direct and continuous experience with the word, they mention the meaning of a new word in a single sentence without an example, or they offer a synonym and continue on to the next word. To understand why this happens, consider the teacher as the expert and the student as the novice. All too often the experts view the vocabulary of their discipline as community language. The novice views the expert's language as foreign. Strange as it seems, the teacher's expertise can hinder the student's learning if vocabulary meaning is not recognized as the first step in building the foundation for understanding the content.

A student with problems in the second category needs remediation in word recognition, although instruction in word meaning should not be ignored. The teacher should capitalize on the student's strength in word meaning, to improve the weakness, word recognition. The teacher can correlate prior knowledge, word meaning, with decoding skills to increase accuracy and fluency in word recognition.

In the third category, a student who exhibits problems in both word recognition and word meaning needs intensive remediation in both areas. However, initial reading remediation should focus on decoding and word recognition skills since the secondary poor or disabled reader needs the tools to decode and recognize words before the meaning of these words can have importance. Once this student has mastered word recognition skills equivalent to the end of the third-grade reading level, then the emphasis of instruction should shift so that word recognition can be linked to word meaning.

INSTRUCTION IN WORD MEANING

For instruction in vocabulary development to be successful, it must provide the poor or disabled reader with extensive opportunities to build new concepts upon old knowledge so that transfer of information is effective. It must also provide the poor or disabled reader with external organization so that these "students develop a flexible mental file for storing and retrieving words. A new word isn't much value if it is filed and lost" (Dale, 1971, p. 7).

Guidelines for Teaching Vocabulary Meaning

The following guidelines adapted and modified from Forgan and Mangrum (1981) are suggested to assist in the instruction of vocabulary development.

- Instruction should be consistent, systematic and continuous.
- Teach words that are part of the student's life so that meaning will be relevant. The lack of relevancy causes disuse and loss of word meaning.
- New words are more efficiently learned when they are part of a first-hand experience.
- Provide the students with varied experiences with the word. The word should be used in many like and different contexts before it can be assumed that meaning has taken place.
- It is best to study a few words in depth rather than a large list of words in a shallow, vague manner. (pp. 132–133. Used with permission.)

To enhance students' learning of vocabulary meaning, more direct and continuous practice with teacher/student interaction must be provided. Instruction must also include various examples, explanations, and several experiences in linking the words to students' experiences.

A general rule to keep in mind is that the more a word is used, the more meaning it tends to have and the more likely the word will be retained. Casual and vicarious experience with a word causes confusion, misconceptions, and vague memories of it. For example, a student may say, "I remember Miss Kennedy talking about that in science last year, but I don't know what it means."

LEVELS OF WORD MEANING

Research indicates that teachers are word mentioners in that they do not teach word meaning but rather they "tell" word meaning. Many teachers realize the importance of vocabulary development but have not been provided with the information or training to develop a systematic approach of instruction in this area. The authors' many years of experience as educators has demonstrated that teachers' performance does improve when teachers understand what they are doing and why they are doing it and are provided with a framework in how to do it.

Three Levels of Word Meaning

The following definitions for levels of word meaning and activities for each level adapted from Forgan and Mangrum (1981) are provided to assist content area teachers in beginning to develop more consistent, systematic, and continuous instruction for the poor or disabled reader.

Level 1: Specific Level

At this level, the student can identify one particular characteristic or feature of an object, event or person. An example of this would be the word *ill*. At this level, the word *ill* would be defined as *sick*. No other fact or event would be related to the word.

Level 2: Functional Level

At this level, the student can express a major use of the word or can define the word by using it in a sentence. At this level the word *ill* might be defined as "someone who isn't feeling good," or the student would exhibit understanding of the word by using it in a sentence such as, "When I was ill, I was in pain."

Level 3: Conceptual Level

At this level, the student has several facts and ideas linked with the word. The student recognizes these linkages and groups them into a common component or common category. When asked to define the word *ill,* the student might respond, "A person who is ill is unhealthy and can be indisposed with a disease."

At the specific level, the student associated a like word with the word *ill.* The word is almost known. At the functional level, the student demonstrated an understanding of the word by using it in a sentence and relating the word to a direct experience; therefore the word is partly known. At the conceptual level, the student demonstrated that he or she has many facts and ideas linked with the word *ill,* and the word is well known (pp. 137–140).

Words entering students' vocabularies do not automatically move from the specific level to the functional level and then upward to the conceptual level of meaning. Word meanings often remain at the specific or functional levels if sufficient activities and instruction are not provided.

Asking students to look a word up in the dictionary generally retains the meaning of the word at the specific or functional level with very little, if any, movement toward the conceptual level. Asking students to define words by using them in a sentence, to state a synonym, or to write a sentence using the particular word generally retains the word at the functional level. To provide adequate instruction in vocabulary meaning for the poor or disabled reader, it is recommended to use the functional level activities to introduce the meaning of words and then proceed to conceptual level activities to expand the meaning of words. Specific level activities are useful as practice and review activities only.

Activities for Each Level of Word Meaning

Specific Level Activities

Activities at this level should be used with caution since specific level activities provide the students with "almost knowing." It is strongly recommended that activities at this level be used as practice or review activities only after the student has had introductory experiences with the word(s) at the functional level.

Frequently teachers limit instructional activities to specific level activities. This approach attenuates the student's learning through their inherent delimiting factors.

Examples of specific level activities are:

- Locate words in the glossary or dictionary and write a definition and sentence without further instruction. This type of activity does not give the student sufficient practice or application to make the word meaningful and sufficiently relevant.

- Match prefixes and suffixes to their most common meanings. Without further instruction, this activity encourages rote memory.
- Play word games such as Scrabble, Word Bingo, and Password. Without further instruction, this activity does not give the student sufficient practice in using the words in a variety of situations.
- Use exercise vocabulary books. This activity should be used only as a review because the words in exercise vocabulary books are generally not relevant to the student's academic or social needs.
- Memorize prefixes and suffixes and link them with single meanings. Without further instruction, this activity does not provide application to root words; therefore no transfer of information takes place.
- Give a simple one-word definition. Without further instruction, this causes stilted understanding of the word and decreases the use of the word. The student is apt to apply this word to only one situation, relating the one meaning to the one situation the student has learned.
- Show a picture of an object. Without further instruction, this activity restricts the student in that the focus is on one characteristic of the object, and therefore, only one feature of the meaning of the word is learned.

Functional Level Activities

It is highly recommended to use activities at this level as introductory activities. Functional level activities lend themselves to student-teacher interaction since they involve the students' active participation in the learning process. These activities are conducive to providing the students with a "hook" to hang prior knowledge.

Some simple functional level activities are:

- Suggest many synonyms for one word. For example, using the word *jailer,* some synonyms are a keeper, a warden, or a guard.
- Suggest antonyms for a word. Using the word *cowardly,* some opposites are brave, bold, or valiant.
- Classify words. Group the words to assist in understanding function. For example, the word *beg* is a verb that expresses action, and it means to request.
- Use similes. For example, a critic is like a censor; a critic is like a judge; or a critic is like a reviewer.

More extensive functional activities are:

- use of visual aids to teach word meaning

- acting out the meaning of words
- explaining, giving examples and discussing words before reading new materials

The latter is an especially effective introductory activity to use with disabled readers since they have difficulty in retrieving meanings of words. This is manifested by substituting words within their general cognitive structure. For example, when asked for the opposite meaning of the word *evening,* the student may incorrectly respond "afternoon." The slow rate of retrieval also affects the student who may comprehend abstract meanings but is only able to produce a simple definition.

The poor or disabled readers also have difficulty in producing or identifying the structural form of words even though they may know the meaning of the words. For example, when the student is asked to define the noun *textbook,* the student will define its function, "it's something to read." When asked to define the verb *to forecast,* the student will define the word as a noun, "a prediction."

Explaining, Giving Examples, and Discussing Words before Introducing New Materials

This activity has four steps Each step is hierarchical in nature. It first provides the poor or disabled reader with examples of word meaning using different structural forms as well as familiar associations of the word for clearer understanding and easier retrieval. The later steps offer the students exercises in applying the word in different contexts and structural forms and then analyzing the meaning according to the contextual and structural changes of the word. The steps are:

1. In step one, the teacher selects words from the reading materials that need explanation. Words should be selected according to their familiarity to the students and the degree of importance in understanding major concepts.
2. In step two, students must present these words in phrases taken from the context or present these words in phrases or sentences that use context clues. Examples of four types of context clues to be used in phrases or sentences are as follows:
   a. definition clue, i.e., "Brush your teeth so they do not decay."
   b. synonym clue, i.e., "Have your dentist check you for tooth decay or cavities."
   c. familiar expression clue, i.e., "If you don't go to the dentist your teeth will decay or rot."

10

    d. comparison and contrast clue, i.e., "Daily brushing will promote health not decay of your teeth."

3. In step three, to expand the use of the word, teacher and students give additional sentences or phrases using several topics. For example, "The decay of the Roman Empire was caused by greed," "Books, papers, clothing, and furniture decay if stored in damp basements for long periods of time," and "Drug abuse can contribute to mental decay."

4. In step four, students explain the different meanings, structural forms, and connotations derived from the sentences or phrases.

Use of Visual Aids to Teach Word Meaning

Pictures, graphs, charts, and other visual aids can be used to teach word meaning. The teacher should show the picture or visual aid and explain uses, special features, and characteristics. The teacher should then compare it with other objects in the same category.

Activities Using Visual Aids

The following examples illustrate the difference between teaching word meaning with visual aids at the specific and functional levels. The lesson objective for both activities is that students will be able to identify, recall, and explain the natural body features of a porcupine that are used for defense.

Visual Activity at the Specific Level

A picture of a porcupine is shown with the following explanation: "This mammal is a porcupine; notice the body covering of sharp quills. Quills are the porcupine's chief defense against other annoying animals."

This activity provides the students with an awareness of one feature of the natural defense mechanism of a porcupine.

Visual Activity at the Functional Level

A picture of a porcupine is shown with the following explanation:

> "This mammal is a porcupine, and it belongs to the rodent family. Notice the quills that are a special body covering for defense against other annoying animals. Notice the arrangement of the quills on the tail. The common belief that porcupines throw their quills like arrows at their enemies is not true. What really happens

is that the porcupine gives a quick flip of the tail and that sinks a mass of quills deep into the enemy's skin. Also notice the shading of body color; this shading of color blends into the forest environment where the porcupine lives. This body camouflage can be considered another natural defense mechanism for the porcupine.''

Next, the teacher shows a picture of another mammal and points out and explains the body features that are used for defense. These body features are then compared with the natural defense features of a porcupine.

The functional activity not only emphasized the importance of the tail as a natural defense mechanism but also expanded the meaning of natural defense mechanism by explaining the importance of the shading of body color. Instruction at the specific level can be considered show and tell, but instruction at the functional level can be considered show and learn.

Acting-Out the Meaning of Words

Verbs are especially conducive to this activity along with utilizing positive and negative examples of the meaning of the word. To demonstrate the word "obnoxious" act it out by demonstrating that it means objectionable or offensive behavior, then act out what it is not by demonstrating pleasing or favorable behavior.

CONCEPTUAL LEVEL

At the conceptual level many ideas and facts are linked with a word. One activity at this level will not ensure a student's use of the word in several different sentences or contexts. Many activities at all levels are necessary to gain this degree of word meaning. Activities at the conceptual level should be used only after words have been introduced through the use of functional level activities.

Conceptual Level Activities

The most effective way in which to guarantee that students will link several facts and ideas with a word is to provide them with real and direct experiences such as field trips. Although this is the most effective technique, it is also very often unrealistic and impossible to achieve. As a substitute for real and direct experiences the following five activities can be effective in expanding vocabulary development:

1. The teacher can use simulation such as mock trials or mock marriages. Teachers can dress in period costumes when lecturing and discussing specific historical events or can demonstrate the special characteristics of a significant historical person by replicating those characteristics through dress. For example, the teacher could wear a stovepipe hat, morning coat, and beard when discussing Abraham Lincoln and the Civil War or deliver the lecture on John F. Kennedy and the 1962 Cuban crisis with a Bostonian accent.
2. Teachers can compare the geographical, historical, social, and psychological significance of words. For example, when teaching the word *tobacco* at the conceptual level, the teacher could discuss the geographical regions where tobacco is grown in America or make a historical comparison of the regions from early America to present day. The historical and social uses of tobacco could be compared with today's uses. The psychological significance of tobacco from early America to present day and the impact of the tobacco industry on the American economy from early America to the present could be discussed.
3. Audio-visual activities, such as movies, filmstrips, or recordings could substitute for real experiences.
4. The teacher can discuss connotations. Since connotations are positive and negative emotional association of words derived from past experiences, they can cause confusion and misconceptions in learning. However, using students' connotations of words to expand word meaning is highly beneficial. A connotation of a word implies relevancy of that word. Consequently, discussing connotations of words increases students' knowledge of word meaning from "almost" or partly knowing to knowing well. To use connotations to expand word meaning, the teacher should start with the dictionary meaning, proceed to more common meanings and then proceed to students' connotations of the word.
5. Teachers should use many reference materials. Once students understand a word at the functional level, pictures and other aids found in reference materials such as encyclopedias or books written on a specific topic help expand the level of meaning.

Although activities at each level of word meaning provide an instructional framework to increase consistent, systematic, and continuous instruction in vocabulary development, these activities alone do not ensure that the words taught will become part of the disabled reader's reading or spoken vocabulary. To ensure this, instructional activities plus repeated practice and review must be provided. For students to obtain flexible mental files in word meaning, it is best to teach a few words in depth rather than several words in a shallow, superficial manner.

PROBLEMS IN CORRELATING WORD RECOGNITION AND VOCABULARY DEVELOPMENT

Learning disabilities teachers and content area teachers all agree upon the need for instruction in vocabulary meaning as well as word recognition. However, when comparing these two groups of teachers, it is found that the secondary learning disabilities teachers emphasize word recognition in instruction whereas the content area teachers focus on vocabulary development. The instructional emphasis of each group is justifiable when considering the nature and training of each position. Much too often the secondary learning disabilities teacher's major responsibility is to increase basic skill levels whereas the major responsibility of the content area teacher is to increase knowledge levels.

Because of this delineation of responsibilities, it is assumed that disabled readers are receiving adequate instruction in both word recognition and word meaning. However, this is not true. Often, the words taught in reading recognition are not the same words that are selected in teaching word meaning, or if the same words are used, time constraints prevent the content area teacher from providing the extensive instruction needed by this population to expand vocabulary meaning. Consequently, the poor or disabled readers fail because they can recognize a word but do not know the meaning or they know the meaning of a word but cannot recognize the word in reading.

A team effort in correlating instruction between content area teachers and learning disability teachers can effectively address this dilemma. Once a set of words is selected and a common instructional objective is established by both teachers, each teacher has a fuller understanding of what is to be taught, how it is to be taught, and who is responsible for what part of instruction. A team effort reduces student failure and teacher frustration.

A MODEL TO CORRELATE INSTRUCTION IN WORD MEANING THROUGH COLLABORATIVE EFFORT

A five-step model that allows for collaboration between content area teachers and learning disabilities teachers in order to increase word meaning and word recognition in the content areas follows below:

1. The first step is the selection of words.
   a. The content area teacher selects the most essential words the student will need to understand the content for that unit of study. The maximum number of words to be taught should not exceed six per week.
   b. The content area teacher and the learning disabilities teacher confer to determine the order in which the words will be taught and to discuss word meaning activities that will be provided in the classroom and resource room.
2. The next step is informal assessment.
   a. The learning disabilities teacher informally assesses the student's level of word meaning and word recognition for each word selected.
3. Feedback is next.
   a. The learning disabilities teacher reports to the content area teacher a list of the selected words, stating the student's level of familiarity and unfamiliarity with each word.
4. The fourth step is instruction.
   a. The content area teacher proceeds with the regularly planned classroom activities but monitors the student's responses to determine levels of progress.
   b. The learning disabilities teacher begins instruction with three out of the selected first six words. Preferably, two of these words should be words that the student "almost knows" or that the student is familiar with and one word that is unfamiliar to the student. After the student has mastered the first three words at the functional level of meaning, the teacher should introduce a new word daily. After each new word is learned, it should be practiced with the words previously learned for that week.
   c. When possible, words should be introduced by using functional level activities. Syllabication and word recognition strategies should be applied to these words.
   d. When the student can recognize the word, can understand the meaning of the word, and can use it out of context, then the student records the word in a vocabulary notebook.
   e. The student keeps a vocabulary notebook. After a word is learned, the student records the word, the meanings of the word, and sample sentences for each meaning in the notebook. The meanings and example sentences for each word should be in the student's own words and not the words of the dictionary.
   f. Once a week, the student should practice using newly learned words along with review words selected from the student's notebook.

5. The last step is follow-up and planning.
   a. On a weekly basis, the content area teacher and learning disabil-
      ities teacher confer to discuss the progress of the student; deter-
      mine the words to be taught for the following week; and discuss
      the activities and modification of activities to be used for further
      instruction.

This elaborate model may not guarantee that "D" students will become
"A" students. However, it is a realistic, practical model that entails only
ten minutes of weekly meeting time; allows for the exchange of instructional methods and ideas between the content area teacher and the specialist; increases student achievement; and lessens student and teacher
frustration by allowing students and teachers to work on common academic objectives.

SUMMARY

This section presented word meaning as a prerequisite to understanding
content. Whenever word meaning is being taught, content is learned.

The vocabulary activities and collaborative team model have been presented so that teachers can increase their awareness of the significance of
vocabulary meaning in the content areas. The instructional strategies presented increase the expansion of word meaning by focusing on the attainment and extension of already known word definitions and word meanings.

READING AND REASONING

What is Reading Comprehension?

According to the unabridged edition of the *Random House Dictionary*
(1971), the definition of comprehension is "the capacity of the mind to
perceive and understand." Most writers agree that understanding is the
fundamental goal of all reading. According to McGuire and Bumpus (1975),
"Comprehension is what reading is all about, it is the aggressive, dynamic
process of applying cognitive skills to what is being read. It requires from
time to time, memory, associative thinking, reasoning, and insight" (p. 1).
Smith (1975) states, "Comprehension means relating new experiences to
the already known . . . Comprehension means making sense" (p. 10).

There is much controversy as to the nature of reading comprehension.
Some writers support the theory in which comprehension is a total of many

222 THE LEARNING DISABLED ADOLESCENT

subskills; others support a more general theory that one factor accounts for all of comprehension.

In this book, reading comprehension is defined as a thinking process that includes deriving meaning from symbols, interpreting the meaning of the symbols, and applying this meaning to previous ideas and experiences. In essence, the thinking process is the major factor that accounts for what people do when they comprehend. According to Raths, Wasserman, Jonas, and Rothstein (1967), "The process is the experience (plus the effort) that a student goes through as he learns" (p. 247).*

READING COMPREHENSION AND LEVELS OF COGNITION

To begin to understand this definition of reading comprehension, it is necessary to realize the relationship between reading comprehension skills and cognitive levels of learning. Each level of cognition requires a specific series of reading/thinking skills. The following defines the reading/thinking skills at each level of cognition.

Knowledge Level of Cognition

This level organizes unorganized information that is explicitly stated by the author. Comprehension skills needed for this level are:

- selecting, listing, and recalling details
- recognizing, labeling, and recalling sequence; comparing and contrasting; and cause and effect relationships
- identifying and recalling main ideas
- identifying and recalling character traits
- grouping events, people, or objects into categories
- paraphrasing details from the reading selection into the reader's own words
- summarizing by using direct or paraphrased statements from the reading material

Comprehension Level of Cognition

At this level, interpretation of data is processed through inductive reasoning, that is forming generalizations or conclusions from implicitly stated information in the reading material.

---

*S. Wasserman, S. Jonas, A. Rothstein with permission from Charles E. Merrill Publishing Co., © 1967.

The additional skills needed to comprehend at this level are:

- inferring supporting details
- inferring sequence, comparison-contrast, and cause and effect relationships
- inferring the main idea
- inferring character traits
- translating figurative language to literal meaning

Application, Analysis, Synthesis, and Evaluation Levels of Cognition

At these levels, conclusions and decisions are arrived at through deductive reasoning, that is forming conclusions and making decisions by comparing ideas presented in the reading selection with internal information provided from the reader's prior experiences, knowledge, and values. The additional skills needed at this level to comprehend are:

- distinguishing facts from fiction
- distinguishing relevant from irrelevant information
- predicting outcomes
- explaining or supporting the outcomes
- verifying the outcomes
- analyzing and evaluating character traits
- solving problems in new situations when no directions or methods have been specified
- producing a new principle not evident before

Although the skills within each level of cognition are not necessarily hierarchical in nature, the levels of cognition are. Knowledge is at the lowest level of learning, and evaluation is at the highest level of learning. Consequently, the demands on thinking skills increase as the levels of cognition increase in rank.

A task that requires the identification of the main idea at the knowledge level is much different than the same task at the comprehension level. At the knowledge level, the task requires that the reader identify and recall the stated main idea; the reader repeats the author's message. However, at the comprehension level, the task requires the reader to identify the main idea that is suggested but not plainly expressed. The reader must form conclusions from what the author has implied and must translate the author's message. Identifying the main idea at the comprehension level is a more complex and difficult task to perform for it increases the demands of the thinking process and requires interpreting as well as retaining and retrieving information. It is critical that teachers realize the relationship between reading skills and the levels of cognition in order to understand the significance of the reasoning process in reading comprehension.

Understanding the requirements of each level of cognition and the series of skills within each of the levels of comprehension improves instruction. The teacher becomes more aware of the demands of the curriculum and what these demands require of the students. Therefore, more accurate instructional objectives can be planned.

Levels of Reading Comprehension

Further clarification of the definition of reading comprehension requires that the complex nature of this topic be simplified. Several writers have delineated levels of comprehension that have begun to give more meaning to the thought process in reading comprehension. In 1960, Gray described the reading comprehension process as:

- reading the lines
- reading between the lines
- reading beyond the lines (p. 17)

Herber (1978) on the other hand, defines reading comprehension as a three-level process:

> *Literal Level*—First the reader examines the words of the author and determines what is being said, what information is being presented. The reader is required to recognize, identify, and recall facts and details at this level.
>
> *Interpretive Level*—Next the reader looks for relationships among statements within the material. From these intrinsic relationships, the reader derives various meanings. The reader distinguishes, extends, translates, and generalizes from the passage and from past experiences.
>
> *Applied Level*—At this level the reader takes the product of the literal—what the author has said—and the interpretive—what the author meant by what he said—and applies this to previously learned knowledge, thereby expanding the understanding. The reader selects, retrieves, and generalizes this information to create a new rule, principle, or idea. (p. 40. Reprinted with permission.)

Spargo and Harris (1978) further explain Herber's levels of comprehension as:

Level 1: Vocabulary comprehension—what do words and expression mean? This level develops:
1. knowledge of word meaning in a given content field
2. the ability to use word analysis skills and context in understanding words and expressions which are used in precise and specialized ways

Level 2: Literal comprehension—what did the author say? This level requires:
1. the identification and recall of factual detail, knowing what the author said
2. the need for the reader to organize the details in some structural form and store the concepts for later recall

Level 3: Interpretive comprehension—what did the author mean? This level requires the reader to:
1. translate significant relationships among details
2. generalize these relationships and interpret their significance

Level 4: Applied comprehension—how can this information be used? This level requires the reader to:
1. extend reasoning abilities beyond the reading
2. develop extrinsic concepts. These are new ideas which extend beyond those identified in the reading selection.
3. deal with meaning stimulated by the passage but extending out from it, applying expressive or creative understanding (p. 7. Reprinted with permission.)

THE THOUGHT PROCESS AS THE MAJOR FACTOR IN READING COMPREHENSION

This final clarification of the definition of reading comprehension presents an understanding of how the levels of cognition affect the thought process at each level of comprehension.

Thought Process at the Literal Level

Thinking is to form or have an idea or image in the mind. At the literal level the student deals only with information that is explicitly stated by the author. Thinking occurs at this level in that a student must identify or recall essential characteristics of an event, concept, or idea. This describes the lowest level of learning, the knowledge level.

At this level, a student is required to assimilate, absorb, and regurgitate information that has been explicitly stated. The reader is required to keep in mind, recollect, or locate details in the reading whether it be the stated main idea; the order or sequence of events or incidents; likenesses and differences between events and ideas; or the causes and effects or reasons for events and incidents.

At the literal level of reading, a reader receives the author's expressed meaning. The reader reads on the line and deals with information that is explicitly stated. At this level, the reader, very much like a lawyer, must obtain the information and locate and acquire the facts that relate to who, what, where, when, why, and how.

Thought Process at the Interpretive Level

At the interpretive level of reading comprehension, the reader must "read between the lines." It is at this cognitive level of learning, the comprehension level, that a student is required to generalize information and to perceive relationships between different concepts. Thinking at this level means to "think through," to ponder or sort relevant from irrelevant information; to distinguish essential from nonessential information; and to develop concepts or conclusions that must be supported by information in the reading material. The reader is required to generalize, translate, and interpret the relationship of past learning and ideas to the present information to form new concepts. These new concepts must be defended through information gained in the reading material. The reader may be required at this level to provide the main idea or produce relationships of details to support this main idea when it is not provided by the author. The reader may have to compare stated likenesses with differences not stated in the reading material but drawn from past learning. The reader may have to provide causes for incidents and events from past experiences when only results are stated.

Thinking Through Evidence

At the interpretive level, the reader adds meaning to the author's message or content by reading between the lines. The reader becomes the judge, one who examines and interprets evidence to determine what is relevant to the case. In order to achieve this, the reader must "think through" or ponder and defend impartial decisions for declaring what is admissible as evidence. The judge must distinguish, translate, interpret, and defend what he or she considers to be admissible evidence.

Thought Process at the Applied Level

At the applied level of reading comprehension, the reader reads "beyond the lines." At this level, the reader must be able to relate the reading information to past experiences and then produce or create a new rule or principle. The term "thinking up" implies thinking up new ideas, thinking up new concepts, and generating and creating new generalizations. The highest levels of cognition—analysis, synthesis, and evaluation—occur at the applied level of learning. At this level, the reader is required to break down, combine, and change information to reconstruct and support the generated new rules or principles. The new conclusions, rules, principles, and value judgments must be based on clearly defined criteria. These criteria are developed from concepts in the reading material as well as past learning. These new rules and principles must be supported by logical evidence. A principle is a primary truth or rule from which other principles are derived. It can be an adopted rule or method for application.

"Thinking Up" Verdicts

At the applied level, the reader reads beyond the lines. The reader becomes the jury. The reader inquires into the written message and extends this message by seeking a balance between his or her own values and the presented evidence. The reader must "think up" the verdict based on presented evidence. The reader must break down, combine, and reconstruct the evidence to support the final verdict. The reader ponders and evaluates the "smoking gun" evidence and circumstantial evidence to render a just verdict.

Gagné (1970) refers to combining information and concepts to develop broader ideas and generalizations as a "chaining" process. Herber (1978) makes the analogy with the chaining process in this way:

> Details (literal level) are chained together to form concepts (interpretive level), which are chained together to form principles (applied level). (p. 47. Reprinted with permission.)

In summary, absorbing details (thinking) is linked together with developing concepts (thinking through) which are connected together to form principles (thinking up).

Table 7-1 provides an overview of the thought processes used in reading comprehension. It outlines the definition, major cognitive processes, and task requirements for the literal, interpretive, and applied levels of reading comprehension.

Table 7-1 Theoretical Model of the Thought Process in Reading Comprehension

	Thinking	Thinking Through	Thinking Up
Levels of Reading Comprehension	Literal Level	Interpretive Level	Applied Level
Definition of Levels of Comprehension	reading the line	reading between the lines	reading beyond the lines
Levels of Cognition	knowledge	comprehension	application analysis synthesis evaluation
Major Task Requirements	locate and recall details explicitly stated	translate, interpret and defend	breaking down, combining, and changing information to construct and support new rules or principles

QUESTIONING AND REASONING

The trademark of teaching is asking questions. According to Cunningham (1971), questioning in teaching is most commonly used to:

- initiate instruction
- create learning situations
- evaluate learning
- manage behavior
- give directions
- manage classroom activities (p. 83. Reprinted with permission.)

Unfortunately, the least common use of questioning in the classroom is to stimulate reasoning. All too often questions are limited to usage as an instructional tool facilitating recall of information rather than generating effective student thinking.

To enhance the thought process through effective efficient questioning, questions should be devised to generate thinking at each level of reading comprehension and stated so that student responses are appropriate and meaningful. Cunningham (1971) recommends that efficient questions should be devised to provide thinking at each level of cognition and should include:

Table 7-2 Examples of Efficient and Inefficient Questions

Question	Inefficient	Efficient
Yes and no questions	Did Molly like living in the new town?	How does Molly's life in the new town compare to her life in her home town?
Indefinite questions	What about Molly's education?	How did Molly's education differ from Mr. Whitesides' education?
Ambiguous questions	What happened to Molly when she came to the new town?	How did fear hurt Molly when she first came to the new town?
Double questions	Who was Molly's father and what did he do to her?	How did Molly's father interfere with her life in the new town?

- clarity of purpose, stated with a sensible word order
- provision for reflective and critical thinking relating meaningfully to the experience of the students being questioned; familiar terms and examples make this possible.
- quality, suitable guidelines for students to form meaningful responses (p. 85. Reprinted with permission.)

Efficient questions are stated with clarity of purpose; provide suitable guidelines for students to form meaningful responses; call for analysis and evaluation; and lead students in the direction of problem solving. Inefficient questions require short, factual answers and guessing because they lack adequate criteria for students to form meaningful responses; fail to communicate the intent of the question; and do not require explanations of relationships or concepts, therefore deterring higher level thinking skills.

Table 7-2 provides examples of efficient and inefficient questions based upon John Steinbeck's (1946) short story "Molly Morgan." The efficient questions are examples of questions used in a senior modified short story course to generate a class discussion regarding Molly's consequences of self-delusion.

EXAMPLES OF EFFICIENT QUESTIONS AT EACH LEVEL OF READING COMPREHENSION

Literal Level

Questions asked at this level of comprehension should pertain only to information that is explicitly stated in the reading selection. Questioning at this level is used to identify, group, and recall information and is considered the first step in developing concepts.

The following are literal level questions based on information that was clearly stated in this reading. How many questions can you answer without looking back?

- List the five characteristics of an efficient question?
- Name four question faults.
- What is the trademark of teaching?
- What is the least common use for questioning in the classroom?

Interpretive Level

At this level of comprehension, questions are designed to increase the thinking process by requiring the reader to interpret, infer, and imply meaning from what has been stated. Questions at this level deal with information implicitly stated in the reading selection. Students should always be directed to support their answers with information from the reading selection. Support the answers to the following questions by using information found in the reading:

- Why is questioning the trademark of teaching? A statement in the first paragraph will help provide an answer.
- Why should teachers learn to ask questions more efficiently? A statement in the second paragraph will help provide an answer.
- Why are "yes and no" questions inefficient? Statements in the third paragraph can help provide an answer.

Applied Level

Questions at this level are designed to direct the reader to analyze, synthesize, and solve problems in new situations and to produce new principles or conclusions not clearly evident before the reading experience. Information from the reading plus prior knowledge and experiences are used to support the responses. There are no right or wrong answers at this level as long as the reader can apply logical information from the reading and prior knowledge to defend and support the answers.

Answer the following questions to evaluate and defend your thinking on questioning and reasoning.

- Compare efficient and inefficient type questions to decide if you believe questions connote evaluation.

- Write two efficient questions and list the characteristics that qualify each question as efficient.
- Questions are effective instructional vehicles for generating thinking. Describe two other effective instructional vehicles that you believe generate thinking. Support your choices.

Students should also understand how questions relate to specific levels of comprehension so that they can establish and clarify the purpose of their own reading. A strategy to increase reading comprehension for poor or disabled readers is to provide them with an understanding of why they are reading and what problem must be solved in this reading. Is it to obtain information, examine and interpret information, or to support a just verdict?

INCREASING REASONING IN CLASSROOM INSTRUCTION

Thinking and reasoning in reading comprehension is not a new idea. For several years, commercially prepared workbooks, ditto masters, and teacher's "how to" guides have been available to educators. Most poor or disabled readers have worked extensively with these materials, frequently provided by the special teacher (reading or learning disabilities specialists). The same students use the same materials year after year, and still the poor or disabled readers cannot successfully achieve in the content areas. Why?

With the recognized need for increasing thinking skills in the reading curriculum came the onslaught of commercial materials. Although these materials do provide thinking and reasoning activities, they have little relevance to the content being learned. Students learn how to do the activities and often enjoy a particular workbook or activity. However, they do not realize how the activities relate to understanding the content areas.

The major shortcoming with programming of this nature is not the materials but the lack of instructional emphasis on application of skills. Students must learn how to apply the skills from the remedial materials to thinking and reasoning in content area textbooks. What good is a hammer if you cannot pound a nail straight?

A guaranteed resolution to this problem is nonexistent. However, to begin to reduce this problem, classroom instruction must first recognize the reasoning skills mastered and then expand these skills by providing ample opportunities that correlate skills with content. Bruner (1960) states that "The process of reasoning is the same for all persons—it differs only in degree of sophistication not in kind" (p. 14).

Criteria for Developing Thinking Related Instructional Activities

Raths, Wasserman, Jonas, and Rothstein (1967) suggest the following four criteria to assist in developing reasoning and thinking in instruction:

1. Determine a purpose for activities.
   a. The purpose must have an easily translatable activity.
   b. The purpose guides the selection of the activity.
2. Activities must relate to operations of thinking.
   a. The activity must signify a relationship to thinking.
   b. The activity must have intrinsic value.
   c. The activity should lead to other operations of thinking.
   d. The activity should help the student improve abilities to discriminate information; interpret information; and analyze, evaluate and apply information.
   e. The activity should represent a wide sampling or variety of experiences.
3. Activities should relate to students.
   a. The activity should lead the student to insights such as "I never noticed this before."
   b. The activity should increase curiosity on the part of the student.
   c. The activity should be interesting for the student.
   d. The activity should not be repeated so often as to cause student boredom.
   e. The activity should be appropriate for the student who is doing it. It should not be too easy or too difficult.
   f. The activity should lead to sharing on the part of the students.
   g. A student's reaction to activities should be used to suggest future activities.
   h. Students should have the opportunity to raise questions.
4. Activities should be related to curriculum.
   a. The activity should be appropriate for the subject matter under study.
   b. The activity should have a significant relationship to the subject matter under study.
   c. The activity should not be too broad or too difficult to study; if so, break the activity down into several smaller activities.
   d. Thinking activities should be done frequently. (pp. 225–256. Adapted and used with permission.)

IMPLEMENTATION OF THINKING AND REASONING IN THE CONTENT AREAS

Most teachers would agree that developing thinking and reasoning is a major goal in education. However, there is less consensus in how to reach this end for there is no "golden rule" to follow that ensures the attainment of this goal.

Guidelines for Improving Thinking and Reasoning in the Classroom

The following are some guidelines suggested by Schmeck (1981) to implement thinking and reasoning in the content area:

- Avoid dictating "sacred" statements to passive "scribes".
- Place greater emphasis on the meanings of concepts than the symbols used to represent meaning.
- Spend much time on presenting examples of concepts. Have students relate their personal meaningful examples to these concepts.
- Ask compare and contrast questions. Have students supply an idea from their personal experiences to be compared and contrasted with the idea presented in class.
- Encourage students to understand the meaning of concepts by describing and defining these concepts in their own words before they record them in their notes.
- Frequently test and assign homework. Tests are vehicles for shaping learning behavior. Test for comprehension of meaning. Assure students that their personal experiences are important and relevant to the topic at hand. Give credit for thoughtful answers. The tests should require that the students give personal examples and relate them to examples given in class. (pp. 225–256. Reprinted with permission.)

Students should learn that there are many alternative ways of expressing a unit of information. Meaning is important and similar meanings can be symbolized in different ways for different people. Only by encouraging students to dredge their memory for related ideas and giving them opportunities to restate these ideas can students become more thoughtful learners.

APPLICATION OF READING/THINKING SKILLS IN SPECIFIC CONTENT AREAS

Content area reading presents numerous problems for the poor or disabled reader. Some problems are created by the technical vocabulary unique to the language of the subject as well as by the extensive amount of abstract concepts. In addition, new facts and concepts are presented faster with fewer repetitions, and as a result, the more facts presented to the reader, the greater the demands on retention. Needless to say, as poor or disabled readers advance through the grades it becomes increasingly more difficult to be a disabled reader and achieve high honors.

An awareness of the major thinking/reasoning skills required in each area of study is essential to understanding the learning problems of the poor or disabled reader at the secondary level. Although there is similarity in most of the skills required in the content area, each area dictates which reading skills are paramount to learning in that subject. Therefore, it cannot be assumed that the poor or disabled reader can apply learned skills to all subjects. Once a skill is mastered, the student must be provided with various experiences in transferring the skill to each content area. For example, a student required to translate implied relationships of abstract ideas in social studies is not performing the same task as the student who is required to translate formulas into significant relationships in math. Both tasks require interpretation but with a separate set of vocabulary and a different set of concept rules. Although the poor or disabled readers may have mastered general reading/thinking skills, content area teachers must share in the responsibility for teaching the reading skills required by the subject.

Reading and Thinking Skills in Specific Content Areas

Social Studies

To highlight the major reading skills needed in understanding written information in social studies, a student must:

- learn a new technical vocabulary
- locate facts
- translate abstract ideas into meaningful concepts
- organize material, identify, distinguish, and translate relationships and interrelationships of the ideas
- recognize, interpret, and distinguish concepts of time, space, and chronological order

Mathematics

Very specialized reading takes place in mathematics. Mathematical reading material is concise, abstract, and presents complex relationships. Mathematical materials have more ideas per line and per page than other subject matter; one concept is built on another. A student can gain meaning from this material only if the previous concepts are fully understood. Mathematics texts have more technical vocabulary than most other texts. For the student to understand mathematical texts, they must:

- translate numerical symbols into verbal symbols
- translate formulas into significant relationships
- read very slowly

Science

Science textbooks introduce technical vocabulary that requires the student to understand the meaning of these words in context. The student may be familiar with these words but may not recognize the meaning that relates the word to science facts. Science texts place a high demand on the student to sequence events and to develop an orderly approach to classifying, categorizing, and memorizing.

Science textbooks require the student to:

- locate the stated problem
- list the facts that relate to this problem
- analyze these facts
- predict outcomes from these facts
- verify the outcomes with the facts distinguished and analyzed

ORGANIZATIONAL PATTERNS

The fact that subject texts conform to different paragraph patterns means that poor or disabled readers must be aware of the types used in order to learn more successfully. Teachers should instruct from the text by using the pattern types as teaching tools. Emphasizing organizational patterns in instruction increases poor or disabled readers' understanding of the structure of the text. They can better understand the component parts and the organization of the concepts presented.

An important skill in reading comprehension is recognizing the language of the author. Most paragraphs in factual writing conform to some organizational pattern. These patterns reveal how a writer groups ideas and the relationship of these ideas to one another. Organizational patterns are the internal cues that assist the reader in understanding the unique language of the author.

When an author has an idea to express in paragraph form, details are stated that will describe or support the idea and are arranged so the reader will clearly understand the message. Recognizing the pattern of the paragraph or the relationship of the main idea to the supporting details, aids the reader in accurately translating the message. The pattern itself is an essential part of the message.

Understanding the Main Idea

Recognizing the importance of the main idea in a paragraph is essential to understanding organizational patterns in expository writing. A paragraph is a group of sentences that fit together to support an idea. The sentences in a paragraph fit together in any one of or in any combination of several patterns. Paragraphs fit together because one sentence conveys a main idea that the other sentences clarify, validate, or support with facts and details. A paragraph without a main idea is like a hammer without a handle; it has no meaning or purpose. The main idea may be implied or explicitly stated and is the most important idea in a paragraph for it provides unity of thought.

The Importance of Details

In many reading situations, it is just as important to note and remember significant facts and details as it is to recognize and understand the main idea of a paragraph. Details have many functions:

- Details furnish a reader with concrete information to clarify a complex concept.
- Details furnish a reader with evidence to translate and support conclusions and judgments.
- Details become a tool to relate newly learned concepts to concepts in other content areas.

Paragraphs fit together because each of the sentences (facts and details) tell something about a single subject (main idea) in a particular pattern. Facts and details that support the main idea may be organized in several patterns such as order of importance, time order, spatial development, cause/effect, comparison/contrast, and a simple listing order. The organizational patterns most commonly found in secondary content texts are simple listing, sequencing events, cause/effect, and comparison/contrast.

Signal Words

Signal words are connective words that are essential to understanding the relationship between facts and details and the main idea. An awareness of signal words is essential to reading comprehension since these words signal the reader as to the relationship between ideas. In addition, the greater the amount of signal words in content reading material, the greater the difficulty students may have in understanding it.

In a comparative study done by Rodgers (1974) to determine the connective load (signal words) of textbooks in the content areas, it was reported that every text examined used signal words frequently and expected the reader to be alert to them. Rodgers concluded that social science texts were less burdened with signal words than textbooks in physical sciences. However, it must be taken into account that textbooks for physics, chemistry and biology have more printed pages.

The signal words most frequently used in content area texts found in Rodgers' study are shown in Table 7-3.

ORGANIZATIONAL PATTERNS IN CONTENT AREA TEXTS

Organizational patterns may be viewed as advanced organizers in reading. Advanced organizers provide the student with an awareness of what is going to be learned and how this learning is related. The predominant organizational patterns in expository writing are listing, sequence, cause and effect, and comparison/contrast.

Listing Pattern

Simple listing of facts and details is the most commonly used paragraph in expository materials and is also the easiest to recognize. There is no special order or relationship to the details; they all support the main idea and are all equally important. However, this pattern can be difficult for poor or disabled readers. The facts and details are presented in an orderly fashion, but the structure and organization of the pattern is not sufficient for this population to retain all the information presented.

In addition, listing information can be associated with a topic or subtopic that relates to a main idea presented in a previous paragraph. This information can be presented over several pages and in several different para-

Table 7-3 Signal Words Common in Textbooks

Geography

Listing	Sequence	Cause/Effect	Comparison/Contrast
also	then	because	but
		thus	however
		therefore	although
		since	while
		if	yet
		so	

History

Listing	Sequence	Cause/Effect	Comparison/Contrast
	then	thus	but
		because	while
		since	although
		therefore	however
		if	yet

Chemistry

Listing	Sequence	Cause/Effect	Comparison/Contrast
also		thus	but
		since	however
		because	although
		therefore	while
		if	yet
		so	

Biology

Listing	Sequence	Cause/Effect	Comparison/Contrast
also	then	however	yet
		thus	while
		since	although
		because	
		therefore	
		so	

Physics

Listing	Sequence	Cause/Effect	Comparison/Contrast
also	then	because	but
		therefore	however
		since	although
		thus	while
		so that	on the other hand
		consequently	in other words
		if	
		so	

Source: Reprinted with permission of Denis Rodgers and the International Reading Association.

Table 7-4 Words Used in Listing Patterns

several	kind(s)	way(s)	one	number words: one, two,
many	type(s)	varieties	another	three
series	style(s)	in addition	still another	types
few	couple	some	an example	third kind

graphs. An understanding of how bits and pieces of information relate cannot be gained until the reader groups the information with the appropriate topic or subtopic. The poor or disabled reader frequently has not developed the skills necessary to provide the internal organization of information needed for this type of reading.

Words and phrases frequently used in this pattern are shown in Table 7-4.

Sequence Pattern

Sequence patterns, also referred to as time order, are used by writers to develop a chronological sequence. Events are usually presented in the same order in which they happen. Newspapers, vocational texts, history books, cookbooks, and ' how to'' books are generally written in some type of chronological or step-by-step order. This pattern is the easiest for most readers to recognize.

However, in science, this pattern is the most difficult for students. Information is explained in a step-by-step process, but students are not in the habit of reading with this degree of precision. The reader must understand each step in its appropriate order, isolate the steps from the nonessential information, and recognize the associations of the steps. If a reader misses one step, the reader will not be able to understand the concept completely since the concept can only be developed through sequentially connected bits of information. Consequently, reading must be slow and cautious.

In social studies, the sequence pattern is not as difficult to deal with as it is in science since, in social studies, this pattern is not used to communicate specific sequences. Instead, it is used to develop time sequences such as movement from one time period to another, as in the movement from the agricultural economy of colonial America to the technological economy of postindustrial America.

Words and phrases frequently used in this pattern are shown in Table 7-5.

Table 7-5 Words Used in Sequence Patterns

first	next	later	in 1943	secondly
second	then	still later	in 1958	thirdly
third	finally	later on	after that	eventually
yesterday	tomorrow	last	to begin	to sum up
today	steps	lastly	procedure	
in conclusion		at last	plans	

Comparison/Contrast Patterns

Comparison/contrast patterns are used when concepts, events, or objects are discussed to explain likenesses (comparison) and differences (contrast) among them. Comparison and contrast are technically two different ways of organizing details. However, most writers consider them both similar in method and often use them in the same paragraph. Comparison is used alone when something difficult to understand must be explained since it allows for greater specificity.

The comparison/contrast pattern is widely used in science and social studies texts. It is an easy pattern to detect because the signal words are generally provided in the introductory sentence at the outset of the pattern. This pattern is widely used in science texts to explain ideas and to clarify an idea already introduced.

Words and phrases frequently used in this pattern are shown in Table 7-6.

Cause and Effect Patterns

Cause and effect patterns are used to present material involving causative relationships, i.e., a paragraph that gives a reason for something. A

Table 7-6 Words Used in Comparison/Contrast Patterns

different	but	compare
different from	on one hand	both
similar	on the other hand	as well as
same	however	not only
alike	contrast	but also
not alike	although	either . . . so
while	than	unless
yet	equally important	on the contrary
in spite of		

Table 7-7 Words Used in Cause and Effect Patterns

why	as a result of	reason	so that
if	the effect of	since	hence
so	on account of	therefore	thus
cause	due to	consequently	
because	outcome	this led to that	

cause is any reason or event that brings about a result. The effect is any outcome traceable to a cause.

The complexity of this pattern makes this paragraph more difficult to recognize. Williston (1974) stated some of these difficulties as:

> More than one cause or one effect can be stated and the two parts may be in opposite ends of the paragraph. The cause may be stated at the beginning of the paragraph and effect at the very end of the paragraph. This structure can also be found in reverse, with the effect stated at the beginning of the paragraph and the result stated at the very end. (p. 18. Reprinted with permission.)

Social studies is a natural subject for the cause and effect pattern. The subject's nature is to discuss events followed by reasons. Cause and effect is the most common pattern in social studies. The reader recognizes the effect and then locates the causes.

Words and phrases used in this pattern are shown in Table 7-7.

Paragraphs have a function; they provide a system for readers to organize information, set a purpose for reading, and foster skills in reading. However, difficulty arises in teaching organizational patterns when the patterns are combined in a paragraph, creating complicated groups of sentences that cannot be easily analyzed. When teaching the poor or disabled reader organizational patterns in reading, it is imperative that this concept be applied only to reading materials that have distinguishable organizational patterns.

INTRODUCING ORGANIZATIONAL PATTERNS

An abstract concept such as organizational patterns is difficult and confusing to the poor or disabled reader. In setting a solid foundation for understanding the concept, utilizing oral activities in introducing each pattern is recommended before proceeding to written material. Once the students can apply the pattern to the text, then introduce a new pattern.

The skills in applying each pattern should be mastered before the next pattern is introduced.

Guidelines for Introducing Organizational Patterns

The following seven guidelines explain the order of instruction and suggest simple introductory activities.

1. The teacher should introduce each pattern separately, explain the purpose of the pattern, and list the signal words for the pattern on the board.
2. With the signal words in viewing range of the students, the teacher should describe an event using three to four sentences containing signal words from the organizational pattern being introduced. The students are instructed to identify the signal words used in the teacher's description. Then students are instructed to describe a situation or event using the signal words in the telling. Students should be viewing the particular set of signal words as they speak.
   Some suggested oral topics are:
   a. listing, i.e., a student orally describes the events and activities from yesterday's English class.
   b. sequencing, i.e., students describe what they did from the time they got up until they arrived at school.
   c. cause/effect, i.e., students discuss reasons why they might be late to class and describe what would happen when they finally arrived.
   d. comparison/contrast, i.e., students describe a car before and after a trip to the carwash.
3. The teacher can select passages from a text that demonstrates the pattern being introduced. These selections must clearly demonstrate the specific pattern being introduced.
4. Students underline the signal words in the passages. The teacher should have students read the passages substituting signal words in the passages with other signal words listed on the board.
5. To reinforce this skill, students could survey newspapers and magazine articles and underline the signal words in these articles.
6. The teacher should provide several activities to practice applying the pattern to the textbook before introducing a new pattern.
7. The same procedure should be followed when introducing the next organizational pattern. However, after practice activities with the new pattern, the teacher should provide practice activities using both of the patterns before introducing the third pattern. Teachers should

continue in this manner until all of the organizational patterns are introduced and applied to textbooks with mastery.

ORGANIZATIONAL PATTERNS USED IN TEACHING

Written Communication

Organizational patterns help the reader understand the message of the author as organizational patterns help the writer convey the message to the reader. In many instances, writing is the reverse process of reading. Whenever possible, reading and writing skills should be taught simultaneously to reinforce and expand the application of these skills.

In writing, organizational patterns furnish the poor or disabled reader with the structure to convey a written message. The majority of these students cannot communicate in writing, not only because they are poor spellers, but also because they cannot organize thoughts on paper in an orderly manner. Organizational patterns used in written communication instruction discourage "copying" and encourage creativity. There can be no creativity without structure.

The following activities demonstrate how the relationship of the concept of organizational patterns, main idea, and details can be taught simultaneously in reading and writing. These activities are recommended as reinforcement or practice activities only after the students have been introduced to the concept that a paragraph contains a main idea with supporting details and only after one or more of the organizational patterns have been introduced and mastered. With both activities, a demonstration exercise including group or class participation should precede the requirement for the activity to be completed individually.

Reading Activity

Students use the outline shown in Exhibit 7-1 while a sample paragraph, reproduced on an overhead transparency or on the blackboard, is read by the teacher. This demonstration should be completed with the entire group or class before another paragraph is presented for individual completion.

After the paragraph has been read, the students are instructed to tell in their own words the one idea the paragraph is about. What is the core of the paragraph? Once the students have identified the main idea, they are to write it in their own words in the appropriate place on the outline. The teacher should start with simple paragraphs in which the stated main idea is at the beginning and then proceed using sample paragraphs with the main idea stated in the middle and end of the paragraphs. An implied main

Exhibit 7-1 Reading Outline

Main Idea: _____
_____
_____
Supporting Details: _____
_____
_____
_____
_____
Organizational Pattern: _____
Signal Words: _____
_____

idea should not be introduced until the students have experienced various reading activities at the interpretive level of reading.

Once the main idea has been identified, paraphrased, and rewritten, the teacher should ask the students to identify the details that describe or explain the main idea. Again, the students should write the details in their own words in the appropriate spaces on the outline. Finally, the teacher should ask the students to identify the organizational pattern and list the signal words used in the paragraph. When the students understand the demands of the task, sample paragraphs from the content texts can be used to provide instructional opportunities that emphasize the transfer and application of the skill.

Writing Activity

The teacher should introduce this activity through demonstration and group or class participation. The same outline is used for both the reading and writing activity; however, in the writing activity, the students receive a completed outline with selections made by the teacher. To increase the difficulty of this task and to encourage creativity, the teacher should gradually allow the students to brainstorm and make the selections. First the students select the main idea; then the main idea and details; and finally the main idea, details, organizational patterns, and signal words. The organizational patterns and signal words should be selected by the teacher to ensure practice with needed skills until the students are proficient in writing organized paragraphs.

Exhibit 7-2 Writing a Comparison/Contrast Paragraph

Main Idea:	wearing red clothes

Details: in the winter

in the summer

turtleneck sweaters

gym shorts

Organizational Pattern: comparison/contrast

Signal Words: however, yet, but, on the other hand

1. The students are instructed to orally state a sentence about wearing red clothes. The students determine which are appropriate main idea sentences; these sentences are then listed on the board.
2. The teacher states example sentences demonstrating how the details relate to one or two of the main idea sentences; then the students are asked for further examples.
3. Next the teacher combines the signal words and the details to demonstrate the use of the organizational pattern. Students give further examples.
4. The students are instructed to individually write a paragraph following the outline and using original sentences or any of the main idea sentences listed on the board.
5. Students are instructed to read the paragraphs aloud. Reading their writing aloud can be an extremely uncomfortable and embarrassing experience for most students, let alone for students who lack confidence in most academic endeavors. If a student refuses or acts too embarrassed or nervous, the teacher should ask the student's permission for someone else, preferably the teacher, to read it aloud. The purpose of reading the paragraphs aloud is not to critique or editorialize but to develop an awareness of how one main idea can generate several different ideas and different writing styles that are all equally effective.
6. The students submit the paragraphs to the teacher for proofreading and editing direction. The teacher does not "red mark" the papers but provides positive comments and asks questions to direct self-corrections.
7. Students edit the paragraph directed by the teacher's comments and questions and rewrite the paragraph for final submittal.

The activity in Exhibit 7-2 illustrates total teacher selection and explains the fundamental instructional steps in teaching poor or disabled readers how to write a comparison/contrast paragraph. The integration of reading and writing skills allows for instructional efficiency, creativity, and maximum student growth.

READABILITY FORMULAS

Readability formulas are used to examine and evaluate the level of difficulty of reading materials. Reading formulas are a predictive analysis that determines whether a designated reader can learn from material based on sentence length and vocabulary difficulty but not on conceptual complexity. It is important to recognize that resulting levels from readability formulas are only approximate or estimated. Users should be aware of the formulas and what they determine. Accurate information relies on the validation procedures for each formula, i.e., the Fry formula suggests a level of reading somewhere between the frustration and instructional reading levels.

However, the use of readability formulas to predict reading ease is a commonly recognized practice since most secondary school instructional materials vary widely in readability. As long as secondary school learning success is contingent upon textbooks and independent reading assignments, improving the match between students' reading abilities and the readability of instructional materials is essential.

Three formulas will be described and one readability graph will be presented that are appropriate for the range of reading levels for secondary students.

Dale-Chall Readability Formula

The Dale-Chall readability formula (1948) is one of the oldest and widely used formula that considers both sentence length and presentation of unfamiliar vocabulary. Many experts consider this formula to be the most precise formula available for secondary and adult level material. It uses a word list consisting of 3,000 words and involves highly specified and detailed procedures employing many structural as well as language factors. The extensive list of rules and the Dale-Chall lists of words are now commercially available as are several computer programs available for computing the Dale-Chall formula.

Flesch Reading Ease Formula

The Flesch Reading Ease (RE) formula (1949) has been one of the most frequently used in evaluating materials for adult readers. Basically, it relies upon the number of words, average sentence length, the relative number of words with prefixes, suffixes, inflectual endings, and the number of personal pronouns and nouns, i.e., mother, aunt, people, lady, and baby. This formula does not produce a grade equivalent but computes the comparative ease with which a passage may be read. The formula for determining reading ease is calculated on the:

- number of syllables per 100 words
- average number of words per sentence

- number of personal words per 100 words
- number of personal samples per 100 sentences

A passage is given a grade from 0 through 100 with the lower numbers indicating the more difficult material.

Fry Readability Graph

The first publication of this graph in 1968 made assessment of reading materials easy and available. It can more accurately be described as an aid that provides a highly efficient means of determining readability levels on the secondary level. Like all formulas that use sentence and word length measures as indicators of reading difficulty, the Fry graph tends to underestimate the reading difficulty of those materials that use a large percentage of short sentences and one-syllable words but are filled with unfamiliar technical concepts.

Fry (1977) extended the estimating range of the readability graph from twelfth grade to grade seventeen and expanded the directions by including proper nouns in the word count to increase grade level correlation with other widely used readability formulas. At the same time, Fry explained and clarified the method used to count initials and numbers in the word and syllable count. According to Fry, this extended graph does not out-mode or render the earlier (1968) version inoperative or inaccurate; it is an extension.

The extended graph and expanded directions are presented here because they provide a highly efficient means of determining readability levels for materials on the secondary level. The graph is shown in Figure 7-1.

Expanded Directions for Working the Readability Graph

Directions for using the graph are provided by Fry (1977) as follows:

1. Randomly select three (3) sample passages and count out exactly 100 words each, beginning with the beginning of a sentence. Do count proper nouns, initializations, and numerals.
2. Count the number of sentences in the hundred [100] words, estimating length of the fraction of the last sentence to the nearest one-tenth.
3. Count the total number of syllables in the 100-word passage. If you don't have a hand counter available, an easy way is to simply put a mark above every syllable over one in each word,

Figure 7-1 Graph for Estimating Readability-Extended

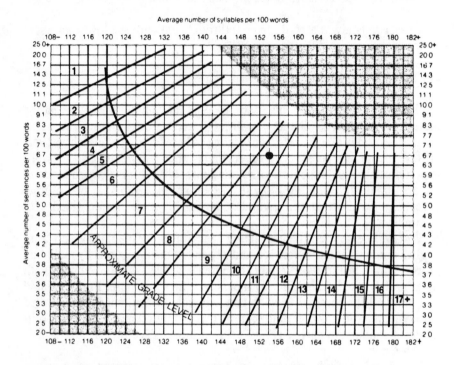

Source: Reprinted from Fry's Readability Graph: Clarifications, Validity and Extension to Level 17. By Edward Fry in *Journal of Reading,* 1977, *21*(3), 242–251.

then when you get to the end of the passage, count the number of marks and add 100. Small calculators can also be used as counters by pushing numeral 1, then push the + sign for each word or syllable when counting.

4. A word is defined as a group of symbols with a space on either side; thus, Joe, IRA, 1945, and & are each one word.

5. A syllable is defined as a phonetic syllable. Generally, there are as many syllables as vowel sounds. For example, *stopped* is one syllable and *wanted* is two syllables. When counting syllables for numerals and initializations, count one syllable for each symbol. For example, *1945* is four syllables, *IRA* is three syllables, and *&* is one syllable.

Example:

	Sentences per 100 words	Syllables per 100 words
100 word sample, p. 7	7.4	148
100 word sample, p. 142	6.3	144
100 word sample, p. 278	6.4	169
	$20.1 \div 3 =$	$461 \div 3 =$
	Average 6.7	Average 154

6. Enter graph with average sentence length and average number of syllables; plot dot where the two lines intersect. [The] area where dot is plotted will give you the approximate grade level. Plotting these averages on the graph, we find that they fall in the sixth grade area, therefore, the book is about sixth grade difficulty level.
7. If a great deal of variability is found in syllable count or sentence count, putting more samples into the average is desirable. (p. 249.)

To expedite the computation involved in this readability formula, an inexpensive scale devised by Fry (1978) is available through Jamestown Publishers. This scale lessens computation time in that after the sentences and syllables in three 100-word passages have been counted and averaged, the average syllable count is aligned on the scale and a grade level is determined. The scale is shown in Figure 7-2.

Readability formulas used alone are not a cure-all for meeting comprehension problems because they frequently yield different results and fail to measure many factors considered important for reading. However, they are useful in giving an estimate of the difficulty of the book and in detecting difficult words in sentences.

READABILITY FORMULAS AND TEXT EVALUATION

Often the primary consideration in the evaluation of a given text is the determination of a reading level. However, the use of a readability formula in evaluating textbooks does not consider other factors that influence readability such as the appeal of the particular writer's style or the reader's interest in a particular subject.

Readability formulas function best when supplemented by the consideration of the author's style. Factors in an author's style that contribute to students' difficulties in understanding reading material include:

Figure 7-2 Fry Readability Scale

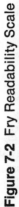

Source: Reprinted from *Fry Readability Scale* by Edward B. Fry with permission from Jamestown Publishers, ©1978.

- Captions under graphs, tables, and diagrams are not clearly written and are not on the same pages as the textual reference.
- Passages are overloaded with technical vocabulary.
- Technical vocabulary is not clearly defined. Clear definitions should be set off by italics; a word or phrase should be inserted in the sentence to define the word; a synonym or pictorial illustration should be provided; or the sentence should be written so there can only be one meaning for the word.
- Long, unfamiliar words are continually used when familiar synonyms would avail.
- Purpose of the writing style may be unclear. Some authors inform, while others persuade.
- Some authors feel that each word is precious, and therefore, concepts and ideas may not be fully explained to the reader. However, when considering the instructional objectives, portions of what the author has included may be irrelevant.
- Syntax should be viewed carefully. The easiest type of sentence to understand is the short declarative sentence such as, "Sammy is going to the movies." Sentences lengthened by additional clauses and phrases can cause confusion and misunderstanding, i.e., "With his pockets full of cash, Sammy the baseball player, who was going to be a politician, went to the museum to see the Picasso exhibit."
- Lack of paragraph design can create difficulty for the reader. When an author intends to discuss an idea or concept, he or she states the idea, explains and describes the idea, and summarizes the idea to offer clarity to the reader. A frequent problem with textbooks is that an idea or notion is mentioned but adequate relationships and summaries are not constructed by the author to provide the reader with sufficient information to gain clear meaning of the concepts presented.
- The amount and variety of signal words must be controlled and used frugally to remain important signals to readers.

Obtaining information through an evaluative survey of the writer's style and combining this information with data from a readability formula produces more conclusive evidence to base decisions for selecting reading material. Combining this information enhances evaluation of material without the necessity for relying on a publisher's analysis.

A Readability Formula with Fewer Than 100 Words

Evaluating the readability levels of teacher-made materials that frequently are composed of passages of less than 100 words by using a

Exhibit 7-3 Selections with Fewer than 100 Words

1. Count the total number of words in the selection and round down to the nearest ten.
2. Count the number of syllables and sentences in the selection.
3. Multiply the total number of sentences and syllables by the number in the conversion graph that corresponds with the number of words in the selection.

Conversion Chart for Fry's Graph for Selections with Fewer than 100 Words

Number of Words in a Selection	Multiply the number of syllables and sentences by
30	3.3
40	2.5
50	2.0
60	1.67
70	1.43
80	1.25
90	1.1

Source: Reprinted from *Teaching Content Area Reading Skills* (2nd ed.) by Harry W. Forgan, & Charles T. Mangrum with permission of Charles E. Merrill Publishing Co., © 1981.

standard readability formula yields inaccurate information since most readability formulas are based on 100-word passages. Consequently, poor or disabled readers fail essay type questions and tests, not because they do not know the information but because they cannot read the questions with understanding. Frequently, teachers assign readings from brief articles that appear to be commensurate with the poor or disabled reader's reading ability; however, they might not be appropriate. Rewriting these articles becomes a futile attempt because there is no recommended means to evaluate the rewritten material if it is less than 100 words.

Forgan and Mangrum (1981) recommend a conversion system using Fry's Graph to determine readability levels for passages with less than 100 words (see Exhibit 7-3). This system is recommended for use when developing teacher-made tests or in modifying materials to a lower readability level for the poor or disabled reader.

Exhibit 7-4 illustrates the use of the conversion chart and Fry's Graph to determine a readability level on a 34-word essay question.

LOWERING THE READABILITY OF READING MATERIALS

When selecting reading materials to supplement the text or for outside reading, the teacher often has problems in trying to locate sufficient material on a particular topic with a lower readability level. Lowering the readability level of reading material may not be as difficult a task as trying

Exhibit 7-4 Example of Determining a Readability Level from a
Selection with Fewer Than 100 Words

Essay Question

Agrèe or disàgrèe with the followìng statemènt:
Undeȑstàndìng the proces̀s of readìng is essèntìal to
undeȑstàndìng how to write, as one is the revèrse proces̀s of
the othèr. Justìfỳ your posìtiòn with specìfic facts.

1. Count the number of words and round this number down to the nearest 10.
   Words in the passage [total] 34, when rounded to the nearest 10
   Total   30
2. Count the number of sentences.
   Total Sentences   2
3. Count the number of syllables.
   Total Syllables   55
4. Locate the number of words from the reading selection on the conversion chart.
   Locate the corresponding number in the right column.   3.3.
5. Multiply the number of syllables (55) in the reading selection by the corresponding
   number of the word count (3.3) to convert them to a scale of 100.
   Total   281
6. Multiply the number of sentences (2) in the reading selection by the corresponding
   number of the word count (3.3) to convert them to a scale of 100.
   Total   6.6
7. Plot the total amount of syllables and total amount of sentences on the Fry Graph
   or the commercial scale to obtain an estimated readability level. Readability level:
   Approximate grade 17+

Source: Reprinted from *Teaching Content Area Reading Skills* (2nd ed.) by Harry W. Forgan, &
Charles T. Mangrum with permission of Charles E. Merrill Publishing Co., © 1981.

---

to locate materials on a specific topic at a lower reading level. Readability
levels can be easily lowered by increasing the sentence count and decreas-
ing the syllable count in a reading selection. The easiest method is to
change the sentence length by increasing the sentence count, and to introduce facts by using many sentences rather than one long complex sentence.
See Appendix A for an example.

Guidelines for Lowering Readability Levels of Reading Materials

The following guidelines adapted from Forgan and Mangrum (1981) are
recommended to lower the readability levels on reading material for the
poor or disabled reader:

1. Carefully scan the selection for difficult or long words, i.e., multi-
   syllabic words and technical vocabulary. However, there are situa-

254   THE LEARNING DISABLED ADOLESCENT

tions when the technical vocabulary cannot be substituted with synonyms such as, phytoplankton or plankton.

2. Substitute as many of the difficult words as possible with easier words by using commonly known synonyms. Use definition clues, familiar expression clues, and comparison and contrast clues to clarify the meaning of words that cannot be substituted with a synonym.

3. Read the selection to determine how the longer, more complex sentences can be divided into shorter sentences. Frequently, a long sentence contains two or more thoughts or concepts. Divide each concept or each thought into a simple sentence.

4. Rewrite the selection utilizing shorter sentences and simpler words. State the main idea at the beginning of the paragraphs and limit the use of signal words. A limited amount of signal words will clarify the relationship of concepts whereas too many signal words confuse the message of the author.

5. Check the readability level of the rewritten selection to determine if the readability level was lowered. (p. 50. Reprinted with permission.)

Whether the word count is the same as the original selection is of no concern. When lowering the readability level of reading materials, the word count can increase or decrease depending upon the change in either or both vocabulary and sentence length. Remember, the goal is to modify reading material so students can read and understand. If the word count increases to 100 or more, use the Fry Readability Graph instead of the Conversion System.

Lowering the readability level of reading material connotes hours of extra work and planning. Modifying reading materials for the poor or disabled readers does take more time than simply assigning readings by directing students to the library. How many poor or disabled readers have ever stood in line waiting to get into a library? A high percentage of these students *will* read when the material is understandable and is provided for them. Lowering readability levels in content reading for the poor or disabled readers is well worth the time and effort spent.

REFERENCES

Bruner, J.S. *The process of education.* Cambridge, Mass.: Harvard University Press, 1960.

Cunningham, R.T. Developing question-asking skills. In Weingard, J.E. (Ed.) *Developing teacher competencies.* Englewood Cliffs, N.J.: Prentice-Hall, Inc., 1971.

Dale, E., & Chall, J.S. A formula for predicting readability. *Educational Research Bulletin.* Ohio State University, 1948.

Dale, E., O'Rourke, J., & Bamman, A. *Techniques of teaching vocabulary.* Palo Alto, Calif.: Field Educational Publications, Inc., 1971.

Durkin, D. What classroom observations reveal about reading comprehension. *Research Quarterly* 1978–79, *14*, 481–533.

Flesch, R. *The art of readable writing.* New York: Harper & Row, 1949.

Forgan, H.W. & Mangrum, C.T. *Teaching content area reading skills,* (2nd Ed.). Columbus, Ohio: Charles E. Merrill Publishing Co., 1981.

Fry, E. A readability formula that saves time. *Journal of Reading,* April 1968, *11*, 513–516.

Fry, E. Fry's readability graph: clarifications, validity, and extension to level 17. *Journal of Reading,* 1977, *21*(3), 242–251.

Fry, E. *Fry readability scale (extended).* Providence, R.I.: Jamestown Publishers, 1978.

Gagné, R.M. *The conditions of learning* (2nd ed.). New York: Holt, Rinehart & Winston, Inc., 1970.

Goodman, K.S. Behind the eye: What happens in reading. In Goodman K.S. & Niles, O.S. (Eds.). *Reading: Process and program.* Champaign, Ill.: National Council of Teachers of English, 1970.

Gray, S. The major aspects of reading. In H. Robinson (Ed.) *Development of Reading Abilities.* (Supplementary Educational Monographs No. 90) Chicago: University of Chicago Press, 1960.

Harris, J. & Sipay, R. *How to increase reading ability.* New York, N.Y.: Longman, Inc., 1980.

Herber, H.L. *Teaching reading in the content areas* (2nd Ed.). Englewood Cliffs, N.J.: Prentice-Hall, Inc., 1978.

McGuire, M.L. & Bumpus, M.J. *Reading comprehension skills—A systems approach.* New London, Conn.: Craft Educational Services, 1971.

Raths, L., Wasserman, S., Jonas, S., & Rothstein, A. *Teaching for thinking theory and application.* Columbus, Ohio: Charles E. Merrill Publishing Co., 1967.

Rodger, S. Which connectives? Signals to enhance comprehension, *Journal of Reading,* 1974, *17*, 462–466.

Schmeck, R.R. Improving learning by improving thinking, *Educational Leadership,* 1981, *38*(5), 384–395.

Smith, F. *Comprehension & learning.* New York: Holt, Rinehart & Winston, Inc., 1975.

Spargo, E. & Harris, R. *Reading in the content fields.* Providence, R.I.: Jamestown Publishers, 1978.

Stein, J., & Urdang, L. (Eds.). *The Random House dictionary of the English language.* New York: Random House, Inc., 1971.

Steinbeck, J. *The portable Steinbeck.* New York: Viking Press, 1946.

Williston, G.R. *Retaining concepts and organizing facts.* Providence, R.I.: Jamestown Publishers, 1974.

SUGGESTED READINGS

Berger, A., & Robinson, H.A. (Eds.). *Secondary school reading.* Urbana, Ill.: National Council of Teachers of English, 1982.

Cebelius, L.S. *Readability: Use, description, discussion.* Unpublished, 1979.

Davis, F.B. Psychometric research on comprehension in reading. *Reading Research Quarterly,* 1972, *7*, 628–678.

Dechant, E.V. & Smith, H.P. *Psychology in teaching reading.* Englewood Cliffs, N.J.: Prentice-Hall, Inc., 1977.

Gallagher, M. & Quandt, I.J. Piaget's theory of cognitive development and reading comprehension: A new look at questioning. *Topics in Learning and Learning Disabilities*, 1981, *(1)*, 21-29.

Joyce, B.R. *Selecting learning experiences.* Washington, D.C.: Association for Supervision and Curriculum Development, 1978.

Klare, G. Assessing readability. *Reading Research Quarterly* 1974, *10*(1), 62-102.

Taylor, O. & Swinney, D. The onset of language. In V. Irwin & M. Marge (Eds.), *Principles of childhood language disabilities.* Englewood Cliffs, N.J.: Prentice-Hall, Inc., 1972.

Weaver, P. & Shonkoff, F. *Research within reach.* Washington, D.C.: Research & Development Interpretation, National Institute of Education, Department of Health, Education, and Welfare, 1978.

Webb, R. Concrete and formal operations in very bright six to eleven-year-olds. *Human Development*, 1974, *17*, 292-300.

Directed Instruction and Study Guides

INTRODUCTION

Chapter 7 explained the major reading ingredients needed for success in teaching the poor or disabled reader in the content area. This chapter describes ways in which the ingredients may be used. Teaching reasoning skills through reading comprehension, teaching reading comprehension through the content area, and developing study guides to teach these skills are not innovative ideas, just as direct teaching is not a unique instructional theory in special education. This chapter attempts to demonstrate how the strengths of special educators, reading educators, and content area teachers can be combined to improve instruction in the content area for the disabled reader.

This chapter is designed to strengthen instructional competencies for content area teachers by expanding and modifying existing instruction and curriculum. Think of the chapter as a specialized cookbook, not the type of cookbook written for the novice cook. It is not for the cook who needs step-by-step guidance on how and what to cook. A novice cook may roast a Cornish game hen with the giblets left in the cavity still wrapped in plastic because there were no directions to tell the cook to remove the giblets, clean the cavity, and fill with bread stuffing before placing in the oven. Or if an experienced cook has eight people coming for dinner, he or she may set the oven at the appropriate temperature but may forget to turn the oven on. This chapter is for the cook who has made all those mistakes and no longer has to stop and think above removing the giblets and turning the oven on at the right time. It's for the teacher who does so many things right but needs to see it in print before a deposit in his or her ego bank can be made. It is for the teacher who is searching for that little extra sprinkle or dash of something to make the adequate lesson more meaningful and more satisfying to the palate. It is for the teacher who is constantly seeking ways in which to provide nutritious instructional diets to enhance academic success.

DIRECTED INSTRUCTION

Directed instruction is a combination approach in which two theories of instruction, the learning theory and the behavioral theory, have been integrated. Major ingredients from each theory have been mixed together and sprinkled with a dash of "what works best for me." It should not be implied that this instruction is a cure-all or that it should be used exclusively with the poor or disabled readers. This plan of instruction works with the poor or disabled reader when used selectively and in a variety of different ways. Although this instructional plan does enhance the poor or disabled reader's academic success in the content areas, it should not be overused or abused. Research indicates (Joyce, 1978) that any one instructional model used daily with no variations leads to unmotivated students and dissatisfied, frustrated teachers. Two aspirin can cure a headache, but three aspirin may cause side effects such as indigestion.

Poor or disabled readers learn more efficiently with structure, consistency, and extensive rehearsal time. Yet these same students need a variety of instruction as well. Variety and structure may superficially appear contradictory. However, content dictates instructional methodology.

Content determines what concepts will be taught. The teacher determines in what order these concepts will be taught and what instructional strategies will be used to ensure that students understand and learn these concepts. There are times when the concepts are such that this instructional model or certain aspects of this model may not be effective in teaching a particular concept. In these instances, the instructional model should be modified or an entirely different model adopted.

Definition of Directed Instruction

The major components emphasized in directed instruction are: (1) teacher directiveness, i.e., the teacher determines the objectives to be learned, monitors student learning, and reinforces activities; (2) program structure, i.e., a well-organized plan of activities to clarify and reinforce new concepts and to relate previous ideas or activities to present learning; and (3) student involvement, i.e., students are encouraged to communicate their thoughts and decisions through problem-solving activities provided by the teacher. This instructional model differs from the model most commonly used on the secondary level in that the textbook is not a substitute for instruction but supplements instruction.

Teacher Directiveness

The instructional model frequently used in the content area focuses on assigned readings in the text followed by teacher-lecture/discussion that clarifies concepts for those students who have read the assignment and provides failure warnings to those students who did not or could not read. After the teacher-lecture/discussions new readings in the text are assigned to introduce new concepts, and the instructional cycle continues.

Directed instruction differs in that the teacher prepares the students for the assigned reading by first previewing the concepts to be learned and emphasizing how these new concepts relate to previous activities and knowledge. Only after the preview has been completed is reading assigned from the text along with teacher-prepared guided activities that correspond to the reading and instructional goals. When the students have completed the reading and guided activities, the concepts and relationships of concepts are clarified and reinforced by group and class discussions. Student responses from the guided activities are the focus of the group and class discussions. New readings are not assigned until all student misconceptions are clarified and concepts relevant to the instructional goals are reinforced through added activities and teacher-guided experiences. Frequently, teacher directiveness consists of explaining, directing, and testing. In the directed instructional model teacher directiveness consists of explaining, directing, probing, testing, listening to responses, and demonstrating new ideas.

Many content area teachers who have attempted to increase teacher directiveness in instruction often resort to the old model in a short period of time. They fear they are pampering their students by providing too much structure and guidance and not providing adequate learning experiences for the students to do their own thinking. The fear that students will not become responsible for their own learning greatly influences the lack of change of instruction on the secondary level. Often this fear is based on personal opinion rather than on personal and professional research.

Carroll (1964) stressed the value of directed instruction as follows:

> We believe that teaching becomes a relatively straightforward and simple operation once an adequate analysis of the behavior to be taught has been made and a program of instruction has been planned which features each separate item to be learned in its

proper order . . . a direct rather than an indirect approach is to be taken. (p. 352. Reprinted with permission.)

PROGRAM STRUCTURE

Research by Ausabel (1960) and Glynn and Divesta (1977) in the area of human learning and memory suggests that people remember and retrieve more efficiently when the organization of information is presented in a structured manner. Students who are told to learn but are not provided with external organization frequently forget what they have learned or do not learn at all.

For students to retain higher order concepts, they must also be provided with systematic reviews spaced at intervals throughout the weeks and months. Spaced repetitions (Gagné, 1974) require that previously learned skills and concepts be retrieved and used thereby becoming a useful tool for problem solving.

External organization in instruction is attained by organizing information in a sequential manner. Sequencing determines an order of instruction that decreases confusion by increasing an optimal order for introducing new information and strategies. The order of presentation of skills and concepts is an essential factor in program structure. Sequencing instruction provides a framework for teachers to more easily monitor student progress and reinforce learning by relating previous ideas and activities to present learning. Sequencing instruction significantly lessens the difficulty poor or disabled readers have in learning and increases students' retention of important information and concepts.

Sequencing Guidelines

The following five guidelines are suggested by Carnine and Silbert (1979) for sequencing instruction in the content areas:

1. Pre-skills of a strategy or relationships of a concept are taught before the strategy itself is presented.
2. High utility skills and concepts are taught before less useful ones.
3. Concepts or skills having similar distinctions should not be introduced at the same time.
4. Easy skills or concepts are taught before more difficult ones.
5. Instances that are consistent with a skill or concept are introduced before the exceptions. (p. 17. Reprinted with permission.)

Preskills of a Strategy

The most critical sequencing rule is teaching components of a strategy or concept before the entire strategy or concept is introduced. For example, in preparing students to understand a chapter or unit in the textbook, a preskill would be to teach the meaning of the technical vocabulary before teaching the concepts. The preskill required in order for students to understand the more complex concepts is the development of an adequate understanding of the technical vocabulary.

High Utility Skills

High utility skills are those skills essential to learning in a specific subject area. In math, simple addition is a high utility skill; a student who has not learned how to compute simple addition problems will find it difficult to compute simple subtraction and multiplication problems. A high utility skill essential in developing vocabulary meaning in the content area is learning how to locate the meaning of words through contextual clues.

Concepts and Skills with Similar Distinctions

The procedure of separating information and strategies likely to be confused can be illustrated by the following example.

In teaching weather, four types of clouds are listed and defined: cumulus, cirrus, stratus, and nimbus. The following day a quiz is given to the class, and a question on the quiz is, "Name the four types of clouds and describe each cloud type." Students may remember the definition but not the names of the clouds, or they may remember the names and definitions but match the names with the wrong definition.

Teaching Simple Skills before More Difficult Ones

The poor or disabled reader can more easily locate organizational patterns of listing, sequencing, comparison/contrast, and cause/effect dealing with explicitly stated information before locating these patterns in implicitly stated information.

Consistent Instances with a Skill or Concept

Introducing examples consistent with a strategy before introducing exceptions increases clarity of presentation and decreases instructional time. The spelling rule, "i before e" should be introduced as a constant, using only words that apply to the rule. Once those words are mastered in spelling then the teacher can introduce the exceptions. For example, when introducing reading/thinking skills at the literal level of comprehension, the student would be asked questions that deal with stated information and not questions that deal with implied information. Questions that require both levels of comprehension should be asked only after the student has mastered answering questions at each level.

Guidelines for Sequencing Instruction

The following three guidelines for sequencing instruction illustrate how the fundamental rules of sequencing are essential in planning directed instruction:

1. The teacher should identify major skills and determine entry level performance. Teacher-made activities and teacher observation are effective instruments to use in gathering this information. Entry level information provides a starting point for instruction; it helps answer the questions: "Where do I start? What do I start with? What should be taught first?"
2. The teacher should modify textbooks. To modify the text, the teacher must first identify the high utility skills the student will need in order to succeed. Often, the poor or disabled reader must be taught more skills than time allows. The teacher should select the skills the student will most frequently be required to use. Content dictates the skills to be taught. However, the teacher must decide what concepts to present and what skills will most help the student understand these concepts.
3. The teacher should order the skills. Content determines the order of skills. The teacher must break complex skills into their component parts and introduce the easy points before the more difficult points.

Guidelines for Providing Directed Instruction

The following guidelines for providing directed instructions are simple to implement if the order of instructions is planned first. Directed instruction without an order of presentation is like doing all of the Christmas shopping on Christmas Eve: buy anything as long as the shopping gets done. Teach anything as long as the teaching gets done.

1. The teacher should use advanced organizers. Advanced organizers provide the framework for illustrating how the major concepts to be studied will interrelate. Advanced organizers are extremely helpful when the students have not had relevant or prior experiences to

relate to the new learning or when students may have the background to understand but do not recognize the relationships. Advanced organizers are a preview of, "what is going to be learned," "why, when, and where it will be learned," and "how it is going to be learned."

2. Students must be active in the instructional learning process. The teacher explains, describes, or shows, and the student responds, does, practices, or makes errors.

3. The teacher should provide feedback. Teacher must provide cues for the student to identify and correct errors.

4. Teachers should provide more practice. However, this practice should not be a repetition of previous practice. Active repetition should be given in many different ways so that the student has many opportunities to arrange this information in a framework that already exists in his or her cognitive structure. Different experiences must be provided to ensure that the student realizes the relationships of the information to his or her own experiences. When this occurs, information becomes relevant and is more efficiently retained and retrieved.

5. The teacher should provide learning experiences in which new information is combined with previously learned skills or concepts. This result can be achieved with very little, if any, teacher assistance. Although it is an essential step for the student to begin to transfer information to other areas, transfer sometimes inhibits learning. This generally occurs when two or more elements of learning are so similar that they not only become associated but they become confused with one another. For example, in using the words *longitude* and *latitude,* most learning disabled students can explain the concept of coordinates but cannot identify which word pertains to length and which word pertains to width.

6. If the student responds positively with the transfer of information, the teacher must make an instructional decision whether to introduce a new skill or concept. Both the student and teacher must be dynamically active in the teacher-learning process. The rate of retrieval depends on the degree of original learning, continual rehearsal, and the availability of cues. Johnson (1979) states, "Teaching . . . becomes the structuring of opportunities for students to gain insight and organize information in ways that rearrange their thought patterns" (p. 165. Reprinted with permission.)

To increase the disabled reader's internal organization of information, the external organization of instruction must also be increased. To accomplish this, commercial material must be modified and complex concepts and skills must be broken into their component parts and ordered in a logical manner. Based on the theory that study guides increase students' thought processes and skill levels, these guides become a natural instructional framework for increasing structure and organization in learning.

DEFINITION AND PURPOSE OF STUDY GUIDES

Brunner and Campbell (1978) state, "A study guide is a teacher-generated paper-and-pencil stimulation that helps students become active and purposeful readers by focusing their attention on the reading/thinking skills being employed and on the content concepts being presented" (p. 154. Reprinted with permission.)

Study guides integrate skill and concept development; promote learning as an active, dynamic process; cultivate reasoning skills; and increase independence in learning. However, they are not the magic cure for all the ills of secondary education. Study guides are practical, relevant aids to assist in meeting the educational needs of students.

Study guides are a major instructional tool in teaching the poor or disabled reader in the content areas. This principle is based on the theory that information is not stored randomly but is routed into memory in an organized way. When new material is organized and grouped with prior information already existing in memory, the new material becomes relevant and instruction becomes more successful. Study guides are the external organization that plan the route for internal organization in learning.

The poor or disabled reader who lacks the motivation, skills, and stamina to complete reading assignments can benefit greatly from study guides that:

- create a purpose for reading
- emphasize the essential information to be learned
- offer the learning of new concepts without extensive reading
- foster motivation in learning
- increase relevancy in learning
- focus on the student's strengths instead of the weaknesses

The poor or disabled reader very often shuns reading because of a fear produced by years of school failure. These students view textbooks in the same manner as many people view a visit to the dentist, i.e., "I'll do it only when I have to," or "I'll do it when I want to." These students assume a defeatist attitude, i.e., "Why read when it doesn't help," or "I spend time studying but I still flunk; there's too much to learn." It is frightening to open a book and see hundreds of words and think that at the end of an hour the words will still be meaningless.

Study guides provide a measure of relief to these readers in that the guides are not overwhelming in size and they include the familiar language of the teacher, not the unfamiliar words of the author. Consequently, the student begins to recognize that learning is not as overwhelming as originally perceived.

The study guide is a special planned travel guide to thinking and learning. It helps students see where they are going, how they are going, and what they need to do to get there. In addition, study guides emphasize the student's strength, the ability to think, and deemphasize the student's weaknesses, recall of bits and pieces of information. What was once trivia to these students becomes important knowledge. Study guides are a vehicle for content teachers and special educators to more effectively correlate the demands of the secondary curriculum with the academic needs of the students.

DEVELOPING STUDY GUIDES FOR THE POOR OR DISABLED READER

Three major steps must be taken to develop study guides for the poor or disabled readers. The first step is to determine the readability level of the section of the text that corresponds with the study guide. The second step is to analyze the content of the unit or chapter, and the third step is to plan and prepare the study guide.

Determining the Readability Level

Developing a study guide for poor or disabled readers without determining the reading level of the text defeats the purpose of the study guide. The readability level assists in determining the extent to which the text can be used to supplement, reinforce, and expand the instructional objectives. The author's style of writing, technical vocabulary, clarity of writing, syntax, organization of information, maps, charts, graphs, illustrations, and captions should also be reviewed when determining a reading level. Often it is these factors that are not measured in a readability formula that dictate the type and amount of activities in the study guide essential to learning the concepts presented.

The next two steps, content analysis and planning and preparing, can be most efficiently accomplished by using the five-point task analysis procedure suggested by Woodward (1981) and adapted as follows. The first three points, reviewing the content, surveying the material and identifying skills, are essential to content analysis. The last two points, planning and preparing, make up the final step in developing a study guide.

Content Analysis

The purpose of content analysis is not to determine what concepts should be taught. Teachers are the experts. They already know what concepts to teach, and they know their students. They have already identified the students' interests, attitudes, study skills, and abilities. A content analysis should not be executed to determine the objectives to be taught. It should be used to determine how the text can best reinforce, expand, and supplement the objectives already selected by the teacher.

The initial step a teacher must take in analyzing the content is to review the unit or chapter so that major concepts and skills can be identified and arranged in an order appropriate to the instructional objectives and teacher presentation. In reviewing the content, the teaching materials available, the specific skills of the students, and the objectives of the lessons must be considered in order to select the appropriate concepts and skills to be emphasized in the study guide.

Next, the teacher must survey the material for words and phrases the students may find difficult to recognize or understand. The teacher must decide which words will be pretaught, which ones will be simply pointed out and pronounced, and which ones are unimportant enough to be ignored.

Due to time constraints, it is recommended that the selection of words be small to facilitate deeper meaning of each word taught. Preferably, not more than 12 words should be included per unit. A large selection of words will consume most of the instructional time and hinder the learning of the total content unit. On the other hand, a large selection of words with insufficient instructional time allotted will result in superficial learning.

Finally, the teacher must identify the skills and processes the students need to complete the learning task successfully.

Planning and Preparing the Lessons and Study Guide

At this point in developing a study guide, lesson goals and objectives should be fully established and should reflect a combination of:

- "teacher's choice" of concepts to be presented
- text presentation including the organization of information and a technical vocabulary
- skill needs of students, both study skills and reasoning skills

The following example demonstrates the planning process for a study guide intended for use in a vocational education class that stresses career preparation. This example illustrates teachers choice of goals, the selection of concepts found in the text that will reinforce these goals, and the specific reading/thinking skills that are essential to understanding the concepts presented.

Example of the Planning Process for a Study Guide Utilizing Reading/Thinking Skills

The teacher's goals in this example are:

- Students will demonstrate increased awareness of themselves and how others perceive them.
- Students will understand that personal qualities have a cause/effect relationship on how they interact with the world, including jobs.

The supporting concepts in the text are:

- People have their own individual needs, preferences, strengths, weaknesses, and abilities.
- Happiness and success are dependent upon an individual's understanding of his or her personal qualities.
- Employers look for people with skills and pleasant personalities.

The reading/thinking skill need of the student is:

- Recognition of a general organization pattern in the text which is causation (if . . . then, what can cause you to succeed or fail).

The next example is another combination of teacher's choice, text offerings, and student skill needs. This example differs in that it emphasizes both study skill development and reading/thinking skills such as inferential comprehension, cause/effect, and comparison skills that will be introduced and practiced.

The planning process was used to develop a study guide for a ninth grade social studies class consisting of 15 poor or disabled readers reading on a fourth or fifth grade level.

Example of the Planning Process for a Study Guide Utilizing Study Skills and Reading/Thinking Skills

The teacher's instructional objectives were that students will be able to:

- name the North Central states and their capitals

- state main rivers, geographical features, and climate
- employ map skills stated above
- describe the pioneer role in settling the frontier
- relate how the Indians were affected by the movement westward
- describe how towns and cities grew into states
- compare past practices in agriculture with present practices
- relate the importance of machinery and transportation both in agriculture and industry
- describe the industries in the North Central states as well as resources
- describe manufacturing and food processing
- relate the effects of the assembly line
- describe the food factories of the Middle West
- make comparisons of today with yesterday

The skills to be developed included:

- the use of maps to locate and label cities, rivers, and lakes
- the use of scales to measure distance
- the use of symbols and colors to obtain specific information
- the use of literal and inferential comprehension through cause/effect, comparison, and listing

The example below is incomplete and cannot be used to develop study guides for the poor or disabled readers. This format only considers information in the text and ignores teacher choice and student skill needs. It would be more appropriate to use this format as a guide for students who have already been taught and have mastered how to learn and read and are now reading to learn.

Example of an Incomplete Format

The purposes of the chapter are:

- to explain how people are able to adapt to, and even prosper in, a harsh environment
- to emphasize that people are often a region's most valuable natural resource
- to explain the relationship between occupations and the environment

PREPARING THE STUDY GUIDE

In preparing a study guide, the types of activities are determined by the goals and objectives of the unit plus the status of the student's reading/

thinking skills. Reading/thinking skills that must be introduced will require more repetitive activities than skills that need to be reviewed. However, reading/thinking skills that need to be expanded will require more diverse activities than review or introductory skills.

A unit study guide should include activities that introduce, review, and expand skills in the development of vocabulary, concepts, organization, and reasoning. Vocabulary exercises provide a strong foundation for developing and expanding concepts. Concept activities organize scattered information into categories for clearer understanding and more efficient retention and retrieval of facts and concepts. Organizational activities provide the reader with patterns to understand the thoughts and logic of the author's message. Comprehension reasoning activities provide the reader with thinking skills that lead the reader to his or her own interpretations.

The following section of this chapter explains and illustrates a variety of recommended activities to use in preparing study guides for poor or disabled readers.

VOCABULARY ACTIVITIES

Vocabulary and concept development is a unitary process in which word meaning is a prerequisite to the reading/thinking process. Vocabulary experiences provide a strong foundation for developing and expanding concepts. The following activities are designed to demonstrate experiences in word meaning that are associated with concept development. These activities are easy to construct, take no more than a half hour to develop, and provide students with meaningful and needed learning experiences.

Activity A

Activity A is an introductory activity that should be used only after the unit or chapter has been previewed with the students. A motivational aspect, the magic square, not only generates interest from the students but acts as a cue for self-correcting. If the numbers do not add up to 15, an error has been made. The student must then "think through" the information. Activity A is shown in Exhibit 8-1.

Activity B

Activity B is an exercise that develops study skills and reasoning skills simultaneously. The student must locate information in the text and then

Exhibit 8-1 Vocabulary Activity A

Directions: Using the vocabulary words below in Column A, match them to their meanings in Column B. Fill in each Magic Square with the number from the matching definition so each column across, down, and diagonally will equal 15.

A.	B.	C.
D.	E.	F.
G.	H.	I.

A. Stamp Act _____
B. Patrick Henry _____
C. Sons of Liberty _____
D. Townshend Acts _____
E. Writs of Assistance _____
F. Boston Massacre _____
G. Samuel Adams _____
H. Boston Tea Party _____
I. boycott _____

1. raid by Sons of Liberty to throw tea into the ocean
2. a law requiring colonists to stamp papers such as wills and deeds
3. fighting in Boston caused by colonists teasing British troops
4. secret group formed to raid Stamp Act collectors' homes and destroy stamps
5. warrants British officials used to search colonists' homes
6. "Father of the American Revolution" who urged people to fight for their rights
7. a law to tax tea, paint, and paper to allow searching of homes
8. the act of refusing to use or buy something
9. a man who did not believe in taxation without representation and urged people not to abide by it

link previous learning with present learning to determine the correct meaning. Activity B is shown in Exhibit 8-2.

Activity C

Activity C, like Activity B, is considered a combination activity. Dictionary skills, recognition of multiple-meanings of words, reasoning skills, and compare and contrast skills are included in this activity. The student must locate the information both in the text and the dictionary. Then, the

Exhibit 8-2 Vocabulary Activity B

Directions: Match these words from the chapter with their meanings. The page and paragraph numbers are provided after each word.

_____ 1. holstein (52,3)   a. to harness a pair of animals
_____ 2. yoke (52,6)   b. a group of animals born at one time
_____ 3. piglet (53,4)   c. large, black and white dairy cattle
_____ 4. mattock (53,4)   d. an adult female pig
_____ 5. brood (54,1)   e. having an ugly or keen nature
_____ 6. sow (54,1)   f. a little pig
_____ 7. stone (55,11)   g. a tool like a pickax but with at least one flat blade, for loosening the soil
_____ 8. ornery (56,9)   h. in England, 14 pounds

student must compare and contrast the two meanings with past learning experiences to be able to select the appropriate synonym. Activity C is shown in Exhibit 8-3.

Activity D

Activity D appears to be a comparatively easy task for students, but it offers much value to the learning process. The purpose of this activity is to understand the meaning of familiar words when used in an unfamiliar manner in the text. It is recommended that students engage in this type of activity before reading the unit or chapter. Activity D is shown in Exhibit 8-4.

PRACTICE AND REVIEW VOCABULARY ACTIVITIES

Practice and review activities are essential to vocabulary development. One experience with a word or set of words will not provide a student

Exhibit 8-3 Vocabulary Activity C

Directions: Find each of your vocabulary words on the page and paragraph listed. Using your dictionary, write the definition that most closely matches the way the word is used in the sentences.

1. capstan (27,4) _____
2. yoke (28,2) noun _____
3. mission (32,4) _____
4. sty (33,8) _____

Exhibit 8-4 Vocabulary Activity D

Directions: Read these sentences from chapter two. Match the underlined word with its synonym below. You may use your dictionary.

_____ 1. "We're beholding to you, Benjamin Tanner," said Papa, "for fetching him home."
_____ 2. "I didn't want to render it up, but they took it."
_____ 3. "When I had took all the sewing to be took, Papa burdened me upstairs to my room."
_____ 4. "I don't cotton to raise a fool."
_____ 5. "Anything'll bite, be it provoked."
     a. agree
     b. grateful
     c. give
     d. angered
     e. carried

---

with sufficient word meaning. However, systematic practice and review provides increased usage of vocabulary and retention of words.

Review Activity A

Review Activity A can serve as a pretest before the introduction of a new unit of study to determine what words and word meanings should be emphasized during the course of study. This activity can also be used as a review exercise toward the end of a unit of study or before a quiz or test. Review Activity A is shown in Exhibit 8-5.

Exhibit 8-5 Review Vocabulary Activity A

Directions: Here are several pairs of words. Based on the experiences you have had with the words related to each pair, place an *S* on the line between them if their meanings are similar. Place a *D* on the line if their meanings are different.

1. navigate	_____ steer	
2. prosperity	_____ poor	
3. garment	_____ minerals	
4. megalopolis	_____ super city	
5. tariff	_____ tax	
6. pollution	_____ cleanliness	
7. corporation	_____ friends	
8. anthracite	_____ coal	
9. bituminous	_____ rocks	
10. communications	_____ T.V., radio, newspapers, magazines	
11. petroleum	_____ oil	

Exhibit 8-6 Vocabulary Review Activity B

Directions: To solve this puzzle, look at the definitions below. Think of a word that fits the definition and has the same number of letters as the number of spaces provided in the lines. The letters in the □ will spell a word going down.

1.   _ □ _ _ _
2.   _ _ _ □ _ _ _ _ _
3.   _ _ □ _ _ _ _ _ _
4.   _ _ _ _ _ _ □ _ _ _
5.   _ □ _ _ _ _ _ _ _
6.   □ _ _ _ _ _ _
7. _ _ _ _ _ _ _ □
8.   □ _ _ _ _ _ _ _ _ _
9.   _ □ _ _ _ _
10.   _ _ □ _ _ _ _ _ _ _ _ _ _ _
11.   _ _ _ _ _ □

The name of our country: □ □ □ □ □ □   □ □ □ □ □ □

Definitions:
a. having a rocky or hilly surface
b. production, distribution, and use of income and wealth
c. a stream feeding into a river or lake
d. the watering of land by artificial means
e. use of machines and modern procedures in industry
f. a dry area with little rainfall and sparse vegetation
g. land formation that rises sharply above the level of the neighboring land areas on at least one side
h. the physical features of an area
i. infertile
j. minerals, soils, water, and other materials occurring in the natural world and used by people
k. rich land that will produce crops

Review Activity B

Review Activity B includes a motivational aspect, the vertical and horizontal puzzle. This puzzle also serves as a self-correcting device. The lines indicating the number of letters in each word serve as a cue for accurate retrieval of information. Review Activity B is shown in Exhibit 8-6.

Exhibit 8-7 Vocabulary Review Activity C

Vocabulary: Follow these directions.

1. Write a three-syllable word that means a person who comes to make his home in a new country.

   I _ / _ _ / _ _ _ _

2. Write a two-syllable word that means a ship that used to be the fastest ship afloat.

   C _ _ _ / _ _ _

3. Write a five-syllable word that means unimportant.

   I _ / _ _ _ / _ _ _ _ / _ / _ _ _ _

4. Write a three-syllable word that means trading or business.

   C _ _ / _ _ _ _ / _ _ _ _

5. Write a three-syllable word that means a person who first settled a region or developed an occupation.

   P _ / _ / _ _ _ _

6. Write a four-syllable word that means delay.

   P _ _ / _ _ _ _ _ / _ _ _ _ / _ _ _

7. Write a two-syllable word that means a pit where stone or slate is obtained.

   Q _ _ _ / _ _

8. Write a two-syllable word that means too much.

   S _ _ / _ _ _ _

9. Write a three-syllable word that means instruments that do fine work.

   P _ _ / _ _ / _ _ _ _

10. Write a two-syllable word that means to increase in size.

    E _ / _ _ _ _

Practice and Review Activity C

Review Activity C is a practice activity that reinforces the meaning of words and integrates a review of structural analysis. The initial consonant and the lines that indicate the amount of letters per word act as a cue or prompt for retrieval of information. Review Activity C is shown in Exhibit 8-7.

CONCEPT ACTIVITIES

Concept guides are information organizers that provide the student with a tool to "chunk" information. "Chunking" can be defined as rearranging information in a more efficient format or order for increased retention. Chunking is what the brain presumably does to store several bits of information so that they can be retrieved. To clarify this concept, say the following numbers, 5298715, several times. If asked two hours from now to recall those numbers, more than likely they would be recalled incorrectly or not at all. However, if the numbers represented a phone number of a friend and were "chunked" in the following manner 529-8715, retrieval would be more efficient.

Concept activities are based on the assumption that learning begins with awareness. Once a student becomes aware of an idea, then this idea must be associated with prior knowledge for retention of information.

Consider the concept guide a mother might develop for a son or daughter going to college for the first time. The point is to prevent clothes from being ruined by colors running or fading in the wash. To accomplish this dirty clothes should be sorted into three piles before going to the laundry as follows:

White Clothes	Medium-Colored Clothes	Dark Clothes
tube socks	plaid shirts	jeans
underwear	pajamas	running shorts
white shirts	T-shirts	dark socks

Quite likely, the student returned with white tube socks.

Concept Activity A

Concept Activity A, as shown in Exhibit 8-8, is an example of an awareness activity to identify proper terms to their specific jobs. The purpose of this activity is to provide the students with an awareness of the relationships of "bits" of information. Note the page and paragraph numbers that are provided to ensure ease in location of information for the poor or disabled reader.

Concept Activity B

Concept Activity B illustrates sorting bits of information into categories or chunks of information to broaden concepts. Familiar items are included to connect the new concepts with prior knowledge to increase the rele-

Exhibit 8-8 Concept Activity A

Directions: Fill in the blanks. Use the page and paragraph number to help you.

1. Name four types of supporting tissue. (page 271, paragraphs 5 and 6; and page 272, par. 1)
   a. _____
   b. _____
   c. _____
   d. _____

2. Muscles are divided into two types. (page 272, par. 3 and 4)
   a. _____
   b. _____

---

vancy of the concepts to the student's life. Concept Activity B is shown in Exhibit 8-9.

Concept Activity C

Concept Activity C, as shown in Exhibit 8-10, is more difficult than Concept Activities A and B since it requires recall of prior knowledge. The strength of this activity is that it requires the student to relate new concepts with prior knowledge to expand the understanding of prior knowledge. Most students understand the meaning of discrimination because they have had emotional experiences pertaining to the word. However, this activity expands the meaning of the word from themselves to the world.

Concept Activity D

Concept Activity D illustrates a graphic structure that serves as a visual framework to assist students in realizing the relationship among words

---

Exhibit 8-9 Concept Activity B

Directions: Matter includes all solids, liquids, and gases. Please categorize this list into the three physical states of matter.

Words:

iron	oxygen	ice	hydrogen
water	chlorine	copper	wine
helium	Cheerios	milkshake	bar of soap

Lists:

solids   *liquids*   *gases*

Exhibit 8-10 Concept Activity C

Women as a Minority Group
Directions: As you know, women are often considered to be members of a minority group. Consider the three areas of discrimination and apply them to women. Using your book and your own knowledge, list specific examples for each area:

Social discrimination: _____

_____

Political discrimination: _____

_____

Economic discrimination: _____

_____

---

and concepts being taught. Such structures also serve as connectors for linking new information with prior knowledge. Graphic structures offer students a visual sense of how the parts fit the whole. The activity illustrates a graphic structure that organizes brainstorming information by using the category words what, where, when, how, and why. Brainstorming is an excellent instructional tool when it is followed up with an activity that structures and organizes the information for efficient retrieval. Concept Activity D is shown in Exhibit 8-11.

ORGANIZATIONAL GUIDES

Organizational guides assist the reader in focusing in on specific points of information by providing a system for readers to group or organize information. The relationships of concepts are emphasized to increase the coherence of the author's message and to facilitate recall. Often the poor or disabled reader has much difficulty with recognizing relationships that are not explicitly stated by the author. A major purpose in using organizational pattern guides is to emphasize these relationships to the reader. The goal is not to have students identify each pattern in each paragraph, but to have students become aware of these patterns and how these patterns can assist them in reading to learn. Organizational guides should be used only for reading material in which a clear pattern exists. The teacher must be sure that the guide reflects as clearly as possible the pattern (relationship) the students are to learn.

Exhibit 8-11 Concept Activity D

Lesson Goal: To relate vocabulary pertaining to consumerism to life situations.				

Steps:
1. Teacher writes the word *consumer* on the board and discusses with the class what the word means. The teacher solicits all the synonyms the class can think of and writes them on the board. Students copy the words into their career notebooks.
2. Next, the teacher lists all the things students can think of that can be purchased. The teacher then asks students to select partners and complete a chart of ten things they could buy. For each item, students must include *what* it is; *where* it could be bought; *when* it could be bought; *how* they could arrange to buy it; and *why* someone would want to buy it.

Sample Chart:

What	Where	When	How	Why
1. house	bank	anytime of year	mortgage— pay monthly	to live in
2. tickets to a movie	theatre	before the show	cash	to be entertained
3. record	dept. store	when they're on sale	cash, check, chg. card	to learn the words to a song

STUDY GUIDE ACTIVITIES FOR ORGANIZATIONAL PATTERNS

Simple Listing Activities

Listed information is seldom complicated to understand but is often the most difficult for the poor or disabled reader to retain and recall. This difficulty occurs because there is no particular order to the information presented, and there is no obvious conceptual association to link with the facts and details. The lack of associative properties of simple listed information combined with the memory problems of the disabled reader results in the necessity for the teacher to provide external organization whenever a task requires retention and recall of listed information.

Listing Activity A

Listing Activity A, shown in Exhibit 8-12, provides practice in familiarizing students with simple facts and at the same time provides a "hook" to grasp understanding by requiring the students to explain in their own

Exhibit 8-12 Listing Activity A

Directions: Pages 102–108 in your text describe and explain the general and enumerated powers of Congress. Read these pages *first,* and then complete the following activities in your study guide. If you cannot remember all of the information, feel free to look back in your book.

Powers of Congress
Part I directions: List the *three* general powers of Congress and *explain in your own words* what each power means.

1. _____

2. _____

3. _____

Part II directions: List six enumerated powers of Congress and *explain in your own words* what each power means.

1. _____

2. _____

3. _____

4. _____

5. _____

6. _____

---

words the meaning of each congressional power. Copying denotes regurgitation, but paraphrasing denotes understanding. Meaningful information is relevant information, and relevancy significantly increases retention and retrieval.

Sequencing Activities

Sequencing activities are recommended when a series of events is not explicitly stated or is stated in a confusing order. An example of a sequencing activity is shown in Exhibit 8-13.

Sequencing Activity B

Sequencing Activity B is recommended when the order of events is not explicitly stated in the text. In Sequencing Activity B, shown in Exhibit 8-14, the years the events occurred were stated but were out of chronological order.

Exhibit 8-13 Sequencing Activity A

Directions: Sequence the order of the digestive system from 1 to 8, with 1 as the first step in digestion and 8 as the last step. Try to do this without the diagram in your book.

Digestive System
_____ food enters stomach
_____ food substances can pass through membranes
_____ food is taken into mouth and broken up
_____ the food goes to the small intestine
_____ liver makes a digestive juice that pours into the small intestine
_____ at the same time saliva is poured onto the food
_____ stomach muscles break food up smaller
_____ food goes down the esophagus

Comparison/Contrast Activities

Writers use the comparison/contrast pattern to clarify an abstract idea or to explain a new idea. For example, a writer could explain downhill skiing by comparing it to skateboarding. This type of writing is generally explicit and is easy to understand. However, when the comparison or contrast is implied, the poor or disabled reader may not understand or recognize that a comparison or contrast has been made. It is especially advantageous to the poor or disabled reader to engage in activities of this nature when the information is implied.

Comparison/Contrast Activity A

This activity is a recommended introductory activity that focuses the reader's attention on the identification of patterns. Activity A is shown in Exhibit 8-15.

Exhibit 8-14 Sequencing Activity B

Directions:
In your text, page 7, paragraph 2, discusses 3 events that led to World War I. List those 3 events in the order they happened:

1. _____

2. _____

3. _____

Exhibit 8-15 Comparison/Contrast Activity A

Directions: On page 76, paragraph 3, is an example of how authors make comparisons. What key words tell you the authors are making comparisons? Clue—one key word is *but*.

Key words:

_____ _____ _____ _____ _____ _____

Comparison/Contrast Activity B

This activity, shown in Table 8-1, is a comparison activity devised to increase the understanding of abstract concepts by comparing these abstract concepts to familiar and concrete information.

Comparison/Contrast Activity C

This activity, shown in Exhibit 8-16, not only encourages students to compare and contrast concepts, but also allows the students to share the "thinking through" process. Whenever group discussions are part of an activity, there is always an increase in reasoning. Group discussions show how the same conclusion can be reached by as many different routes as there are members in the group. Conversely, as many different conclusions as there are members in the group may be reached even though each member travels the same route.

Cause/Effect Activities

Cause and effect patterns in reading materials can be complicated for the poor or disabled reader when:

Table 8-1 Comparison/Contrast Activity B

Directions: The book calls elements the alphabet of matter. You can better understand chemical elements by comparing them to the alphabet. Complete this chart that compares the two.

Alphabet	Chemical Elements
26 letters in the alphabet	
26 letters make up all the words	
x, q, z are not frequently used	
letters composed of shapes	
can reduce words to letters	

Exhibit 8-16 Comparison/Contrast Activity C

Lesson Goal: To encourage students to compare and contrast ideas related to consumerism.

Grouping: The class is arranged in groups of 3, and each student has a copy of the activity sheet.

Directions: On the line in front of each pair of words, write either *alike* or *different*, depending on what your group decides fits the pair. Each person in your group must agree with the answer before it is written on the activity sheet. If there is no total agreement within your group, refer back to your book for help in reaching a group decision.

_____ 1. staying within your budget/competing with your neighbors

_____ 2. Monopoly (game)/monopoly (real life)

_____ 3. content labeling on a package/horsemeat and ground beef sold as hamburger

_____ 4. peer pressure/supply and demand

_____ 5. mechanic replacing good parts/car manufacturer purposely making defective parts

_____ 6. buying what you need/buying what you want

_____ 7. propaganda/false advertising

_____ 8. Federal Trade Commission/Better Business Bureau

- the causes are stated at the beginning of a paragraph and the effects at the end of the paragraph;
- the causes are stated in one paragraph, the effects in another paragraph; or
- the effects are stated before the causes.

In these instances it is recommended to develop cause/effect activities to provide the poor or disabled reader with a clearer understanding of the reading material.

Cause/Effect Activity A

Activity A is an introductory activity that explains the concept of cause and effect in an effective manner. Activity A is shown in Exhibit 8-17.

Cause/Effect Activity B

Activity B demonstrates the overwhelming amount of information that poor or disabled readers are required to recall and understand. This activity assists the disabled reader in recalling and understanding an overwhelming amount of information by emphasizing the cause/effect relationship. The student is further assisted by the page and paragraph numbers listed for easier location of information. Activity B is shown in Exhibit 8-18.

Exhibit 8-17 Cause/Effect Activity A

Directions: Using pages 259–262, fill in the missing causes and effects.

Example: Cause—If I do not complete this worksheet (cause), my grade will go down (effect).

Causes	Effects
1. Before the Industrial Revolution, businesses were small.	They only employed _____ and they knew _____ .
2. After the Industrial Revolution, the owners thought _____	Working conditions for employees became a problem.
3. Many mines and factories weren't safe.	Workers were often _____ _____
4. Workers formed a union, the Knights of Labor.	The work day for adults and children ___ _____
5. Skilled laborers _____ _____	The A.F.L. only _____ _____
6. Businesses were very strong but unions _____ _____	_____ _____

Cause/Effect Activity C

Activity C demonstrates the relationships and interrelationships of cause and effect situations and is shown in Exhibit 8-19.

Cause/Effect Activity D

Activity D is a practice review exercise demonstrating the use of several patterns in one exercise. This activity is recommended for use after the students are well acquainted with and have had much practice with organizational patterns. It is recommended that this activity be used toward the end of a unit as a review lesson before a quiz. Activity D is shown in Exhibit 8-20.

DEVELOPING STUDY GUIDES FOR THE THREE LEVELS OF READING COMPREHENSION

In 1970, Harold Herber introduced the three-level guide to reading comprehension in the content areas. Since then much controversy has

Exhibit 8-18 Cause/Effect Activity B

> **Directions:** Here are sets of words or phrases. Each set shows a separation between words and/or phrases. Each set represents a possible relationship expressed or implied by the author. Place a check on the list before each cause/effect relationship you can support from the text in some way. Be ready to identify your evidence. The numbers in parentheses give you an idea of where to look in the text. The first number is the page number, and the second number is the paragraph number.
>
> _____ 1. humid subtropical/southeastern United States (238,2)
> _____ 2. humid subtropical/summers are hot and the winters mild (238,2)
> _____ 3. humid subtropical/cotton, tobacco, peanuts (238,5)
> _____ 4. humid subtropical/long, cold winters (238,5)
> _____ 5. humid subtropical/little rainfall (238,5)
> _____ 6. humid continental/southwestern United States (239,1)
> _____ 7. humid continental/unpredictable type of climate (239,1)
> _____ 8. humid continental/plenty of rainfall and long growing season (239,1)
> _____ 9. steppe/Great Plains (239,2)
> _____ 10. desert/intermountain region (239,3)
> _____ 11. desert/plenty of rainfall (239,3)
> _____ 12. marine/Pacific Northwest (239,4)
> _____ 13. Mediterranean/Southern Pacific Coast (240,2)
> _____ 14. Mediterranean/warm, dry summers (240,2)
> _____ 15. Mediterranean/moist winters (240,3)

arisen about the instructional methodology for using these guides. Some experts believe all students can deal with the three levels of comprehension that correlate with the levels of cognition. Others believe that students should only deal with the levels of comprehension that are commensurate with their cognitive abilities. Therefore, an above-average student should be required to complete activities at three levels whereas a poor student should only be required to complete activities on the knowledge or literal level of comprehension. These minimal requirements for the poor or dis-

Exhibit 8-19 Cause/Effect Activity C

> **Directions:** Match the cause to the effect by drawing a line from the *Cause* to the *Effect*. Brainteaser!! Pollution and mass production are listed as causes AND as effects. Take your time in thinking through the answers. This is TRICKY!!
>
> | Cause | Effect |
> |---|---|
> | 1. assembly | increased production and cheaper products |
> | 2. many mineral resources in the North Central states | pollution |
> | 3. automobiles | great manufacturing region |
> | 4. pollution | mass production |
> | 5. mass production | some diseases |

Exhibit 8-20 Cause/Effect Activity D

Directions: Listed below are sets of terms. Each set has a special relationship. If it is a simple listing relationship, label the set with an L. If it is a sequence of events, label the set with an S. If it is a comparison/contrast relationship, label the set with C/C, and if it is a cause/effect relationship, label the set C/E. Be prepared to explain your choices, and *remember* there are no wrong answers if you can support your conclusion with facts.

Page 11   Ferdinand Magellan/Spain .... _____

Pages 11–12 Cortez/Ponce de Leon/Columbus .... _____

Pages 11–12 Spanish/Indians/slavery .... _____

Pages 11–12 gold/silver/Spanish .... _____

Pages 12–13 cities of gold/Extevancio .... _____

Pages 12–13 horses/cattle/sheep .... _____

Pages 12–13 disease/escape/Africans .... _____

Page 15   kings/Divine Right/God .... _____

Page 19   representative Government/Divine Right .... _____

Page 19   Magna Carta/Divine Right .... _____

Page 24   Roman Catholic/Protestant Revolution .... _____

---

abled reader are based on the assumption that these students cannot reason beyond the knowledge level of cognition (literal level of comprehension) due to lack of intelligence.

Poor or disabled readers can, in most instances, reason at all levels of cognition, and their cognitive abilities often surpass their reading skills. This assumption is based on years of experience that shows that most poor or disabled readers have difficulty in word recognition and therefore in understanding the printed word. For the secondary disabled reader, this difficulty increases and reasoning abilities appear to decrease due to inadequate and insufficient instruction. Restricting the disabled reader to the literal level of comprehension is like watering household plants once a month and expecting them to grow.

The three-level reading comprehension study guides are significantly effective instructional instruments with disabled readers when each level is introduced separately and mastered before the next level is introduced. A major goal in using three-level comprehension activities in a study guide is to incorporate study skills with reasoning skills. To achieve this goal with poor and disabled readers, it is essential to provide students with prerequisite skills before the strategy itself is presented. Many learning disabled students have had several years of remedial instruction in the mastery of study skills and reading comprehension skills in which the bulk of practice was accomplished through the use of exercise worksheets and workbooks. This type of instruction tends to isolate skills and does not offer the poor or disabled student the needed experiences in how to implement and apply these skills to learning in the content areas.

Even though these students may have some skills in locating and selecting information from reading materials, there is no guarantee that these students can consistently apply these skills to content area texts. Therefore, when introducing the three-level study guide to the learning disabled population, it is recommended to begin activities at the literal level to ensure that the students understand the transfer and application of skills to the textbook.

USE OF QUESTIONS IN THE THREE-LEVEL COMPREHENSION GUIDE

Although there is agreement among the reading experts that the use of statements in the three-level guide generates more thinking and reasoning, when introducing each reading level to the poor or disabled reader, it is preferable to use questions first and then statements. The rationale for this approach is based on the theory that new concepts are more effectively learned if they are linked with prior experiences. The new concepts are the varied significant uses of the comprehension guides, and the prior experiences are years of instruction through questioning. Questioning is the trademark of teaching. For students, questioning is the most familiar instructional instrument in learning. Consequently, introducing each level of comprehension with questions accelerates a clearer understanding of what comprehension guides are all about, how to use them, why they are used, and what will be learned by using them.

Once the understanding of the literal level is grasped and skills in locating and selecting information from a text are mastered, then the teacher can shift to using true/false statements at the literal level to strengthen reasoning skills in reading. The teacher should proceed by introducing each level of comprehension first through questions and then statements until all levels are mastered. Questioning in comprehension guides is only the first step in a long journey.

GUIDELINES TO DEVELOP QUESTIONS FOR COMPREHENSION/THINKING ACTIVITIES

The following three guidelines can be used to develop questions for comprehension activities:

1. The teacher should start with simple questions stated in the language of the author to locate explicitly stated information. These questions

should include page and paragraph numbers to assist students in locating the information with as little frustration as possible.

  a. Questions should be designed so that students can locate the information in an orderly fashion. At this point, the teacher should not have the student skip through the pages to locate the information.

  b. The words, *who, what, where, when, why* and *how* are recommended for use in these question activities.

2. The questions should be designed so that information can be located in one part of a paragraph. The teacher should gradually develop questions that will guide the student in locating information that is found in different parts of the paragraph. Some information may be at the beginning of the paragraph, and some information may be at the end of the paragraph. The teacher should then design questions that require information from more than one paragraph.

3. Questions should be designed to paraphrase the author's language. When the students can locate information from different areas of the paragraph, the teacher should introduce declarative statements instead of questions. Some of these declarative statements should be true, and some should be false. There is a two-fold purpose in using true/false statements. First, the student must decide if each statement reflects "what the author says." This develops accuracy in sorting the information. Second, students develop an ability to distinguish important from nonimportant information provided by the author. (Herber, 1978)

In general, the same guidelines should be followed for developing statements as for developing questions. However, the teacher should start by "lifting" the statements from the text and then rapidly moving to paraphrased statements. Whenever possible, positive statements rather than negative statements should be used.

Questions and Statements for Each Level of Comprehension

The passage from Conlin, Herman, and Martin (1966) demonstrates the development of questions and statements at each level of comprehension. This is a more difficult passage for the poor or disabled reader to understand because there is more information implicitly stated in this passage than explicitly stated and because the passage demonstrates a writer's attempt to persuade the reader rather than to inform. However, these same characteristics are favorable in a reading selection when teaching reading as a thinking process.

This passage was selected by an eighth grade English teacher to develop an awareness of the following concepts:

- Communication exists in several different forms and styles.
- Styles of written communication may be diametrically opposed but equally respected.

The English Language and How It Grew

Conlin et al. (1966) state:

> Where do you think language is really made? Some say it is the classroom. Others say it is in the dictionaries. Well, I say it is made in the buses and on the streets. When the 400,000,000 people who speak English talk, they make the language. Hearing a clever word or phrase, the average person turns around. Then he knows that language is being made. Do grammar books make language? Grammar, in the opinion of the linguists, describes how language works.
>
> Don't make a judgment, however, until you hear me out. Why is newspaper writing so fascinating? Writing is communication, and communication is the translation of experience and observation into words. Since the reporter has a deadline, some interesting and strange forms appear in the daily paper.
>
> The writer who doesn't have time to consider how Shakespeare would have said it must write in contemporary style. Shakespeare, by the way, didn't take time off to check how others would have written something. It must always be remembered, however, that Shakespeare knew how to use language effectively. Good reporters are, in my opinion, equally knowledgeable. (Reprinted with permission.)

Exhibit 8-21 provides a list of questions and corresponding statements. The discussion that follows explains and clarifies the purpose of each question and statement.

AN EXPLANATION AND DESCRIPTION OF QUESTIONS AND STATEMENTS AT EACH LEVEL OF COMPREHENSION

Literal Level

At the literal level, the objective of questioning is to have students locate, recall, paraphrase, or summarize ideas that have been explicitly stated by the author.

Exhibit 8-21 Questions and Statements at the Three Levels of Comprehension

Literal Level	
Questions	**Statements**
1. Who makes language?	1. Language is made by people who speak English.
2. What is writing?	2. Writing is a form of communication.
3. What are the different forms of communication?	3. Talking, writing, and grammar books are forms of communication.
Interpretive Level	
1. Do newspaper reporters and Shakespeare use the same style of writing?	1. Newspaper reporters and Shakespeare use the same style of writing.
2. Do linguists describe how language works?	2. Linguists describe how language works.
3. A better title for this passage might be: a. "Reporters and Shakespeare" b. "Communication Does Not Have to be Eloquent to be Understood" c. "Newspaper Reporters Talk to People"	3. A better title for this passage might be "Newspaper Reporters Talk to People."
Applied Level	
1. Is a picture worth a thousand words?	1. A picture is worth a thousand words.
2. Your English teacher and the author of "The English Language and How It Grew" are having a debate. What are the issues they would dispute, and what issues would they agree upon? Who would you agree with, your English teacher or the author?	2. the great debate: style vs. form.
3. Is it easier to be blind or deaf?	3. The blind and deaf can communicate.

Comprehension/thinking questions and statements should be read by the student before reading the text. The questions and statements create a purpose for reading and provide a preview of the reading content. Reading the questions and statements beforehand provides the student with a structure to sort out relevant from nonrelevant information and gives the student an awareness of the relationship of concepts.

Questions at this level direct the student to explicitly stated information provided by the author to develop the concepts in the instructional goals.

Literal Level Questions

The following are examples of reading comprehension/thinking activities ranging from simple explicit questions to paraphrased questions.

Exhibit 8-22 Declarative Statements at the Literal Level

Directions: Read these statements before you read the passage. Some of the statements are true and some are false. If the statement is true, write the paragraph number where you found the information on the blank in front of the statement. If the statement is false, do not write in the blank.

  __1__   Language is made by people who speak English.
  __2__   Writing is a form of communication.
  _____   Talking, writing, and grammar books are forms of communication.

- Question 1: Who makes language? Student's response: People who speak English.
- Question 2: What is writing? Student's response: Writing is communication. Questions 1 and 2 are examples of direct questions that require the reader to locate or recall information from one or two sentences located in the same section of the paragraph.
- Question 3: What are the different forms of communication? Student's response: The forms are talking and writing. Question 3 requires the reader to locate or recall information from different paragraphs in the passage.
- Question 4: Name two different styles of writing. Student's response: Two styles are the contemporary style and the Shakespearean style. Question 4 requires the reader to paraphrase the response. The author discusses Shakespeare as a writer but does not label his style of writing. Therefore, the reader is forced to use words other than the author's.

Declarative Statements at the Literal Level

An example of declarative statements at the literal level is shown in Exhibit 8-22. The quotation from Conlin et al. (1966) is used as the reference.

Statements one and two simply require the reader to locate information and make a decision based on one fact. The difficulty of the task increases with statement three in that the reader is first required to locate three different pieces of information from three different paragraphs in the reading material. Then, the reader must sort the information into categories of true and false and finally make a decision based on how the information was categorized. Increasing steps in a task of this nature increase the reasoning process but also increase the chance of error if each step is not clearly emphasized with the poor or disabled reader.

The following example in Exhibit 8-23 illustrates a different format for comprehension thinking activities at the literal level. This format generates

Exhibit 8-23 A Comprehension Activity As an Advanced Organizer

> **Directions:** Read the following statements about communication. Put a check before each statement you believe is true. After reading the page, check those statements supported by the reading.
>
> **Before reading**   **After**
> _____   _____   1. Language is made by people who speak English.
> _____   _____   2. Writing is a form of communication.
> _____   _____   3. Talking, writing and grammar books are all forms of communication.

an awareness of specific prior knowledge before the reader is involved with the new information for the reader must compare thinking before and then after the material has been read. This activity provides the reader with a hook to hang new ideas, and it directs the reader to the appropriate existing cognitive structures with which to link the new ideas. In essence, it can be considered an advanced organizer.

INTERPRETIVE LEVEL OF COMPREHENSION/THINKING ACTIVITIES

At this level, the student develops skills in translating what the author is implying. The reader must link information presented by the author to prior knowledge in order to "think through" or translate what the author means.

To develop comprehension guides at this level, the teacher must survey the reading material and ask the following questions: What does the author mean by what he has written? What information can be implied or induced from what the author has stated? Can this implied information be supported by facts or ideas in the reading passage?

When writing questions and statements for this level of comprehension, it is important to stress that student responses must *always* be supported by some information in the reading material.

In devising questions and statements for the interpretive level of reading, teachers should follow the preceding guidelines for developing questions and statements at the literal level.

Two additional guidelines that are specific to this level are as follows:

1. Teachers should explain the concept of interpretive reading to students. Students understand what they are doing and why they are doing it.

2. Teachers should start with questions and then proceed to statements that are related to several facts and ideas in the passage. The difficulty level of the questions and statements should be gradually increased by devising questions and statements that are related to the less obvious information implied by the author.

An Activity to Introduce the Concept of Implied Meaning in Reading

An activity to introduce implied meaning in reading includes the following steps:

1. The teacher clips magazine or newspaper advertisements.
2. The teacher then shows the students an ad from the magazine or newspaper.
3. As the students are looking at the picture, the teacher reads the words in the ad.
4. The teacher writes two statements on the board. The first statement uses words, phrases, and sentences that are directly stated in the ad. The second statement relates to what is implied in the ad.
5. The teacher reads the first statement and asks the students if that idea was stated in the ad.
6. The teacher reads the second statement and asks the students if it was stated in the ad. The teacher asks the students if the ad conveys the message in any way at all. Then the teacher asks the students to find something about the picture or something in the words that support the unstated message.
7. The teacher shows a new advertisement and reads the ad. The students devise statements relating to what the ad implies. The students must support the implied meaning with information from the ad. This information can include words or parts of the picture that support the implied message.

At the interpretive level of comprehension, task demands on the thinking/reasoning process are increased. Therefore oral introductory activities as suggested above are necessary instructional steps in providing the poor or disabled readers with prerequisite skills essential to learning at this level. At the onset of instruction, students must have an understanding of what these tasks require and what is involved in the process to solve problems.

Interpretive Level Questions

At this level, the purpose of questioning is to direct students to ideas implied by the author that are not explicitly stated in the passage. A yes or no response is not acceptable. Answers must always be supported and defended by logical information from the passage as follows:

- Question 1: "Do newspaper reporters and Shakespeare use the same style of writing? Find information in the passage to support your answer."
- Student's response: "No, the passage states that reporters have to write fast because of deadlines. People who write fast do not have the time to think how Shakespeare would have said it, so they write in a contemporary style so the contemporary style and Shakespearean styles must be different."

Question 1 requires the reader to compare and contrast information that is not stated by the author. The reader must translate the author's information by utilizing prior knowledge to make the comparison before arriving at a conclusion. Another example is provided as follows:

- Question 2: "Do linguists describe how language works? Find information in the passage to support your answer."
- Student A: "No, grammar describes how language works."
- Student B: "Yes, linguists could describe how language works. They study the history of a language, the rules of the language, and how words and phrases make up sentences. The passage states that, in the opinion of the linguists, grammar describes how language works. Linguists are experts who probably help write grammar books."

Question 2 is difficult to answer at the interpretive level of comprehension since it requires the reader to use more information from prior knowledge than information from the passage. Student A probably did not understand the meaning of the word *linguist*. However, is this a vocabulary problem or a reading comprehension problem? Student B obviously had the prior experience to translate the author's implication. Because the word *linguist* was meaningless to Student A, that information was omitted from the concept, and a different conclusion was reached. However, both responses are correct, and both responses were defended by logical information from the passage. Another example is shown below:

Exhibit 8-24 Declarative Statements at the Interpretive Level

---

Directions: Check the items below that you feel represent ideas that the author presents. These statements may be phrased differently than in your book. Be prepared to defend your conclusions with information from the passage.

_____ 1. Newspaper reporters and Shakespeare use the same style of writing.
_____ 2. Linguists describe how language works.
_____ 3. A better title for this passage might be, "Newspaper Reporters Talk to People."

- Question 3: "Choose another title for this passage. Support your choice with information from the passage."
  1. "Reporters and Shakespeare"
  2. "Communication Does Not Have to be Eloquent to be Understood"
  3. "Newspaper Reporters Talk to People"
- Student's response: "Communication does not have to be eloquent to be understood. Talking is communication. Not all people who talk use correct grammar, yet they're understood. Reporters communicate, yet they write in a simple way compared to Shakespeare's writing style."

Question 3 requires the reader to determine the relationship among important facts in the passage, to compare and contrast explicit and implicit information with prior knowledge, and to support a conclusion.

Statements at the Interpretive Level of Comprehension

Exhibit 8-24 shows an example of a statement activity at the interpretive level.

When comparing the question and statement issue at the interpretive level, it can be concluded that questions do not lessen the thought process at this level as long as the student is directed to justify conclusions by using information from the reading material. Training the student to defend and support conclusions by information in the reading material is the most significant strategy to develop at this level of comprehension.

Applied Level Questions

At this level, the objective of questioning is to guide students in combining what is known with what is being learned so that creative comprehension develops. Comprehension can be considered creative when new concepts, rules, or principles are formed by relating the author's meaning with the reader's preexisting concepts.

It is common to include "do you think" statements in questions at this level. There are various levels of knowledge and various value systems within a classroom, among students, and among teachers. Hence, the answer often depends on the question (Howell & Kaplan, 1980). "Do you think" implies a request for an opinion. The student's opinions will vary, and often there will be significant dissonance between the student's and teacher's way of thinking. Acceptable responses to "do you think" questions must be supported with information from the text as well as from the student's previous knowledge and experiences.

At this level, common quotes, metaphors, slogans from bumper stickers, posters, and popular TV slogans can be used to assist the student in linking the information from the reading passage to his or her own life. Some examples of questions at this level are:

- Question 1: Is a picture worth a thousand words? Use the reading passage to support your answer.
- Student's response: Pictures are communication. The author talks about strange forms that appear in the daily newspapers. Lots of times there are all kinds of pictures in the newspaper. They tell more about the event than what's actually in the article. Lots of times when I am reading in a textbook, I can't understand the words but I can really understand better when there are graphs or maps or pictures to view.
- Question 2: Your English teacher and the author of "The English Language and How it Grew" are having a debate. What are the issues they would dispute, and what issues would they agree upon? Who would you agree with, your English teacher or the author?
- Student's response: They might agree that Shakespeare and newspaper reporters both communicate in writing. However, the author thinks that both newspaper reporters and Shakespeare are equally good writers, but my English teacher would say that isn't true. The teacher would say that much more talent goes into the Shakespearean style of writing and that not all newspaper reporters use good grammar, and if you don't use good grammar, you are not a good writer. The author would reply that grammar is not language or communication; grammar only tells you how language works and it doesn't have to be the best grammar to communicate. I agree with the author, but I also think that it's harder to communicate in writing than to communicate through talking.
- Question 3: Is it easier to be blind or deaf? Use information from the reading passage to support your answers.

Exhibit 8-25 Declarative Statements at the Applied Level

Directions: Check those ideas you believe relate in some way to the ideas in the reading passage. Be prepared to defend your choices.

_____ 1. A picture is worth a thousand words.
_____ 2. The great debate: style vs. form.
_____ 3. The blind and deaf can communicate.

- Student's response: I think it is easier to be blind. Communication occurs when people talk and write. If I'm blind, people can still talk to me, and I can hear and talk back. If I'm deaf, I can only receive communication through my eyes and answer with my hands. It would be harder to talk if I was deaf, and therefore, more difficult to communicate.

  The purpose of Question 3 is to broaden the concept of communication, and to guide the student in realizing the relevancy of newly formed principles and how these principles relate to other concepts and to the world outside of school.

In all three responses, information from the passage, prior experience, and personal values were used to support the student's opinions and ideas. Whether the teacher agrees with the responses is unimportant. What is important is that the responses are logically supported with information from the reading as well as prior experiences to form generalizations, new rules, and new principles.

Statements at the Applied Level

Exhibit 8-25 presents an activity using statements at the applied level.

Questions at the applied level are directly associated with evaluation and imply that there is a right or wrong answer. Declarative statements are more effective in developing the thought process in reading since they eliminate the threat of being right or wrong. Without this threat, the poor or disabled reader becomes more secure in offering responses, consequently regenerating reasoning skills that have been dormant due to years of fear. If students are required to reason, make judgments, and decide alternatives, they must be given the opportunity to practice these skills. The type of questions and statements used in the three-level comprehension guides can also be developed to generate reasoning in class discussions and on quizzes and tests.

STUDY GUIDES AND INTRACLASS GROUPING

Well-planned lessons that include intraclass grouping often fail when problem solving and decision making are required. Products of these groups usually reflect the work of one student in the group. The other students were too busy discussing the Saturday night dance or the upcoming social events of the week or were generating ways to be suspended from class. In these situations, teacher directiveness becomes teacher management; few students learn; and few teachers attempt intraclass grouping again.

For those teachers who are brave enough to try again and who want the most mileage out of study guides, study guide activities can be used as discussion energizers with intraclass groups. Study guide activities followed by small group discussions significantly increase thinking and reasoning skills.

Intraclass groups using study guides should be groups of three or four members randomly selected by the teacher to stimulate thinking and reasoning and provide structure to the group task with specific assigned activities and rules. The activities are prepared by the teacher and are assigned to the students to be independently completed either in class or for homework. Students are not allowed to respond with yes or no answers. All responses, including personal opinions, must be supported and defended with information from the text and/or logical prior experiences.

After the groups are selected, the teacher should set a time limit for the task. Students should then be instructed to discuss each task in order of appearance. Each student must respond to each item by stating the answer and explaining the facts that support and defend the answer. If there are conflicting responses, the group cannot proceed to the next item until the group arrives at a consensus of opinion. Conflicting responses are resolved by continuing to explain reasoning and providing supporting information.

When the time limit has ended, the teacher should ask a member from each group to report to the class the group's response and reasoning for each item. Each group responds to the same item before proceeding to the next item. When there are conflicting responses from the groups, the teacher should intervene by requesting from the conflicting groups further information to clarify and defend their answers. If the positions are logically explained, the teacher should again intervene to emphasize how and why each response is acceptable. If either position is not logically presented, the teacher must restate questions back to the class until a logical conclusion can be reached. The purpose of intraclass grouping is to encourage thinking and reasoning and to discourage "right or wrong."

After the groups have been selected and have begun their discussions, it is the teacher's responsibility to observe the groups and intervene whenever a group needs further information, encouragement, procedural suggestions, or assistance in evaluating decisions.

The responsibilities of the teacher and students change when study guides are used with intraclass groups. Although the teacher continues to maintain control over the planning and preparation of the lesson, the students are forced, by the nature of the task, to become more actively involved in the learning process, therefore assuming more responsibility for their learning. The teacher's responsibilities are to:

- assign students to groups
- specify the criteria for success
- seek information and opinions
- defend and support decisions
- support group consensus

As the observer, moderator and evaluator, the teacher is responsible for keeping the groups on task, influencing the direction of the groups by restating questions back to the groups, and assisting the groups in evaluating their decisions.

The students assume more responsibility for learning because the rules for performing in the group increase the incentive to complete the assigned study guide activities, thereby increasing group performance. The rules that increase the incentive to achieve require each student to participate by adding to the group decision and require that each student must define his or her responses by citing supportive evidence from the text as well as personal opinion. Preparing for the group by independently completing the assigned activities greatly increases the student's chances of becoming a respected performing member of the group, and therefore, peer approval increases.

Benefits from intraclass groups for the poor or disabled reader are innumerable. As stated before, poor or disabled readers can reason, although their reasoning skills may be somewhat dormant due to the lack of expectation and challenge. Poor or disabled readers who participate in intraclass groups become aware that they are more like than unlike their peers in that their thinking processes are much the same. For this population, participation in intraclass groups builds confidence and regenerates thinking and reasoning.

Intraclass discussion groups are as valuable as the follow-up activities that are suggested in the class text but are rarely used due to lack of time. These follow-up activities are frequently designed to increase thinking and reasoning by providing opportunities for the students to generalize content to other life situations. Substituting study guide activities for suggested follow-up activities, although often not as creative or extensive in design, achieves the same goal with less use of time and more emphasis on the student's present learning needs.

When study guide activities are used as a structure for intraclass group discussions, students gain the opportunity to share one another's reasoning, to compare and discuss reasons for their responses, and to reflect and react to what they have read. These small group discussions also foster indirect results such as an understanding of peer opinions and of alternative choices made by others. These indirect results should not imply that the purpose of study guides in intraclass groups is to develop skills in interpersonal relationships and group dynamics. Rather, the primary purpose is to increase reasoning skills through orally sharing ideas by explaining the thought process entailed in the development of the idea. However, when two or more people are in a discussion, interpersonal communication skills cannot be avoided or ignored. For further information regarding communication skills, see Chapter 3.

CORRELATING CLASSROOM AND SPECIAL EDUCATION INSTRUCTION THROUGH STUDY GUIDES

A time and communication problem exists in correlating instruction between content areas and special education. Consequently, serious and well-intended individual instructional attempts in both disciplines often produce few results. Instruction is "hit or miss;" teachers are frustrated, and students fail. To maximize learning achievement for the poor or disabled reader, reinforcing and supporting each other's instructional endeavors is essential. The special educator must recognize the student's skill needs in relation to the demands of the secondary curriculum. The content area teacher must recognize the increased amount of classroom instructional structure and organization the disabled reader needs to begin to achieve the goals of secondary education.

The following four guidelines present a systematic approach for special educators and content teachers to reinforce and support one another's instructional efforts through the use of study guides:

1. A content analysis is applied by the content teacher to determine:
   a. content objectives
   b. organizational patterns of the unit or chapter
   c. new vocabulary to be taught

  d. instructional classroom activities
  e. homework assignments
2. The content teacher and special educator must meet to clarify:
  a. content objectives
  b. classroom instruction
  c. homework assignments
3. The special educator develops a study guide based on the content analysis and the student's skill needs.
4. The content teacher and special educator meet to refine the study guide and determine teacher responsibilities.
  a. The special educator's instructional responsibilities are to:
    • introduce new skills
    • provide sufficient activities for practice of new skills
    • provide sufficient activities that transfer the new skills to the text
    • provide feedback to content teacher on student's progress biweekly
  b. The content teacher's responsibilities are to:
    • develop instructional activities whenever possible to reinforce the skills emphasized in the study guide
    • modify the readability level of quizzes and tests
    • set realistic academic goals for achievement
    • emphasize thinking skills in instruction
    • provide feedback to special educator on student's progress biweekly

The intent of using study guides for instructing the poor or disabled readers is not to burden teachers with more planning and preparation but rather to encourage a process in which information may best be obtained. The intent of study guides can best be summed up by Bruner (1964), "We teach a subject not to produce little living libraries on the subject but rather to get a student . . . to embody the process of knowledge getting. Knowledge is a process, not a product" (p. 335. Reprinted with permission)

ANNOTATED BIBLIOGRAPHY

Estes, T.H., & Vaughn, J.L. *Reading and Learning in the Content Classroom*. Boston, Mass.: Allyn & Bacon, Inc., 1978.
  This book is a comprehensive work that views reading in the content areas as a process of learning and suggests that content and reading skills be taught concurrently. Various units of study in the content areas

illustrate creative study guides in science, social studies, business education, health, and math.

Gerhard, C. *Making Sense: Reading Comprehension Improved through Categorizing*. Newark, Del.: IRA, 1975.

This source provides a clear understanding of the organizational skills that are interrelated in the reading/writing process. It presents a sequential program in integrating the components necessary to organize ideas in reading and writing. The sample lessons and activities provide the teacher structure in expanding reasoning skills in the reading/writing process.

Herber, H.L. *Teaching Reading in the Content Areas*. Englewood Cliffs, N.J.: Prentice-Hall, Inc., 1978.

This book is highly recommended for anyone wishing to develop or expand the use of study guides in group instruction. It combines indepth information about the nature and purpose of study guides and intraclass grouping along with practical activities to employ this approach in the content areas.

Lyons, V. (Ed.). *Structuring Cooperative Learning: The 1980 Handbook*. Minneapolis, Minn.: A Cooperative Network Publication, 1980.

In this book, the rationale and definition of cooperative learning is reviewed, and the specifics of structuring a classroom cooperatively are summarized. Lesson plans, submitted by teachers from all grade levels and areas of the United States, emphasize cooperative learning as an instructional approach to maximize the student's cognitive and affective learning outcomes. The lesson plans include goals, group procedures, and content activities in writing skills, vocabulary lessons, business education, social studies, science, and math. This handbook is recommended as a teacher's aid for adapting group procedures to use with intraclass grouping and study guides.

Piercy, D. *Reading Activities in Content Areas*. Boston, Mass.: Allyn & Bacon, Inc., 1982.

This book emphasizes reasoning skills through instructional activities and teaching techniques in the content area. It is an excellent source to use in developing study guides and reinforcement activities.

Spargo, E., & Harris, R. *Reading the Content Fields Series*. Providence, R.I.: Jamestown Publishers, 1978.

The goal of this series of workbooks is to teach students how to comprehend reading material in the content areas. Vocabulary development and the three levels of comprehension are emphasized through sample reading selections from math, science, practical arts, social studies, and English. This series is self-contained in that clearly defined instruction is given throughout the individual books to direct students through the activities. However, the lessons and exercises can be easily modified by combining the exercises with directive instruction for use as introductory or reinforcement activities.

Tierney, R.J., Readence, J.E., & Dishner, E.K. *Reading Strategies and Practices: Guide for Improving Instruction.* Boston, Mass.: Allyn & Bacon, Inc., 1980.

This book is a practical reference offering various examples of instructional techniques, reading strategies, and activities. The instructional procedures are clearly defined and easy to follow. Included are practical suggestions for constructing and developing study guides.

Williston, G.R. *Comprehensive Skills Series.* Providence, R.I.: Jamestown Publishers, 1974.

This resource is a series of comprehensive skills booklets, each providing a clear definition and sample exercise for the specific skill presented in the booklet, preceded by 30 practice activities. The clearly defined and mature student introduction and preview technique in section one of each booklet provides teachers with a valuable reference for adapting effective instructional strategies in explaining and introducing new skills to the learning disabled reader.

REFERENCES

Bruner, J.S. Some theorems on instruction illustrated with reference to mathematics. In E.R. Hilgard (Ed.), *Theories of learning and instruction, The sixty-third yearbook of NSSE.* Chicago, Ill.: National Society for the Study of Education, 1964.

Brunner, J.F. & Campbell, J.J. *Participating in secondary reading, A practical approach.* Englewood Cliffs, N.J.: Prentice-Hall, Inc., 1978.

Carnine, D. & Silbert, J. *Direct instruction reading.* Columbus, Ohio: Charles E. Merrill Publishing Co., 1979.

Carroll, B. The analysis of reading instruction: Perspectives from psychology and linguistics. In E.R. Hilgard (Ed.), *Theories of learning and instruction, The sixty-third yearbook of NSSE.* Chicago, Ill.: National Society for the Study of Education, 1964.

Conlin, D.A., Herman, G.R. & Martin, J. *Our language today 8, Teacher's annotated edition.* New York: American Book Co., 1966.

Gagné, R.M., & Briggs, L.E. *Principles of instructional design.* New York: Holt, Rinehart & Winston, Inc., 1974.

Glynn, S.M., & Divesta, F.L. Outline and hierarchical organization as aids for study and retrieval. *Journal of Educational Psychology,* 1977, 67, 89–95.

Herber, H.L. *Teaching reading in the content areas.* Englewood Cliffs, N.J.: Prentice-Hall, Inc., 1970.

Herber, H.L. *Teaching reading in the content areas, (2nd ed.).* Englewood Cliffs, N.J.: Prentice-Hall, Inc., 1978.

Howell, K.W., & Kaplan, J.S. *Diagnosing basic skills: A handbook for deciding what to teach.* Columbus, Ohio: Charles E. Merrill Publishing Co., 1980.

Johnson, D.W. *Educational Psychology.* Englewood Cliffs, N.J.: Prentice-Hall, Inc., 1979.

Joyce, B.R. *Selecting learning experiences.* Washington, D.C.: Association for Supervision and Curriculum Development, 1978.

Woodward, D.M. *Mainstreaming the learning disabled adolescent.* Rockville, Md.: Aspen Systems Corp., 1981.

SUGGESTED READINGS

Ausabel, D.P. The use of advance organizers in the learning and retention of meaningful verbal material. *Journal of Educational Psychology,* 1960, *51,* 267–272.

Cowan, R. Remedial reading in secondary schools: Three-fourths of a century. In H.A. Robinson (Ed.), *Reading and writing instruction in the United States: Historical trends.* Newark, Del.: International Reading Association, 1977.

Estes, H. & Vaughn, J.L. *Reading and learning in the content classroom.* Boston, Mass.: Allyn & Bacon, Inc., 1978.

Glatthorn, A. *A guide for developing an English curriculum for the eighties.* Urbana, Ill.: National Council of Teachers of English, 1980.

Herber, H.L. & Nelson, J. Questioning is not the answer. *Journal of Reading,* 1975, *18,* 512–517.

Johnson, D.W. & Johnson, R. Conflict in the classroom: Controversy and learning. *Review of Educational Research,* 1979, *49,* 51–68.

Levin, T. & Long, R. *Effective instruction.* Alexandria, Va.: Association for Supervision and Curriculum Development, 1981.

Tobacco Unit: A Prepared Booklet Written to Lower Readability Level, Including a Correlated Study Guide and "Hands-On" Activities

Janet Merkent

PURPOSE OF THE UNIT

In this particular school system, the science curriculum requires that units on tobacco, alcohol, and drugs be taught in the eighth-grade science classes. However, the science text not only has a readability level of tenth grade but also designates few pages to the topic of tobacco. The pages that are designated offer vast information with little explanations and repetitions causing confusion and misconceptions for poor or disabled readers. Thus, the primary objectives of this unit were to:

- offer a clear, concise, and comprehensive overview on the study of tobacco at a sixth-grade reading level
- integrate reading/thinking skills with content

The first objective was accomplished by writing a booklet on tobacco, even though Fry's readability formula disputes this effort. According to Fry's readability formula, the readability level of the booklet is tenth grade. This is an inflated calculation due to the extreme high syllable count dictated by the various science terms used in this topic of study. However, this booklet reflects criteria that decrease readability levels of written material that cannot be measured through the use of readability formulas. This booklet demonstrates how to lower readability levels through controlling the use of signal words and by developing simple sentences that use as few clauses as possible.

The second objective was accomplished by correlating the study guide activities with reading/thinking skills required by the three levels of reading comprehension and the organizational pattern used in the booklet. The study guide provides vocabulary exercises, comprehension questions or statements, and organizational exercises for each section in the booklet. The majority of organizational activities adhere to the cause-effect pattern. However, sequencing, classification, and comparison-contrast patterns are also used.

To supplement and reinforce concepts introduced in the booklet a 16mm film and a filmstrip were included. A content analysis of the film and filmstrip are offered to demonstrate the concepts reinforced. Comprehension questions relating to the films are also included to assist students in focusing on the significant facts and concepts being presented and to be used as a format to generate a productive discussion after the viewing of each film.

TARGET POPULATION

This unit on the study of tobacco was developed for an eighth-grade homogeneous science class. The class consisted of eight students, all identified as learning disabled with reading levels ranging from second to seventh grade. The students with the higher reading levels had severe deficits in organization of thought, writing, and spelling but did not receive service from the learning disabilities specialist. The students with the lower reading abilities were being serviced by the learning disabilities specialist to increase word recognition and spelling skills. Several of these students had severely depressed receptive vocabularies.

METHOD OF INSTRUCTION

A cooperative effort among the science teacher, learning disabilities specialist, and English teacher was informally developed to correlate content with the skills needed by these students to achieve in the content areas. The Tobacco booklet and study guide were written by the learning disabilities specialist Janet Merkent, with the intent that it be used by the science teacher in the science class. The science teacher presented the content and taught the reading/thinking skills through the use of the study guide and hands-on activities. The learning disabilities specialist taught the class one period each week to model instruction by introducing new reading/thinking skills and to review and reinforce previously learned skills.

At the same time, these skills were being reinforced and applied in a modified English class (reading and writing) with the majority of the students from the eighth-grade science class. The success of this unit of study can be measured by its continued use in the science class over the past two years.

ORGANIZATION OF UNIT

Section I   Tobacco
Section II   Study Guide—Vocabulary words, vocabulary exercises, comprehension questions, and organizational exercises for each section and content analysis and comprehension activities for a filmstrip and film
Section III Recommended Hands-On Activities

Table of Contents

Tobacco

LESSON 1. A HISTORY OF SMOKING

People did not smoke in Europe when Columbus discovered America in the late 1400s. However, the Indians of the New World were already smoking. The Indians used smoking for religious and healing purposes. They also used it as a sign of peace and friendship.

About 50 years after Columbus' voyage, explorers introduced tobacco seeds into Europe. Between 1559 and 1565, people began growing the tobacco plant in Portugal, France, Spain, and England.

During the late 1500s and early 1600s, the use of tobacco became very common in Europe. Some people thought that tobacco could cure sicknesses such as toothaches, deafness, and even cancer. Other people believed the use of tobacco was sinful.

In 1607, John Rolfe began planting tobacco in Jamestown, Virginia. His work in growing good quality tobacco helped make tobacco farming become one of America's first industries. During this time tobacco was used by smoking it in pipes, chewing it, or sniffing it.

During the 1800s, cigars became popular. Cigarettes also became popular during this period. British soldiers learned about these "paper cigars" from Turkish soldiers. Afterwards, cigarettes became the most popular way to smoke tobacco. As a matter of fact, cigarettes were so popular that the Red Cross passed out cigarettes to our soldiers during World War II. However, at this time, people were not aware of the health dangers that cigarettes can cause.

Today, research has shown tobacco use to be dangerous. Although many Americans have stopped smoking, millions continue to use tobacco in many different ways.

LESSON 2. WHAT IS TOBACCO?

Tobacco is a member of a family of plants known as the Solanacae or potato family. The group is sometimes referred to as the nightshade family. This family contains about 1,800 species or types of herbs, shrubs, vines, and trees. Other members of the family are the garden pepper, Irish potato, eggplant, tomato, and petunia. Although tobacco is related to these plants, it does not look like any of them. It is also different because its leaf is the valuable part of the plant and it has habit-forming properties.

Tobacco is a flowering annual plant. It grows easily in moist and fertile soil, but it needs much care and attention to grow the finest quality leaf. A full grown leaf is about one to one and a half feet in area. About 50 species of the tobacco plant are found throughout the world. Most of our tobacco comes from the species Nicotiana tobacum.

The species Nicotiana tobacum grows from a tiny seed. A single pod contains between 300,000 to 400,000 seeds. If all the seeds from one year's pods were planted at one time, the earth's land would not be large enough to grow all the plants. Nicotiana tobacum is native to South America and also grows in North America. It grows to be about six feet tall and is an attractive plant. The flowers of the plant bloom in July and August and are pale pink. The seeds ripen in September and October.

LESSON 3. TOBACCO SMOKE, HARMFUL COMPOUNDS, AND TOBACCO SMELLS

When a person inhales on a cigarette, the hot smoke attacks tissues in the mouth, throat, breathing tubes, and lungs. After the smoke passes the mouth, the lungs keep in between 85 and 99 percent of almost all the compounds you inhale or breathe in. There are hundreds of chemical substances in cigarette smoke and tobacco. Three of the most harmful are nicotine, tars, and carbon monoxide.

Small amounts of nicotine are found in tobacco leaves. Nicotine is a colorless liquid that stains paper, though the marks are usually light. It has a bitter taste. In its pure form, nicotine is one of the most poisonous substances of the plant world. A lethal or deadly dose of nicotine is one-third of a grain or 1/1200 of an ounce. It kills like cyanide. It is the nicotine in tobacco that causes a slight narcotic effect when it is smoked. This makes tobacco a depressant, that is it relaxes the central nervous system.

Tar is a substance that damages delicate lung tissues. There are billions of tiny particles in cigarette smoke. When they cool inside the lungs, some form a brown, sticky mass. This tar mass contains chemicals that cause cancer in tests with animals.

Carbon monoxide is a colorless, odorless gas that drives the oxygen out of the red blood cells. There is four to fifteen times more carbon monoxide in the blood of smokers than nonsmokers. Carbon monoxide stays in the blood stream for about six hours after the person stops smoking.

Tobacco Smells

In addition in containing harmful compounds, tobacco also gives off an unpleasant smell. This odor is caused by elements in tobacco smoke such as ammonia and pyridine. The odor lingers or lasts for long periods of time because the tars hold them to the skin and clothes.

LESSON 4. DIFFERENT WAYS OF USING TOBACCO AND SOME OF ITS EFFECTS

There are several ways to use tobacco. The most popular way is to smoke cigarettes. Although more than 30 million Americans have quit smoking (100,000 of them are doctors), almost a million teenagers take up smoking every year. Each year 300,000 Americans die prematurely from the effects of smoking. Cigarette smoking is a major cause of emphysema, chronic bronchitis, lung cancer, and heart disease. The longer a person smokes, the deadlier it is.

Two different ways of smoking tobacco are to smoke a pipe or a cigar. People who smoke pipes or cigars, instead of cigarettes, decrease some dangers to their health. If the smoker does not inhale, he or she is less likely to develop heart disease or severe lung diseases than a cigarette smoker. However, people who smoke pipes or cigars increase other hazards to their health. For example, if the pipe or cigar smoker does inhale, he or she has a *greater* chance than a cigarette smoker of developing serious heart and lung diseases. Because tobacco smoke still enters the mouth, the pipe or cigar smoker is just as likely as a cigarette smoker to develop cancer of the throat, larynx (voice box), mouth, and stomach. Lip cancer also seems to be caused by pipe smoking. Finally, experiments with mice show there are more cancer-causing substances in cigars and pipe tars than in cigarette tars.

A fourth way of using tobacco is to chew it. In 1960, more than 25,000,000 pounds of chewing tobacco was made in the United States. The tar in chewing tobacco has been found to cause cancer of the mouth. In one study, 26 out of 40 men who chewed tobacco had cancer of the mouth. Cancer of the mouth causes four percent (4%) of the cancer deaths. These figures are very important because chewing tobacco seems to be increasingly popular today.

It is quite obvious that tobacco has many effects on the user's health. Because cigarette smoking is the most common way of using tobacco, its effects will be discussed more thoroughly later in the unit.

LESSON 5. HOW SMOKING AFFECTS THE BODY

5A. Effects on the Respiratory System

An important job of the respiratory or breathing system is to allow the body to get oxygen from the air. The body must have oxygen in order to live. Air is taken into the body when the lungs are expanded by a large muscle called the diaphragm. (See Figure A-1.) After the air passes through the nose or mouth and the throat, it is passed through the trachea or windpipe. At the end of the windpipe are two tubes called bronchial tubes. Both the windpipe and bronchial tubes have tiny hairs called cilia and a liquid called mucus that keeps the respiratory system clean. The bronchial tubes lead into the lungs. At the very end of the bronchial tubes are millions of tiny balloonlike air sacs called alveoli. The alveoli let the air or gases pass through the body.

When tobacco smoke is inhaled, it follows the same path that the air does. However, many of the substances that make up the smoke are trapped by the mucus and cilia. The substances not trapped there move into the alveoli. Choking, coughing, and a tickling feeling in the throat and chest are signs that the tobacco smoke bothers the respiratory system. Because the respiratory system must work harder to allow a smoker to breathe, the smoker often experiences more strain and loss of breath when he or she exercises.

5B. Effects on the Circulatory System

The job of the circulatory system is to use the blood vessels, the heart, and other body parts to pass blood throughout the body. (See Figure A-2.) The blood contains oxygen and nutrients that allow the organs to work. The circulatory system also gets rid of wastes such as carbon dioxide.

When smoke enters the body, much of it is passed through the alveoli to the circulatory system. It then follows the same path as oxygen and is absorbed by the organs and tissues.

Studies show that this smoke causes several changes in the circulatory system. First, the heart beats faster than before. It may beat 15 to 20 times

Figure A-1 The Respiratory System

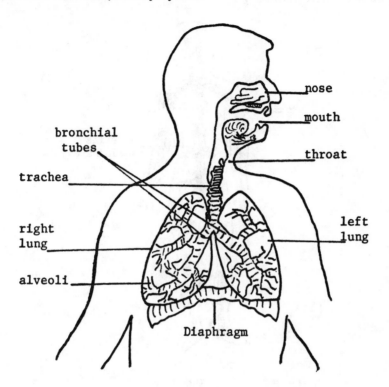

A Group of Alveoli

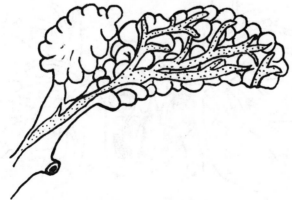

Figure A-2 The Circulatory System

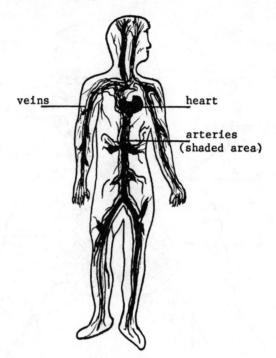

The Heart

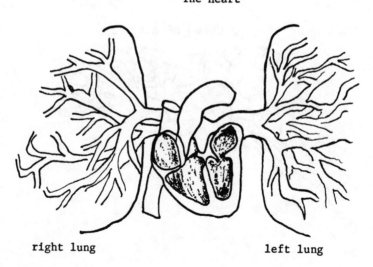

faster. Secondly, some of the blood vessels contract or become narrower. Thus, the blood pressure rises. Finally, the blood carries less oxygen than usual from the lungs to the organs and tissues of the body. Most of these changes are thought to be caused by nicotine.

5C. Effects on the Nervous System

The nervous system gives the body an awareness of both the world and the body itself. It also controls the other systems so that they all work together. The most important parts of the nervous system are the brain, the spinal cord, and all the tiny nerves in the body. (See Figure A-3.)

The nervous system is one of the body parts where smoke in the blood stream is carried. The smoke substances reach the brain quickly so the smoker feels its effects almost immediately. For example, when a beginning smoker inhales smoke, he or she often becomes dizzy. He or she may also get an upset stomach. These effects may be caused by the carbon monoxide, the nicotine, or the lack of oxygen to the brain. Although a regular smoker does not usually experience dizziness or an upset stomach, the smoke substances continue to affect his or her nervous system.

5D. Effects on Pregnant Women and Their Babies

Smoking is a double danger for pregnant women and their babies. Studies show that cigarette smoke in the mother's blood stream also changes the heart rate, blood pressure, oxygen supply, and acid balance for the unborn infant. Pregnant women who smoke tend to have babies that weigh less than those of nonsmoking mothers. They also have more miscarriages and stillbirths.

5E. Effects on Nonsmokers

Recent research has shown that tobacco smoke may also be dangerous to the nonsmoker. The smoke that a smoker exhales or breathes out still contains many harmful substances such as a gas called carbon monoxide. Nonsmokers are also exposed to cigarettes that are left burning in ashtrays. This smoke smells and can be irritating to the eyes and respiratory system. For these reasons, many health organizations and individuals are now fighting for nonsmokers' rights.

LESSON 6. MINOR HEALTH PROBLEMS THAT ARE EXPENSIVE

Smoking is a very expensive and dangerous habit for many reasons. First, cigarettes are quite expensive today. This is especially obvious when

Figure A-3 Brain and Nervous System

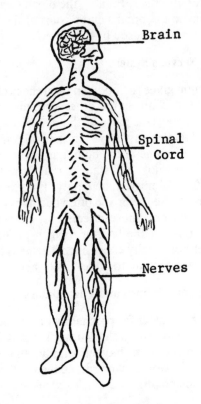

Brain

Spinal
Cord

Nerves

Arteries in the Brain

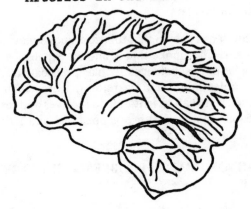

a smoker adds up all the money spent on cigarettes for one year. Second, smokers often burn clothing, furniture, carpets, etc. Other types of accidents such as forest and house fires and automobile and work accidents are often related to smoking. These accidents are both costly and dangerous.

Other minor health problems have been related to smoking. For example, studies show that, overall, smokers are sick in bed about 88 million more days each year than nonsmokers. Other research shows that smokers more often have a chronic or continuous cough than nonsmokers. They also have more phlegm, which is a liquid found in the lungs.

Finally, the fingers, fingernails, and teeth are all affected by smoking. They become discolored or yellowed by the nicotine in the tobacco. Although this coloration does not seem to cause any harmful effects, teeth should be cleaned by a dentist to remove these stains.

LESSON 7. SMOKING AND DISEASE

7A. Chronic Bronchitis and Emphysema

Certain health researchers believe that they have evidence that smoking is related to certain diseases. Two of these diseases are chronic bronchitis and emphysema.

Chronic bronchitis is a long-term inflammation of the bronchial tubes. This swollenness and redness causes the tubes to produce phlegm. The phlegm and coughing can make breathing very difficult.

Emphysema is another disease that makes breathing difficult. Many of the alveoli or air sacs in the lungs become clogged with phlegm. This congestion prevents fresh air from entering and stale air from leaving.

Many doctors believe that chronic bronchitis and emphysema may be related because so many people develop both diseases together. More and more people are dying from these two diseases. Studies show that about six times more smokers die from emphysema and/or bronchitis than nonsmokers.

7B. Lung Cancer

Cancer is a growing mass of abnormal or unusual cells in the body. These cells destroy normal body tissues and functions. Lung cancer often causes death because it interferes with breathing and destroys important tissues in the lungs.

Studies show that about ten times more smokers die from lung cancer than nonsmokers. Research also shows that nonsmokers rarely develop lung cancer. Many scientists believe that there is a *strong* link between lung cancer and smoking.

7C. Coronary Heart Disease

Coronary heart disease is associated with the circulatory system. This disease happens when not enough oxygen-carrying blood can get to the heart. This may cause a heart attack. Almost two times more smokers die from coronary heart disease than nonsmokers.

7D. Other Serious Diseases

Chronic bronchitis, emphysema, lung cancer, and coronary heart disease are not the only serious health problems that have been linked with smoking. Other diseases include cancer of the larynx or voice box, stomach ulcers, cirrhosis of the liver, and several diseases of the circulatory system.

LESSON 8. CIGARETTES AND THE MEDIA

For many years, cigarettes were advertised in all the major forms of the media, including television, radio, and magazines. However, on January 2, 1971, the advertising of cigarettes on television and radio was banned. Today, cigarettes may still be advertised on billboards and in newspapers and magazines. Cigarette manufacturers are also required by law to write the following warning on all cigarette packages: "Warning: The Surgeon General Has Determined that Cigarette Smoking Is Dangerous to Your Health."

Cigarette companies have spent billions of dollars in advertising, trying to link the beautiful things in life to smoking. For example, the advertisements often show a beautiful man or woman smoking a cigarette on a beautiful beach. However, many antismoking campaigns by the American Lung Association and other organizations now show smoking to be a smelly, expensive habit that is very dangerous to your health.

LESSON 9. WHY DO PEOPLE SMOKE?

For many years, psychologists have been interested in finding out why certain people smoke. Some believe that parents who smoke unintentionally influence their children to smoke. Other psychologists feel that many people take up smoking because they have friends who smoke. Many researchers think that there is something about young people's attitudes toward smoking that encourages them to smoke. For example, some teens report that they feel smoking makes them look grownup. Finally, some people feel that certain kinds of personalities may be more likely to smoke.

LESSON 10. MAKING YOUR DECISION

It becomes obvious that deciding whether or not to smoke can be a difficult decision. It is also an important decision because smoking is an addictive habit that is hard to quit. There are forces at work to encourage you to smoke just as there are forces at work trying to get you not to smoke. *You* must weigh the evidence and know your own reasons for deciding whether to smoke or not smoke.

Study Guide

EXERCISES FOR LESSON 1: A HISTORY OF SMOKING

Vocabulary Exercise A

Directions: Please note the following words when you are reading. Try to determine the definition from the meaning of the sentence. After your class discusses the definitions, please write them in your own words.

I. 1. Europe
    2. New World
    3. healing
    4. voyage
    5. explorers
    6. Portugal, France, Spain, and England
    7. Jamestown, Virginia
    8. industries
    9. Turkish
    10. research
II. List all the vocabulary words that are places. Find them on the map in your classroom.

Vocabulary Exercise B

Directions: To solve this puzzle look at the definitions below. Think of a word from the vocabulary list that has the same number of letters as the spaces given. If you do this puzzle correctly, the circled word will be another word from the vocabulary list!

1. _ _ □ _ _ _
2. _ □ _   _ _ _ _ _

3.   _ _ _ _ ☐ _ _ _ _ _
4. _ _ _ _ _ _ _ ☐ _ _
5.   _ _ _ _ ☐ _
6.   _ _ ☐ _ _ _ _
7.   _ _ _ _ ☐ _
8.   ☐ _ _ _ _ _ _

a. a continent of the earth
b. the area that Columbus discovered, including America
c. a business concerned with manufacturing or producing something
d. people who travel to new or strange places
e. a trip
f. a person who is born in the country Turkey
g. a country in western Europe
h. curing a sick person, making a person feel well

Comprehension Exercise

Part A

Directions: Check the sentences or statements you think the author says. Sometimes the exact words are used. Sometimes other words are used.

_____ The Indians of the New World were smoking before Columbus discovered the New World.
_____ In 1607, John Rolfe began planting tobacco in Virginia.
_____ After Columbus discovered the New World, explorers brought tobacco back to Europe.
_____ Cigarettes and cigars became popular during the 1800s.
_____ The Indians smoked only during the marriage ceremony.
_____ Turkish soldiers learned about "paper cigars" from British soldiers.
_____ Everyone who lived in Europe during the 1600s thought tobacco was wonderful.
_____ Not many Americans have quit smoking.
_____ Tobacco became popular in Europe during the late 1500s and early 1600s.
_____ During the 1600s, tobacco was used by smoking it in pipes, chewing it, and sniffing it.
_____ When the Red Cross passed out cigarettes to our soldiers, they knew cigarettes were dangerous to our health.

Part B

Directions: Check the statements that tell what the author means. Be ready to tell why you did or did not check an item.

_____ People in Europe did not smoke before the 1500s because they had not had tobacco before that time.

_____ The Indians believed smoking tobacco was harmful.

_____ People smoked tobacco in pipes for many years because they had not invented or known about cigarettes.

_____ The Americans began smoking tobacco before the people in Europe began smoking.

_____ Tobacco farming became an important business in parts of America.

Part C

Directions: Check the items you think are correct. You should use Lesson 1 to help support your answers.

_____ The Red Cross would not have given cigarettes to the American soldiers if they had known they were harmful.

_____ Cigarettes might have become popular sooner if Americans or Europeans had known about them.

Organizational Exercise—Sequencing Pattern

Part A

Directions: Read the statements below. Then write the number of each statement in the correct order. The first one is done for you.

__8__ 1. Cigars and cigarettes became popular.

_____ 2. Tobacco use becomes popular in Europe.

_____ 3. Columbus discovered America.

_____ 4. People began growing tobacco in Portugal, Spain, France, and England.

_____ 5. Research showed tobacco to be dangerous.

_____ 6. Explorers introduced tobacco in Europe.

_____ 7. John Rolfe planted tobacco in Virginia.

_____ 8. Indians in New World smoked tobacco.

Part B

Directions: The line below is a time line. A time line represents or shows when certain events happened in history. Fill in the events from the first exercise in the correct place on the time line. Be sure to ask your teacher for any dates you are not sure of. The first answer is given to you.

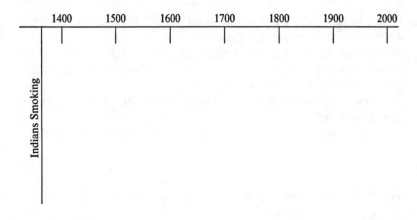

FILM ON SMOKING

Smoking: Past and Present is a 16mm color film published by Wexler Films and the American Cancer Society. It reviews many of the ideas presented in the history of smoking lesson in the booklet. It also serves to introduce the concepts covered in the lesson on the effects of tobacco. This film could be used to review the history of smoking and/or as a preview of the material introduced in the lesson on the effects of tobacco chapter.

OUTLINE OF CONTENT

1. Tobacco was begun with pipe smoking over 1500 years ago. The Indians used tobacco in ceremonies.
2. Tobacco is native to the Americas.
3. In 1492, Columbus discovered tobacco use when he met the Indians.
4. When tobacco was introduced to Europe, it was viewed as evil by some people and as socially acceptable by others. Some people in England even attended lessons to learn how to smoke!
5. Tobacco became America's first large crop. This industry brought our country a great deal of money through sales abroad.
6. In the 1800s British soldiers learned about cigarettes from the Turkish and French soldiers.
7. Between 1910 and 1930, the number of Americans smoking cigarettes multiplied 10 times.
8. During World War II, the American Red Cross sent cigarettes to our men in the armed forces.
9. At this time, people were unaware of the health hazards posed by smoking tobacco.

10. During the last 20 years, a relationship between diseases and smoking has been established.
11. The film also reviews how tobacco smoke is ingested by the body, the parts of the respiratory system, and three major diseases associated with tobacco use (lung cancer, emphysema, and coronary artery disease).

COMPREHENSION QUESTIONS

The following are questions to use after the film is shown:

1. When did people begin smoking tobacco?
   a. over 1500 years ago
   b. less than 25 years ago
   c. in 1864
2. Tobacco grows naturally or is native in which place?
   a. Europe
   b. Iceland
   c. America
3. Who was the first person from Europe to see Indians smoking tobacco?
   a. Columbus
   b. Ponce de Leon
   c. King George
4. Why did some people attend classes in England?
   a. to learn to roll cigarettes
   b. to learn how to protest against tobacco
   c. to learn how to smoke
5. Circle the best statement.
   a. Everyone in Europe believed smoking was an evil, dirty habit.
   b. Some people in Europe were against smoking, but other people liked and approved of it.
   c. Everyone in Europe believed smoking was good only for special occasions.
6. Circle the correct statement.
   a. Tobacco was America's first large crop.
   b. Tobacco was not planted in America until 1950.
   c. Columbus planted tobacco in America before he returned to Europe.
7. When did British soldiers learn about cigarettes?
   a. 1400s on Columbus' voyage

    b. 1800s during a war

    c. 1600s from John Rolfe

8. What increased the production of cigarettes (the number of cigarettes that could be made)?

    a. the invention of a machine

    b. the invention of a paper with a new glue

    c. women rolling the cigarettes faster

9. Who did the Red Cross send cigarettes to during World War II?

    a. our enemies—to slowly kill them

    b. only the British and American generals

    c. our own men in the Army, Navy and Air Force

10. When did people begin to discover that tobacco use may be hazardous or harmful to a person's health?

    a. during the last 20 years

    b. in 1978

    c. during the last 455 years

EXERCISES FOR LESSON 2: WHAT IS TOBACCO?

Vocabulary Exercise

Directions: Please note the following words when you are reading. Try to determine the definitions from the meaning of the sentence. After your class discusses the definitions, please write them in your own words.

1. Solanacae
2. petunia
3. valuable
4. habit-forming
5. annual
6. species
7. Nicotiana tobacum
8. moist

Match these vocabulary words with their meanings.

_____ 1. petunia   a. something that needs to be taken over
_____ 2. habit-forming   and over again, to become addicted
_____ 3. species   b. a family of plants known as the potato
_____ 4. Solanacae   family
_____ 5. moist   c. a species of the tobacco plant
_____ 6. valuable   d. wet
_____ 7. Nicotiana tobacum   e. every year
_____ 8. annual   f. types of plant
                                    g. worthwhile
                                    h. flower

Comprehension Exercise

Part A:

Directions: Answer the following multiple choice questions based on Lesson 2 of your booklet. Circle the correct answer.

1. What is the species from which most of our tobacco comes?
   a. Solanacae
   b. petunia
   c. Nicotiana tobacum
2. Which of these plants does *not* belong to the same family as tobacco?
   a. radish
   b. eggplant
   c. Irish potato
3. What is the most worthwhile part of the tobacco plant?
   a. leaf
   b. stem
   c. vine
4. How large is a full grown tobacco leaf?
   a. 1 to 1½ yards
   b. 1 to 1½ feet
   c. 1 to 1½ inches
5. In what type of soil does the tobacco plant grow well?
   a. wet and fertile
   b. fertile and dry
   c. sandy and moist
6. How many seeds does a single tobacco pod contain?
   a. 30,000 to 40,000
   b. 300,000 to 400,000
   c. 300 to 400,000

7. How tall does the tobacco plant grow?
    a. 16 feet
    b. 6½ feet
    c. 6 feet
8. When do the flowers of the tobacco plant bloom?
    a. September and August
    b. July and August
    c. September and October

Part B

Directions: Answer the following questions by circling the answer that tells what the author means.

1. Circle the statement that is true.
    a. The leaves of the garden pepper, Irish potato, eggplant, tomato, and petunia are *not* the most valuable part of the plant.
    b. The leaves of the garden pepper, Irish potato, eggplant, tomato, tobacco and petunia *are* the most valuable part of the plant.
    c. Both the Irish potato and tobacco plant's leaves and stems are very valuable.
2. Circle the statement that is true.
    a. There are many families in each species of plants.
    b. The Solanacae family contains about 180 species of plants.
    c. There are many species of plants in each family.
3. Which statement describes the conditions a tobacco plant needs to grow a good quality leaf?
    a. wet, fertile dirt with much care
    b. moist, sandy soil with much attention
    c. fertile, dry soil with much care
4. Which statement best describes the seeds of the tobacco plant?
    a. Because there are a few large seeds in each tobacco pod, they must be used sparingly.
    b. Because there are a few thousand seeds in each pod they can be thrown all over the earth.
    c. Because there are a few hundred thousand tiny seeds in each tobacco pod, there are plenty of seeds to plant all the tobacco we want.
5. Which statement best tells where tobacco grows?
    a. Nicotiana tobacum is native to South America, North America, and Europe.
    b. Our tobacco grows naturally in South America and will grow when planted in North America.

c. Nicotiana tobacum grows native in both North and South America.

EXERCISES FOR LESSON 3: TOBACCO, SMOKE, HARMFUL COMPOUNDS, AND TOBACCO SMELLS

Vocabulary Exercises

Part A

Directions: Please note the following words when you are reading. Try to get the definition from the meaning of the sentence. After your class discusses the definitions, please write them in your own words.

1. inhale
2. tissues
3. compounds
4. nicotine
5. tar
6. carbon monoxide
7. lethal
8. narcotic
9. depressant
10. odor

Part B

Directions: Using the vocabulary words, match them to their meanings. Fill in each magic square so that each column across, down, and diagonally will equal 15 when you *add*.

A	B	C
D	E	F
G	H	I

a. narcotic
b. compounds
c. depressant
d. tar
e. lethal
f. odor
g. nicotine
h. inhale
i. carbon monoxide

1. to breathe in
2. dangerous drugs that can become habit-forming become habit-forming when not used correctly
3. a smell
4. a drug that relaxes the central nervous system
5. deadly, something that can kill
6. a poisonous, bitter, colorless substance found in tobacco
7. a substance found in tobacco that becomes a brown, sticky mass
8. a colorless gas with no smell
9. a chemical substance

Comprehension Exercise

Directions: Answer these questions using the information from Lesson 3 of the booklet.

1. What does hot smoke do to a person's tissues?
2. How much of the harmful compounds found in smoke stay in the lungs?
3. List three of the most harmful compounds found in tobacco smoke.
4. List four characteristics of nicotine.
5. What effect does nicotine have on the body?
6. What does tar look like when it cools inside the lungs?
7. What effect does tar have on animals in experiments?
8. List two characteristics of carbon monoxide.
9. What effect does carbon monoxide have on red blood cells?
10. Why do tobacco smells stay on people's skin   and clothes?

Organizational Exercise—Listing and Cause-Effect Patterns

Part A

Directions: Fill in the following diagrams with the help of your teacher. List the three harmful compounds found in tobacco smoke.

3 harmful compounds in tobacco smoke

1. _____

2. _____

3. _____

These three harmful compounds or
substances cause bad effects in
people and in experimental
animals.

Part B

Directions: Fill in the missing information by listing the harmful compounds and their effects.

Cause		Effect
1. _____	⟶	drives oxygen out of red blood cells
2. _____	⟶	_____
3. _____	⟶	causes cancer in animals

EXERCISES FOR LESSON 4: DIFFERENT WAYS OF USING TOBACCO AND SOME OF ITS EFFECTS

Vocabulary Exercise

Directions: Please note the following words when you are reading. Try to determine the definition from the meaning of the sentence. After your class discusses the definitions, please write them in your own words.

1. prematurely

_____

2. decrease

_____

3. increase

_____

4. hazards

_____

Comprehension Exercise

Part A

Directions: Write True or False in front of these statements. Refer to Lesson 4 for the correct answers.

1. _____ This chapter lists four ways to use tobacco: cigarettes, pipes, cigars, and chewing tobacco.
2. _____ More than 30 million Americans have quit smoking.
3. _____ Only a few hundred teenagers begin smoking each year.
4. _____ The later a person begins smoking the deadlier it is.
5. _____ Cigarette smoking causes these diseases: lung cancer, heart disease, emphysema, and bronchitis.
6. _____ A person who smokes a pipe or cigar does not damage his body in any way.
7. _____ Experiments with mice show that there are more cancer-causing substances in cigar and pipe tars than in cigarette tars.
8. _____ Pipe smoking can cause lip cancer as well as other diseases.
9. _____ Although cigarette, cigar and pipe smoking can cause cancer, chewing tobacco does not cause any type of cancer.
10. _____ Cigarette smoking is the most popular way of using tobacco.

Part B

Directions: Write True or False in front of each statement. Be able to support your answers from the information in Lesson 4.

1. _____ Although many people are quitting smoking, many young people begin smoking each day.
2. _____ It is more dangerous to smoke for a short period of time than a long period of time.
3. _____ Inhaling on a pipe or cigar *can* be more hazardous than inhaling a cigarette.
4. _____ Serious heart and lung diseases have been related to smoking cigarettes, pipes, and cigars.
5. _____ Cancer of the mouth can only be caused by chewing tobacco.

Part C

Directions: Do you think these statements are true or false? Help support your answers with information from Lesson 4.

1. _____ Many doctors have quit smoking because they know how dangerous it is.
2. _____ More chewing tobacco will be manufactured in the future.
3. _____ Chewing tobacco is the safest way to use tobacco.

Organizational Exercise

Directions: This section lists four ways to use tobacco: cigarette smoking, pipe smoking, cigar smoking, and tobacco chewing. We are going to list the effects from three of these ways (pipe smoking, cigar smoking, and tobacco chewing). All the effects are listed at the bottom of the page. You must list the correct effects beside each cause. You may use the effects more than once.

Causes		**Effects**
1. smoking cigars	$\longrightarrow$	1. _____
		2. _____
		3. _____
		4. _____
		5. _____
		6. _____
2. smoking pipes	$\longrightarrow$	1. _____
		2. _____
		3. _____
		4. _____
		5. _____
		6. _____
		7. _____
3. chewing tobacco	$\longrightarrow$	1. _____

A List of Effects

mouth cancer   lung disease
heart disease   throat cancer
lip cancer   stomach cancer
larynx cancer

Vocabulary Review for Lessons 1 through 4

Directions: Using the vocabulary words from the following lessons: "A History of Smoking," "What Is Tobacco," "Tobacco Smoke and Harmful Compounds" and "Different Ways of Using Tobacco and Some of Its Effects," complete the following crossword puzzle.

Vocabulary Review for Lessons 1 through 4

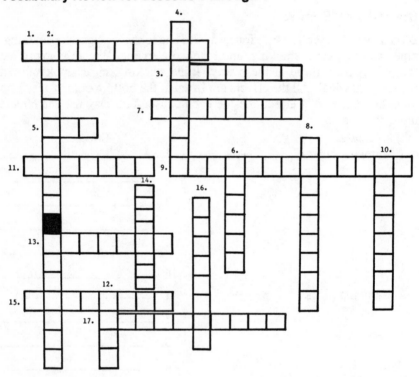

Across   1. businesses
          3. types
          5. a harmful brown, sticky substance in tobacco smoke
          7. worthwhile
          9. something that needs to be done over and over again can become addictive
        11. dangers
        13. a group of cells forming a part of the body
        15. dangerous drugs that can become habit-forming
        17. a drug that relaxes the central nervous system

Down   2. the species of tobacco most often grown and used
        4. to do experiments or study something
        6. to breathe in
        8. a chemical substance
      10. a poisonous, bitter substance in tobacco that can stain objects brownish yellow
      12. smell
      14. to make less; to make smaller
      16. to make greater; to make larger

EXERCISES FOR LESSON 5A: EFFECTS ON THE RESPIRATORY SYSTEM

Vocabulary Exercise

Directions: Please note the following words when you are reading. After your class discusses the definitions, write the meaning in your own words. Also, please write the job (what it does) of any word with a star beside it.

1. ★ respiratory system: _____

_____

2. ★ diaphragm: _____

_____

3. expanded: _____

_____

4. trachea: _____

_____

5. ★ cilia: _____

_____

6. ★ mucus: _____

_____

7. ★ alveoli: _____

_____

Directions: Read the sentences below. Using the vocabulary words, find the word that has the same meaning as the underlined word. Fill in the blanks with the answer.

1. The <u>liquid</u> in the respiratory system keeps lungs clean. _____ is found in the bronchial tubes and windpipe.
2. Tiny <u>air sacs</u> are found in the bronchial tubes. The _____ let gases pass through the body.
3. Air passes through the <u>windpipe</u>. The _____ leads into the bronchial tubes.
4. The <u>breathing system</u> lets air enter the body. The _____ is affected by inhaling tobacco smoke.
5. Tiny <u>hairs</u> line the bronchial tubes and trachea. Keeping the respiratory system clean is the job of the _____.
6. This large <u>muscle</u> expands the lungs. The _____ helps allow air to enter the body.
7. The air had <u>blown up</u> the balloon. The diaphragm _____ the lungs.

Comprehension Exercise

Part A

Directions: Check the statements you think are stated in Lesson 5A of the booklet. Sometimes the same words are used. Other times different words are used.

_____ The respiratory system allows the body to get oxygen from the air.
_____ The air passes through the nose, mouth, and throat immediately to the bronchial tubes.
_____ The alveoli are found at the end of the bronchial tubes.
_____ The alveoli allow air to pass through the body.
_____ Smoke follows a slightly different path than air when it goes through the body.
_____ Harmful substances can enter the alveoli.

Part B

Directions: Check the statements that tell what the author means. Be ready to tell why you did or did not check a statement.

_____ Oxygen is necessary for life.
_____ The lungs depend on the diaphragm to expand.

_____ The nose, throat, mouth, windpipe, diaphragm, lungs, bronchial tubes, and alveoli are all parts of the respiratory system.

_____ The only effects of inhaling tobacco smoke are a choking, coughing, and tickling feeling in the chest.

_____ The respiratory system works equally hard for a smoker and nonsmoker.

Part C

Directions: Check the items you think are correct. You should use Lesson 5A to help support your answers.

_____ Without cilia and mucus, the respiratory system might become clogged and unable to perform.

_____ Coughing and choking are two warning signs that the body gives to tell the person to stop smoking.

Organizational Exercise—Cause-Effect Pattern

Directions: Trace the route of smoke through the respiratory system by matching the causes (numbers) with the effects (letters).

Cause	Effect
_____ 1. person breathes	a. so air can then enter the bronchial tubes
_____ 2. diaphragm works	
_____ 3. air passes through throat and trachea	b. allows gases to pass through to the body
	c. expands lungs
_____ 4. cilia and mucus in windpipe and bronchial tubes	d. coughing, tickling feeling in chest and throat
_____ 5. alveoli work in lungs	e. keeps system clean
_____ 6. smoke irritating entire respiratory system	f. lets oxygen into the body for life

EXERCISES FOR LESSON 5B: EFFECTS ON CIRCULATORY SYSTEM

Vocabulary Exercise

Directions: Please note the following words when you are reading. After your class discusses the definitions, write the meaning in your own words. Also, please write the function or job of the word with a star beside it.

1. ⋆ circulatory system: _____

   _____

2. blood vessels: _____

   _____

3. absorbed: _____

   _____

Comprehension Exercise

Directions: Please answer the following questions. Use Lesson 5B to find or support your answers.

1. What is the job of the circulatory system? _____

   _____

2. List two things that the blood contains. _____

   _____

3. How does smoke enter the circulatory system? _____

   _____

4. What absorbs the oxygen and harmful substances from smoke? ___

   _____

5. List three effects or changes on the circulatory system caused by the harmful substances in tobacco smoke.

   a. _____

   b. _____

   c. _____

EXERCISES FOR LESSON 5C: EFFECTS ON THE NERVOUS SYSTEM

Vocabulary Exercise

Directions: Please note the following words when you are reading. After your class discusses the definitions, write the meaning in your own words. Also, please write the function or job of the word with a star beside it.

1. ★ nervous system: _____

2. spinal cord: _____

3. nerves: _____

Comprehension Exercise

Directions: Please circle the correct or best answer. Use Lesson 5C to help you answer the questions.

1. What is the function of the nervous system?
   a. to give the body an awareness of itself and the world
   b. to control other systems and to make the body aware of itself and the world
   c. to use the brain, spinal cord, and tiny nerves so that they all work together
2. What are the most important parts of the nervous system?
   a. the arteries in the brain
   b. the nervous system and brain
   c. the nerves, spinal cord, and brain
3. How do the harmful substances in smoke reach the nervous system?
   a. They reach the brain.
   ·b. The tiny nerves make them aware.
   c. The bloodstream carries them there.
4. What part of the nervous system is affected first by the smoke?
   a. brain
   b. spinal cord
   c. nerves
5. What effects on the nervous system are caused by smoking?
   a. upset stomach
   b. dizziness
   c. both a and b
6. What may cause these effects?
   a. carbon monoxide and oxygen
   b. nicotine, a lack of oxygen to the brain, or carbon monoxide
   c. nicotine, a lack of oxygen to the brain, and tar

Organizational Exercises—Cause-Effect Pattern (For Lessons 5B and 5C)

Directions: Below are two phrases that are separated by a slanted line (/). Put a check on the line if the first phrase is a *cause* of the second phrase.

The second phrase should be the *effect* (example: sugar/cavities). Lessons 5B and 5C will help you answer the questions.

_____ nicotine in circulatory system/heart beats faster
_____ smoke in nervous system/high blood pressure
_____ smoke in nervous system/upset stomach
_____ blood vessels contract in circulatory system/blood pressure rises
_____ carbon monoxide, nicotine or lack of oxygen to brain/dizziness
_____ smoke in nervous system/nerves tingle
_____ nicotine in circulatory system/less carbon monoxide taken to organs and tissues
_____ nicotine in circulatory system/less oxygen carried in the blood

EXERCISES FOR LESSONS 5D, 5E, AND 6: EFFECTS ON PREGNANT WOMEN AND THEIR BABIES, EFFECTS ON NONSMOKERS, AND MINOR HEALTH PROBLEMS

Vocabulary Exercise

Directions: Please note the following words when you are reading. After class discussion, write the definitions in your own words.

1. infant: _____
2. acid balance: _____
3. miscarriage: _____
4. stillbirth: _____
5. carbon monoxide: _____
6. chronic: _____
7. phlegm: _____
8. health organization: _____

Comprehension Exercise

Part A

Directions: Write True or False in front of these statements. Refer to Lessons 5D, 5E, and 6 for the correct answers.

_____ 1. Cigarette smoke in the mother's blood stream changes the heart rate, blood pressure, amount of oxygen, and acid balance for the unborn baby.

_____ 2. Studies show tobacco smoke is not dangerous to the non-smoker.
_____ 3. Tobacco smoke that is exhaled is pure and safe.
_____ 4. Tobacco smoking can be an expensive habit because of accidents, illness, and the price of cigarettes.
_____ 5. Fingers, fingernails and teeth can become yellowed by the nicotine in tobacco.

Part B

Directions: Write True or False in front of each statement. Be able to support your answers from information in Lessons 5D, 5E, and 6.

_____ 1. Smoking is twice as dangerous for a pregnant woman than it is for a woman who is not pregnant.
_____ 2. If a mother smokes, she may have a baby which weighs less than normal.
_____ 3. Miscarriages and stillbirths happen more often in women who smoke than in nonsmoking women.
_____ 4. Nonsmokers tend to be healthier than smokers.
_____ 5. Discoloration (yellowing) of the teeth by nicotine can cause cavities.

Part C

Directions: Do you think these statements are True or False? Help support your answers with information from Lessons 5D, 5E, and 6.

_____ 1. Pregnant women should not smoke.
_____ 2. Nonsmokers have rights about tobacco smoke.
_____ 3. Smoking does not seem expensive from one day to the next.

Organizational Exercise—Cause-Effect Pattern

Directions: Match the cause with the effects. Use pages 15 and 16 to help you complete the assignment.

	Causes		Effect
_____ 1.	smoke in mother's blood stream	a.	have babies that weigh less than normal
_____ 2.	person smokes in front of nonsmoker	b.	causes accidents
_____ 3.	smoker puts cigarette in mouth and holds it with fingers	c.	nonsmoker breathes in carbon monoxide and other harmful substances
_____ 4.	pregnant women who smoke	d.	fingers, fingernails, and teeth become yellow
_____ 5.	smoker is careless with cigarette	e.	changes baby's heart rate, blood pressure, oxygen supply, and acid balance
_____ 6.	smoker exhales tobacco smoke in front of non-smoker	f.	has cough, is sick more often than nonsmoker, has more phlegm in lungs
_____ 7.	person smokes cigarettes on regular basis	g.	smoke irritates nonsmoker's eyes and respiratory system

VOCABULARY REVIEW FOR LESSONS 5D, 5E, AND 6

Directions: Use your vocabulary words from Lessons 5D, 5E, and 6 to complete the following crossword puzzle.

Vocabulary Review for Lessons (A–E)

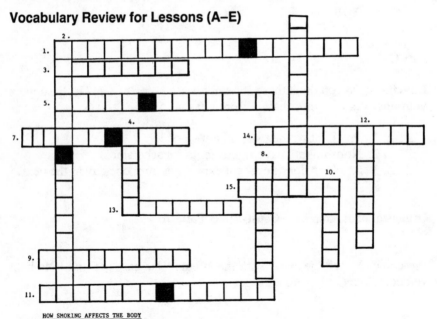

HOW SMOKING AFFECTS THE BODY

Across 1. the system that uses the heart, blood vessels, and other body parts to pass blood through the body
      3. soaked up
      5. arteries or veins that blood passes through
      7. part of the nervous system that goes down the back
      9. the muscle that expands the lungs
    11. the system that makes the body aware and controls other systems
    13. small air sacs that let air pass through the body
    14. a baby that is born dead
    15. a liquid that is found more in nonsmokers than smokers

Down 2. a gas from tobacco smoke
      4. small hairs that keep the respiratory system clean
      6. a developing baby (fetus) that is born too early to survive
      8. continuous
    10. a liquid that keeps the respiratory system clean
    12. a baby

EXERCISES FOR LESSON 7: SMOKING AND DISEASE

Vocabulary Exercise A

Directions: Answer the following questions in complete sentences. Use Lessons 7A-D to find and support your answers.

1. bronchitis: _____

2. emphysema: _____

3. inflammation: _____

4. congestion: _____

5. cancer: _____

6. associated: _____

7. abnormal: _____

8. ulcers: _____

Vocabulary Exercise B

Directions: To solve this puzzle look at the definitions at the bottom of the page. Think of a word from the vocabulary list that has the same number of letters as the spaces given. If you do this puzzle correctly, the circled word will be another word from the vocabulary list.

1. _ _ _ _ □ _ _ _ _ _ _
2. □ _ _ _ _ _ _ _ _ _
3. _ _ □ _ _ _ _ _ _ _
4. _ _ _ □ _ _ _ _ _
5. _ _ _ _ □ _
6. _ □ _ _ _ _ _ _
7. _ □ _ _ _ _
8. _ _ _ _ _ _ _ □

Definitions:

   a. swollenness and redness of tissues
   b. a disease in which the bronchial tubes are always inflamed
   c. being clogged
   d. related, linked
   e. sores, often found in the stomach
   f. a disease in which the air sacs are clogged
   g. a disease in which abnormal cells grow and destroy the body
   h. unusual, not regular

Comprehension Exercise

Directions: Answer the following questions in complete sentences. Use Lessons 7A-D to find and support your answers.

   1. What are three respiratory or breathing diseases that have been related to smoking?
   2. Why may a person cough if he or she has chronic bronchitis?
   3. What happens to the alveoli if a person has emphysema?
   4. Why do many doctors believe chronic bronchitis and emphysema may be related?
   5. How can cancer cause death?
   6. Who does *not* develop lung cancer very often?
   7. What may cause a heart attack?
   8. What three other diseases besides bronchitis, emphysema, lung cancer, and heart disease have been linked to smoking?
   9. Which disease do you think smokers are most likely to get and why?

Organizational Exercise—Cause-Effect Pattern

Directions: Below are two phrases that are separated by a slanted line (/). Put a check on the line if the first phrase is a cause of the second phrase. The second phrase should be an effect. Lessons 4 and 5A will help you complete the assignment.

_____ smoking tobacco/some respiratory diseases
_____ inflammation of bronchial tubes/produces phlegm
_____ breathing is difficult/emphysema
_____ phlegm and coughing/breathing difficult
_____ cells clogged/destroys tissues
_____ air sacs clogged or congested/stops fresh air from entering and stale air from leaving
_____ cancer cells growing/body tissues are destroyed
_____ smoking/lung cancer
_____ smoking/heart disease
_____ not enough oxygen in blood taken to heart/heart attack
_____ stomach ulcers/smoking
_____ smoking/tooth decay

EXERCISES FOR LESSONS 8 THROUGH 10

Vocabulary Exercise A

Directions: Please note the following words when you are reading. After your class discusses the definitions, please write the meanings in your own words.

1. media: _____

2. banned: _____

3. psychologist: _____

4. unintentionally: _____

5. influence: _____

Vocabulary Exercise B

Directions: Read the sentences below. Using the vocabulary words, find the word that has the same meaning as the underlined word. Fill in the blanks with the answers.

1. Cigarettes are <u>not allowed</u> to be advertised on television. Cigarettes were also _____ from being advertised on radio.
2. Television, radio, and newspapers are modern <u>ways to communicate</u>. The _____ lets us know what is happening all over the world.
3. Advertising has an <u>effect</u> on our lives. Parents can _____ their children.
4. The <u>doctor who studied personalities and minds</u> graduated from college. The _____ wanted to find out why the girl smoked.
5. <u>Without meaning to</u>, the boy dropped the glass of milk. The smoker _____ dropped his cigarette and caused a fire.

Comprehension Exercise

Directions: Please answer the following questions in complete sentences. Use Lesson 8 to help find the support for your answers.

1. When were cigarettes banned from television and radio?
2. Why do you think cigarettes cannot be advertised on radio and television but can be advertised on billboards and in newspapers and magazines?
3. What image do cigarette companies often use in advertising?
4. Health organizations show a different image of smoking than cigarette companies. How are these images different?
5. List three reasons why psychologists believe people smoke.

   a. _____

   b. _____

   c. _____

6. What type of person do you think would be likely to smoke?
7. What types of evidence would you consider when deciding whether or not to smoke?

FILMSTRIP ON SMOKING

"Cigarette Smoking: Take It or Leave It" is a ten minute color sound filmstrip published by the American Cancer Society. It presents several teenagers' views about smoking cigarettes. Their opinions are given during informal, everyday situations and conversations. The final scene leaves a main character undecided about whether or not to smoke. The overall objectives are to have teenagers identify various concerns about smoking, explore the implications and attitudes associated with smoking, and make a decision.

Discussion Questions for the Filmstrip

Some of the following questions are taken from a guide provided with the filmstrip.

1. Do the characters in the filmstrip remind you of people you know? How?
2. Who were the main characters?
3. What things were most important to each of these characters?
4. How were the eating habits of Henry, Frances, and Sheila different? What did their eating habits tell about what was important to them?
5. Do you think Frances was right to throw away her sister's cigarettes? If you disapproved of someone else smoking, how would you deal with it?
6. Sheila pointed out that it is hard to know what "too much" is when deciding whether to smoke. Do you agree with her? How would you decide what "too much" is?
   Do you agree with Helen's comment that smoking five or six cigarettes a day isn't too much? Why?
7. Is Frances right in saying that not every choice people make is okay, that some are riskier than others? Why? What things do you choose to do that involve risk?
8. How did Sheila say cigarettes may affect an unborn baby?
9. Do you agree with a lot of points that Frances made or do you consider her a "goody goody"? Why?
10. Why do you think Nick smoked? Are his reasons the same as most people's?
11. Do you agree with Frances that smokers have a responsibility to take other people into account? Why?
12. Where would you go for information about smoking? How do television and magazines affect people's information about cigarette smoking? Do advertisements affect people's decision about whether to smoke?
13. What facts or feelings might influence whether or not you decide to smoke?

Hands-On Activities

ACTIVITIES

Activity A

Objective: To introduce the tobacco unit by brainstorming all positive and negative thoughts about smoking.

Procedure: Make two columns on the blackboard: good, bad. Have student state as many words or phrases as possible for each column. List all contributions.

Discussion: Discuss each contribution briefly. At close of activity, give a brief overview of what will be studied in the tobacco unit.

Activity 2

Objective: To observe the residue caused from cigarette smoke.

Procedure: Have a person light a cigarette, inhale and exhale through a clean, white handkerchief.

Results: A yellowish-brown stain should be quite noticeable on the handkerchief.

Discussion: Discuss what caused the stain, how much of these compounds remain in the body, and their noticeable effects on the body, e.g., stains on hands, teeth, etc.

Activity 3

Objective: To contrast the various levels of tar and nicotine found in many popular brands of cigarettes.

351

Procedure: Collect at least 20 different brands of cigarettes ranging from low to high levels of tar and nicotine. Chart or graph the levels of tar and nicotine, being sure to label each brand.

Results: Charts should show a significant discrepancy between brands according to tar and nicotine content, e.g., Merit vs. Camel nonfilters.

Discussion: Discuss the advantages of smoking a low tar and nicotine cigarette rather than a high tar and nicotine cigarette. How many of one type of cigarette would a person have to smoke to equal a second brand in terms of tar and nicotine content? Are low tar and nicotine cigarettes truly a solution?

Activity 4

Objective: To provide a total picture of the three major systems that are affected by smoking.

Procedure: Have students work in twos and threes. Try to place one pupil with average artistic talent in each group. Trace two outlines of a student's body on large brown paper. Using all diagrams provided in the tobacco unit, fill in the parts of the respiratory, circulatory, and nervous systems. Sew or tape the paper mannequin together while stuffing it with crumpled newspapers and hang it from the ceiling.

Discussion: Discuss how the systems are connected, e.g., oxygen enters respiratory system, passes through alveoli in red blood cells to circulatory system, travels to organs including brain in nervous system.

Note: Full Color Transparencies from Milliken's *Systems of the Human Body* may also be used.

Activity 5

Objective: To determine how costly it is to smoke cigarettes on a regular basis.

Procedure: Determine the average cost of a package of cigarettes. Determine how much it costs to smoke one pack a day for one week, one month, and one year.

Discussion: Do you consider this amount to be much money? What else could be purchased with this sum of money? Do you think most smokers realize they are spending this amount on cigarettes? Why or why not?

Activity 6

Objective: To analyze the image that cigarette advertisements attempt to portray.

Procedure: Collect advertisements and write questions or statements that evaluate the image, e.g., all men who smoke Marlboros are hardy, rustic, good-looking cowboys who appeal to women.

Discussion: Discuss the images and *try* to classify which brands present a more idealistic image.

Activity 7

Objective: To contrast the image of cigarette smoking promoted by the cigarette manufacturers with the image promoted by health organizations.

Procedure: Gather cigarette advertisements. Also gather pamphlets printed by health organizations. Antismoking television commercials may also be recorded. Make a chart contrasting the images.

Results: The chart should list numerous differences between the positive and negative images projected about smoking cigarettes, e.g., girl with a beautiful smile vs. yellow teeth.

Discussion: Discuss the differences. Are any of the images distorted? How could they be made more realistic?

BIBLIOGRAPHY

Milgram, G.G. *The Teenager and Smoking*. New York: Rosen Press, Inc., 1973.

Needle, R. *Basic Concepts of Tobacco and Smoking*. River Forest, Ill.: Laidlaw Brothers, Pub., 1971.

Pamphlets on smoking published by The American Lung Association: New York.
Cigarette Smoking is Harmful
Cigarette Smoking
Lung Cancer
Me Quite Smoking? Why?
No Smoking—A Magazine Written By Kids For Kids
No Smoking—Lungs at Work
Pipe and Cigar Smoking
Questions and Answers of Smoking and Health
Second Hand Smoke

Reprinted from *The Teenager and Smoking* by Gail Milgram with permission of Rosen Press, Inc., © 1973.

Reprinted from *Basic Concepts of Tobacco and Smoking* by Richard Needle with permission of Laidlaw Brothers, A Div. of Doubleday & Co., Inc. © 1971.

Reprinted with permission of The American Lung Association.

Appendix B

Educational Information Systems

Education Abstracts. Washington, D.C.: American College Public Relations Association.

The *Abstracts* summarize articles and booknotes on higher education topics from newspapers, periodicals, and education journals.

Education Index. Bronx, N.Y.: H.W. Wilson Co.

The *Index* reviews 250 of the more valuable and accessible English language education periodicals. Subjects include education and curriculum in all subjects (preschool to adult) plus school administration and finance, guidance, and counseling.

Herickes, S. (Ed.). *Audio-Visual Equipment Directory.* Fairfax, Va.: National Audio-Visual Association, Inc., 1975–76.

This guide, published annually, is based on information provided by manufacturers. More than 2,000 models of audio-visual equipment are listed by type of equipment (74 categories).

Improving Materials Selection Procedures: A Basic "How To" Handbook. New York: Educational Products Information Exchange Institute.

This book provides a brief, comprehensive summary of recommendations for systematizing selection procedures.

Markham, L. *New Educational Materials.* (4th Ed.) New York: Citation Press, 1970.

This book describes selected films, professional guides, tapes, kits, charts, maps, recordings, filmstrips, etc. by grade level.

Merrimack Education Center. *A Directory of Selected Resources in Special Education.* Chelmsford, Mass.

This is an annotated guide to products designed to meet the needs of students with different learning styles through diverse programs and materials. Provides a directory of resources covering testing and assessment, teacher training materials, classroom techniques, etc.

Perkins, F.L. *Books and Non-Book Media: Annotated Guide to Selection Aids for Educational Materials*. Urbana, Ill.: National Council of Teachers.

This book provides a comprehensive listing of more than 250 guides and selection aids for all types of educational materials. Annotations address purpose, subjects, scope, and usefulness.

Resources in Education (RIE). Superintendent of Documents. U.S. Govt. Printing Office, Washington, D.C. 20402.

This resource includes resumes of documents selected by ERIC clearinghouse located throughout the country: conference papers, research reports, school district documents, etc. They are indexed by author and institution and by subject descriptions.

Wilson, C.M. *Sources of Teaching Materials*. Columbus, Ohio: Ohio State University, 1971.

The first part of this guide describes 190 basic reference and research sources. Other sections cover media, publishers, and distributors as well as references to materials and methods of instruction.

Indexes to Educational Media

AAAS Science Film Catalog. New York: R.R. Bowker Co., 1975.

Brown, J.W. *Educational Media Yearbook 1975–76*. New York: R.R. Bowker Co., 1975–76.

This book covers the entire media field: theory and practice, trends and machines, jobs, curricula, and projects.

Connecticut State Drug Advisory Council. *Inventory of Drug Services and Programs*. Hartford, Conn.: Connecticut Drug Advisory Council, 1973.

Film User's Handbook: A Basic Manual for Managing Library Film Services. New York: R.R. Bowker Co., 1975.

Index to Instructional Media Catalogs. New York: R.R. Bowker Co., 1974.

These catalogs of more than 600 hardware and software producers are indexed by subject/media and by product/services.

Landers Associates. *Landers Film Reviews*. Los Angeles, Calif.: Landers Associates, 1974–79.

Limbacker, J.L. *Feature Films in 8mm and 16mm*. New York: R.R. Bowker Co., 1974.

Parlato, S. *Films—Too Good for Words*. Ann Arbor, Mich.: R.R. Bowker Co., 1974.

Annotated Bibliography for Individualizing Secondary Instruction in the Content Areas

Bechtol, W., & Conte, A. *Individually Guided Social Studies,* Addison-Wesley Publishing Co., Inc., 1976.

This book includes objectives, assessment techniques and management.

Danielson, E.R. The cassette tape: An aid to individualizing high school English. *English Journal,* 1973, *62,* 441–445.

Tapes are suggested as study guides and enrichment; as a guide to independent study; to provide teacher feedback (evaluation) on student papers; and to enhance student-oriented seminars.

Educational Structures for Individualized Progress (2nd ed.). Helios Individualized Learning, 1976.

An overview of a number of established systems for individualizing instruction on the secondary level.

Keys to Good Language: Keys to English Mastery. The Economy Co. (grades 4 through junior high)

This book presents nongraded, individualized materials for teaching essentials in speaking, writing, and thinking with emphasis on grammar, vocabulary, spelling, dictionary skills, and reference skills.

Kline, A.A. Individualizing chemistry—A method used in an open high school. *Science Teacher,* 1972, *39,* 61–62.

In this instructional model, students are responsible for establishing their own academic goals. Daily schedules are predicated on 15-minute modular bases. Students select from 60 investigations those which they are interested in pursuing. Laboratory use is available on a flexible basis. Teachers and students collaborate in the student evaluations, which are narrative or criterion-based.

Marusek, J. A program providing individualized instruction for slow learning math and science students. *Science Education.* 1969, *53,* 217–219.

Study topics are presented to students; appropriate resource material is made available to students; assignments are completed by students at their individual rate. The teacher's role is as a resource, monitor and evaluator.

700 Science Experiments for Everyone. New York: Doubleday and Co., Inc., 1962.

These activities compiled by UNESCO for intermediate through high school grades.

Shuman, R.B. English instruction can be individualized. *Peabody Journal of Education.* 1972, *69,* 307–313.

The essence of this author's approach is to utilize peer interaction and group discussion. The teacher contributes writing assignments along with the students. Free written expression along topics of student interest is encouraged.

Study Skills. McDonald Publishing, 1979 (Remedial grades 9–12).

In Book A, students learn how to use reference material, take notes, outline, summarize, organize material, and retain information.

In Book B, students learn the following skills: understanding technical materials (maps, graphs, tables); locating specific information (index, glossary, table of contents); retaining information; organization of material; and library skills.

Writing Techniques in the Subject Areas

Delman, R.J. Composition and the High School: Steps toward faculty-wide involvement. *The English Journal,* 1978, *67*(8), 36–38.

This article argues in favor of incorporating writing skills into a variety of subjects. Sample writing assignments are illustrated for biology, home economics, art, health, mathematics, and music; these assignments reflect the processes of outlining, revising, analyzing/illustrating, comparing, interviewing, and persuading/analyzing.

Petrini, G.C. Teach Johnny How to Write for Social Studies Essay Tests. *The Clearing House,* 1976, *48*(9), 394–396.

This article discusses approaches to helping students, including those with learning difficulties, prepare written responses for social studies essay questions. The author's personal experiences may serve as an inspiration to other educators.

Ross, F.C. & Jarosy, M.H. Integrating Science Writing: A Biology Instructor and English Teacher Get Together, *The English Journal,* 1978, *67*(4), 51–55.

This article describes cooperative efforts to integrate science and writing. A biology instructor and an English teacher present individual narratives concerning how they developed initial commitments to meshing their fields of study. Afterward, a number of joint ventures are discussed.

Sanacore, J. Interdisciplinary Strategies, Independent Study and Career Planning, *Phi Delta Kappan,* 1978, *59*(6), 403–404.

This article describes an innovative program that guides high school seniors to explore careers and to develop competencies as researchers and as writers. Educators representing different fields of study meet with career-oriented students and help them complete comprehensive projects consisting of a foreword, a table of contents, a statement of purpose, an introduction, a number of chapters, an appendix, and an extensive bibliography.

Wilkes, J. Science Writing: Who? What? How? *The English Journal*, 1978, *67*(4), 56–60.

This article distinguishes science writing from scientific writing and suggests the implementation of units, courses, and programs that focuses on teaching the principles of mass communication to students of science. The author suggests the writing of dialogues to dramatize conversations about developments in science, and he provides six approaches to writing effective dialogues.

Annotated Bibliography for Writing Competency Skills

Basic Elements of Writing. Jonesboro, Ark.: ESP, Inc., 1977. (grades 4–9; remedial 10–12)

This is a practical, student-oriented composition series that moves from creativity to creativity under control. This series includes 24 lessons on 12 cassettes with a spirit duplicating master workbook. The book of masters contains a variety of practical assignments and actual student writing samples.

Do It By Letter. Kalamazoo, Mich.: Interpretive Education, 1977 (grades 7–10; remedial 11–adult)

The hands-on kit includes almost everything needed to teach a unit on letter writing. The workbook gives explanations and associated activities that explain in detail the ins and outs of personal and business letters, as well as the mechanics of how to write them.

Learning Mechanics of Written Expression. Baltimore, Md.: Hampden Publications, 1978–1979. (grades 7–10)

This series of cassette skill packs was designed for students having problems expressing themselves in writing. The ten lessons help develop understanding of the use of capital letters, punctuation, abbreviations, and spelling. Lessons are designed to give skill development, reinforcement, review, or enrichment.

Lessons for Better Writing. North Ballerica, Mass.: Curriculum Associates, 1976–1979. (grades 7–12; remedial–adult)

The focus of the text and the exercises is on practical situations. The learning process stresses individual writing and editing and pupil-team evaluation of both student and professional writing.

Lessons in Report Writing. Exeter, N.H.: Learnco, Inc., 1978–1980.

The objective of this workbook is to help students build observation skills, organize observed information, and present this information in a purposeful manner. This goal is achieved by leading students through a wide spectrum of activities that range from following the daily progress of a comic strip character in a journal to learning how to convert a graph into a paragraph.

Lessons in Writing and Rewriting. Exeter, N.H.: Learnco, Inc., 1978–1980. (grades 5–8; remedial–adult)

This workbook consists of 36 single unit exercises and multiunit exercises, each focusing on a specific aspect of writing and providing opportunities to practice various skills and techniques. The individual units deal with writing practice, point of view, parts of speech, structure, and organization. Spaced throughout the workbook are self-correcting questions that require students to review their own writing and perform self-tests.

Outline Building. North Ballerica, Mass.: Curriculum Associates, 1977. (grades 5–9; remedial 10–12)

This text provides a manipulative approach for learning and practice in organizing outlines. It is ideal for students who have difficulty in organizing their thoughts on paper. Since it is self-correcting as well as self-directing, students learn to distinguish between main topics, subtopics, and details.

Using Basic Parts of Speech. Exeter, N.H.: Learnco, Inc., 1978–1980. (remedial grades 9–adult)

This 80-page skills book contains lessons and review exercises that introduce, explain, and provide intensive practice in the use of the basic parts of speech. Activities emphasize the function of nouns, verbs, adjectives, adverbs, and prepositions within the context of the sentence and include opportunities for reinforcement through student writing.

Index

About the Authors

DOLORES M. WOODWARD has had extensive experience with exceptional adolescents. In addition to teaching, she has served as an educational diagnostician, educational director, and school principal. Her accomplishments include the creation of two residential education centers (one a national model) under her educational leadership and guidance. As a graduate level lecturer in special education at Saint Joseph College in Connecticut, she has for several years been involved in the training of special educators. Dr. Woodward has served as a consultant to the Connecticut State Department of Education and has presented workshops and in-service training to several school systems throughout Connecticut on mainstreaming.

Residing in Connecticut with her husband and two daughters, Dr. Woodward is presently the Assistant Superintendent of Schools for the Special School District of the State of Connecticut, Department of Children and Youth Services.

DOLORES PETERS is an Assistant Professor of Special Education, Coordinator of the Graduate program in Secondary Special Education and Chairperson of the Educational Division at St. Joseph College in West Hartford, Connecticut. She has also served as a consultant and in-service trainer to school systems, private facilities, and parent organizations in the areas of educational assessment and curriculum and program development. Her background includes teaching experiences in elementary education as well as special education in both elementary and secondary schools.

She is married and the mother of three grown children.